LAWNMOWER MANUAL

Haynes

A practical guide to choosing, using and maintaining a lawnmower

Brian Radam

Contents

About the author

Ex-racing champion Brian Radam, often referred to as 'The Lawn Ranger', became involved in our great British lawnmower engineering industry in the early 1960s, an interest which culminated in him opening the British Lawnmower Museum, with its amazing rooms full to capacity with over 200 restored vintage lawnmowers, part of a total collection of over 1,000 machines otherwise destined for the Lawnmower Heaven scrapyard.

The museum is situated in the classic Victorian seaside town of Southport, on the golf coast of Lancashire. Rather strangely, Southport is not in the south nor is it a port. It doesn't even have a harbour, but it does boast the second-longest pier in the UK, which for the majority of the time stretches across the beach with the sea a distant mirage. However, Southport does boast 11 pristine golf courses (including Royal Birkdale, just round the corner) and, more importantly, a place where you can immerse yourself in lawnmowers. People visit the multi-award-winning British Lawnmower Museum from all over the world, just to enjoy the unique experience, and it is often referred to as one of the 100 places you have to visit before you die!

Brian Radam's father started Southport's first DIY shop in the early 1940s, repairing lawnmowers and locks after the family shop in Liverpool had been bombed during the Second World War. By the age of ten Brian was enjoying regrinding cylinder lawnmower blades on his father's lathe. After leaving school he served as an apprentice for The Atco Lawnmower Company, which repaired and serviced 425 lawnmowers every week, and the original engineers sold and repaired lawnmowers from Rudge motorbikes with sidecars. Over a 50-year period he has personally sold and maintained

many tens of thousands of lawnmowers and grasscutters of all types. He has appeared on many TV and radio programmes, been a consultant to major manufacturers and, becoming fascinated with all types of mechanical devices, developed a comprehensive understanding of how things work. He has also become one of the elite Fellows of The British Locksmiths Institute, excelling in the mysteries of safes, locks and keys.

▲ The author demonstrating a Greens of Leeds and London 24in pony-drawn lawnmower. Note the examples of leather horse-boots.

▼ Besides being famous for TT racing, Rudge motorbikes were fitted out with sidecars and tools and used by Atco salesmen and engineers for maintenance and repair work, and for demonstrating lawnmowers on potential customers' lawns.

Introduction

Although lawnmowing has become a great British obsession, it all started 1,500 years ago before the English word 'lawn' (meaning 'open clearing in woodland') had even been invented; a more modern definition of lawn would perhaps be 'closely cut grass around a house'. In fact it was a Roman called Pliny the Younger who had the first recorded garden in AD 62, which can still be seen in the famous city of Pompeii, which in Pliny's time was more famous for earthquakes, volcanic eruptions and brothels.

There are 15 million lawns in the UK, and despite the British purchasing nearly a million mowers every year, and the Americans using nearly 70% of their water on grass, lawnmowing is, ironically, not the sexiest of subjects – despite the breathtaking aroma of freshly cut grass being voted the best smell in a national UK survey, and the fact that Robbie Coltrane, when visiting the British Lawnmower Museum for BBC TV, said 'Do you know, people spend more time cutting grass than making love!' And yet when Stephen Fry asked colleagues at his local pub about lawnmowers for a TV programme, not one person would even admit to owning one!

But the British people have a unique obsession with the lawn. A 2012 survey found that 100% of people loved a lawn, but that 90% of people didn't know the difference between a lawnmower and a grasscutter; 6% of people saw mowing the grass as a necessary chore and didn't enjoy doing it; 29% didn't mind, but still didn't enjoy cutting the grass; 44% quite enjoyed cutting the grass, but without too much emphasis on the finish so long as it looked tidy; and 21% of people enjoyed cutting the grass and focussed on the finish they'd achieved.

▼▶ **Edwin Beard Budding patented a machine for cutting grass on 30 August 1830. 'Gentlemen may find my machine an amusing and healthy exercise plus do the work of eight men.'**

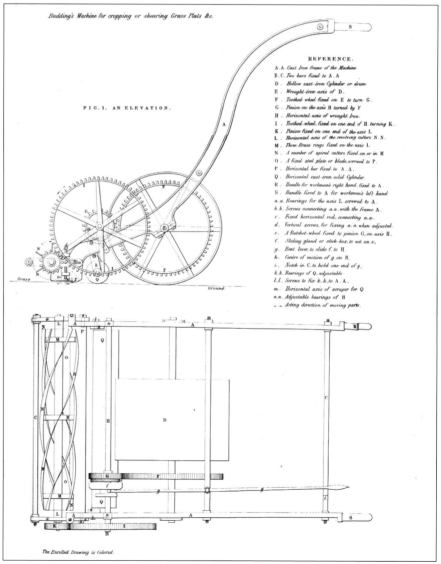

▼ **Roman author and magistrate Pliny the Younger recorded the first 'lawn' in AD 62.**

N° 6081.

Machine for Mowing Lawns, &c.

BUDDING'S SPECIFICATION.

TO ALL TO WHOM THESE PRESENTS SHALL COME, I, EDWIN BUDDING, of the Thrupp, in the Parish of Stroud, in the County of Gloucester, Machinist, send greeting.

WHEREAS His most Excellent Majesty William the Fourth did, by His Letters Patent under the Great Seal of the United Kingdom of Great Britain and Ireland, bearing date at Westminster the Thirty-first Day of August, in the first year of His reign, give and grant unto me, the said Edwin Budding, my executors, administrators, and assigns, His especial licence, sole privilege, full power, and authority that I, the said Edwin Budding, my executors, administrators, and assigns, should and lawfully might, during the term of years therein expressed, make, use, exercise, and vend, within England, Wales, and the Town of Berwick-upon-Tweed, my Invention of "A NEW COMBINATION AND APPLICATION OF MACHINERY for the purpose of CROPPING or SHEARING the VEGETABLE SURFACE of LAWNS, GRASS-PLATS, and PLEASURE GROUNDS, CONSTITUTING A MACHINE WHICH MAY BE USED WITH ADVANTAGE INSTEAD OF A SCYTHE FOR THAT PURPOSE;" in which said Letters Patent there is contained a proviso, that if I, the said Edwin Budding should not particularly describe and ascertain the nature of my said Invention, and in what manner the same is to be performed, by an instrument in writing under my

2   A.D. 1830.—N° 6081.

Budding's Mowing Machine.

hand and seal, and cause the same to be enrolled in His said Majesty's High Court of Chancery within two calendar months next and immediately after the date of the said Letters Patent, that then the said Letters Patent and all liberties and advantages whatsoever thereby granted should utterly cease, determine, and become void, as in and by the same, relation being thereunto had, may more fully and at large appear.

NOW KNOW YE, that in compliance with the said proviso, I, the said Edwin Budding, do hereby declare that the nature of my said Invention, and the manner in which the same is to be performed, are particularly described and ascertained in and by the drawing hereunto annexed, and the following description thereof; that is to say, Figure 1, in the drawing is an elevation of the left side, and Figure 2, is a ground-plan of the same machine, drawn to a scale one fourth of the real dimensions; the same letters refer to the same parts of the machinery in both figures. A, A, is the cast iron frame; B, and C, are two wrought iron bars, with screws at their extremities, for connecting the opposite sides of the said frame; D, is a hollow cylinder or drum of cast iron, fixed on the horizontal axis E, having its bearings in the under edge of the frame A, A; and F, is a toothed wheel fixed on the same axis E, to drive the pinion G, when the drum D, is made to roll on the ground. H, is a horizontal wrought iron axis, turned round by the said pinion G, when the machine is in action. I, is a toothed wheel fixed on one end of the axis H, to drive the pinion K, which is fixed on one end of the horizontal axis L; three brass rings, M, M, M, are fixed on this axis L, to carry the revolving spiral cutters N, which are made of thin steel plates, tempered, fixed on by screws or let into grooves in M; the number of the said spiral cutters so fixed may be from four to eight, or more. O, is a rectangular steel plate, tempered, having its front edge towards N, and a little bevelled like a blunt chisel; this steel plate O, is fixed by screws against the under side of the horizontal cast iron bar P, which is fixed by its extremities to the sides of the frame A, A, at bottom. Q, is a horizontal solid cylinder of cast iron, having its bearings k, screwed against the insides of the frame A, A, by the screws l, which pass through chase mortices in k, in order to allow an ad-

A.D. 1830.—N° 6081.   3

Budding's Mowing Machine.

justment of the height of the cutting plates N, O, above the ground; the whole machine bearing on the cylinders D, Q, when in action, as well as when at rest. R, is a wood handle for the right, and S, is a similar one for the left hand of the workmen; a, a, are bearings for the axis L, screwed to the outsides of A, A, by the screws b, which pass through chase mortices in a, to allow an adjustment of the edges of N, to O; vertical screws d, d, pass through projecting parts of A, A, and bear against the upper and lower edges of a, a. In order to fix a, when adjusted, c, is a front horizontal bar connecting the opposite pieces a a. The ratchet wheel e, is fixed to the pinion G, the sliding gland or box f, fixed by a feather to the axis H, with which it therefore always turns, contains a click or pall for taking into the teeth of the ratchet wheel e, when f, is pushed over it by the lever g; the centre of motion of this lever is at h, on the bar B. A notch in the bar C, at i, serves to lock the end of the bent lever g, when f, by acting on e, compels G, to drive H, I. The bearings of H, are n, n, which are screwed against the outsides of A, A, the screws passing through chase mortices in n n, to allow an adjustment of I, to K, after adjusting the pieces a, a, when f, is moved from e, e, and G, will turn loose on H, and the machine may be rolled along on D, Q, without communicating motion to the cutters round the axis L. Operation of the machine. The various parts being adjusted, and the upper end of the lever g, placed in the notch i, the workman takes hold of the handles R, S, and by pushing forward the machine the drum D, rolls upon the ground like the wheel of a wheelbarrow, at the same time turning F, which drives G, and I, and this wheel I, drives K, L, M, making the revolving cutters N, act rapidly by their smooth outer edges against the edge of the fixed cutter O, so as to crop or shear the grass or vegetable surface. At the same time the cylinder Q, rolls on the ground to regulate the height of O, and consequently the closeness of the cutting or short-ness of the grass left. To keep the roller Q, sufficiently free from any adhering substances, the horizontal bar m, connecting the opposite pieces k, k, serves as an axis for a thin iron scraper curved so as to form a portion of a cylinder or arch, having its lower edge bearing on the surface of Q. The speed with which the machine is pushed forward when at work is not material, because the number of cuts will always be in

A.D. 1830.—N° 6081.

Budding's Mowing Machine.

the same ratio with the space rolled over by the drum D. The revolving parts may be made to be driven by endless lines or bands, instead of teeth. It is advisable to employ the machine when the grass or vegetable surface is dry; and when high grass is to be cut, it is best to shear it twice over, lowering O, N, by adjusting k, k, previous to the second course or kerf. Grass growing in the shade, too weak to stand against a scythe to be cut, may be cut by my machine as closely as required, and the eye will never be offended by those circular scars, inequalities, and bare places, so commonly made by the best mowers with the scythe, and which continue visible for several days. Country gentlemen may find in using my machine themselves an amusing, useful, and healthy exercise. I do not claim as my Invention the separate parts of my machine, considered without reference to the effects to be produced by them; but I do claim as my Invention the described application and combination for the specified purpose.

In witness whereof, I, the said Edwin Budding, have hereunto set my hand and seal, this Twenty-fifth Day of October One thousand eight hundred and thirty.

EDWIN BUDDING. (L.S.)

BE IT REMEMBERED, That on the same Twenty-fifth Day of October the year above-mentioned the aforesaid Edwin Budding came before our Lord the King in His Chancery, and acknowledged the specification aforesaid, and all and everything therein contained in form above written, and also the specification aforesaid was stamped according to the tenor of the Statute in that case made and provided.

Enrolled the Thirtieth Day of October in the year above written.

LONDON;
Printed by GEORGE EDWARD EYRE and WILLIAM SPOTTISWOODE, Printers to the Queen's most Excellent Majesty. 1853.

A lawnmower is one of the few machines in life (besides a car) that people will ever bond with. The fact is, whichever side of the garden fence you sit on, whether your lawn is your pride and joy or mowing gives you a pain in the gr-ass, it will still keep growing. Provided, that is, the weather is above the magic figure of 11°C (or 51.8°F). Another survey concluded that, love it or hate it, over a lifetime a man will walk on average 220 miles, and a woman 48 miles, just cutting grass!

Currently the world is divided regarding the joy of lawns, but if you're one of those who subscribe to the Law of Sod that says, 'I fought the lawn and the lawn won!', this book may just be the tonic you need to achieve that wonderful, satisfying feeling that mowing grass is good for the body and mind, and lifts the spirit. Besides adding value to our properties, mowing creates memories of freshly cut grass and happy, sunny days spent relaxing on our beautiful lawns that make the rest of the world go green with envy!

Being at the sharp end of cutting edge technology, the great British invention of the cylinder lawnmower hasn't changed in principle since the day it was invented and patented on 30 August 1830, and it has remained the favoured lawnmowing machine for traditional formal lawns throughout most of the last two centuries. The lawnmowers of yesteryear were built to last more than a lifetime. Indeed, one manufacturer, Greens of Leeds and London, unknowingly found themselves achieving *Guinness Book of World Records* status by producing a lawnmower in the 1870s that was so good that they were able to market the model unchanged for the next 70 years! They said their machine was perfect, so why change it? So they never did. However, nowadays a lot of things are changing. Yesterday's lifetime products are today's disposables.

Whilst you're reading this you could potentially be using your smartphone to watch your robot mower cutting the grass whilst you're relaxing on the beach somewhere else in the world on holiday; or you could be asleep at night whilst the robot mower silently does its job mowing the lawn. You could even, dare I say it, be walking on artificial plastic grass, perish the thought! Some people say this borders on obscenity, and artificial grass is often spoken of by gardeners and groundsmen with some very unparliamentary language. It makes me shudder to think of it ever replacing one of Nature's finest surfaces to walk, relax and sleep on. Some people say it's like covering your home with plastic cladding and plastic doors. Some people can't even think of polite words to describe it. But don't get me wrong. There's a place for artificial grass, especially where it isn't practical to have the real thing, and it's ideal on balconies, roof areas, poolsides, indoor displays, sports grounds, car drives and heavy foot-traffic areas. But it has no place in this book.

This informative manual will be an asset to your lawnmower armoury, saving you frustration and providing greater understanding of how they work, whilst also saving you time and money by explaining that all lawnmowers aren't the same, and proving that they're far more than just different colours!

Brian Radam
April 2014

Chapter 1

The history and future of lawnmowers and grasscutters

◀ **The author with an American-style scythe, with a curved shaft.**

▶ **Early Edwin Budding lawnmower, 1830s.**

▼ **Representation of Edwin Budding and his lawnmowing machine, based on a contemporary advertisement.**

The pictures on the following page show the British Lawnmower Museum's unique replica of the very first lawnmower, patented by Mr Edwin Beard Budding of Stroud, Gloucestershire, in August 1830, when it was described as 'A machine for cutting grass plats, cropping or shearing vegetable surfaces of lawns and pleasure grounds.' The patent survives today, and is just one of over 600 that, along with hundreds of blueprints dating from 1799 onwards – some of them written on parchment – are housed in the British Lawnmower Museum archives.

Budding's invention may look simple in terms of its components, but it took three top engineers over 300 hours to produce this replica, even aided by modern machinery and computer technology, plus painstaking hours of fine lawn-tuning to give that perfect cut. The mind boggles when you think back almost 200 years – just how long did it take Mr Budding and his business partner John Farabee to produce their prototype? Especially with no electricity, no lathes, no welding, no plastic, no telephone, no Internet ... I could go on; besides the fact he'd never even seen a lawnmower, and didn't know if his idea would work!

This reproduction of Edwin Budding's 1830 'Mowing machine for grass' has its chassis and all the gearing cast in iron, weighing in at 176lb (80kg), with

▲ The author (right) with a traditional straight-shafted British scythe, and TT motorcycle champion Guy Martin (left) with an American scythe.

▶ Gang of scythe men.

a hardwood roller and handles. Yet the practicality of his unique innovative design is such that its assembly or disassembly could be achieved with a small adjustable spanner (another patented Edwin Budding invention) in less than ten minutes.

Designed to be pulled by one or two men or boys whilst steered and pushed by another, the simple design comprises four cast iron gears and a drive clutch to the blade, allowing the cutters to be disengaged at will when in transport mode. Its adjustable grass-height roller is positioned directly in front of the rear roller so that the grass isn't flattened before the cutters contact the grass, which minimises any scalping effect. The ease with which the complete machine could be assembled or dismantled, enabling all the moving parts to be easily accessed, cleaned and lubricated, ensured a lifetime of service. This iconic labour-saving 'strange mechanical automaton contraption', as it was called at the time, could easily do the work of eight men, and it changed the way grass was cut throughout the world – just one reason why 'lawnmowerists' have been drawn to the British Lawnmower Museum in Southport from all over the globe.

In the museum, visitors often ask

▶ Anatomy of the first lawnmower and its component parts.

us how people cut grass before the lawnmower was invented. Well, skilled men with scythes cut grass in gangs of six or eight, often followed by women and children collecting and sweeping the cuttings with brooms. The scythes were often made to measure, consequently young men didn't get a scythe until they'd stopped growing. They also worked very unsociable hours, as the best time to scythe is when the grass

is slightly moist, either very early in the morning or late in the evening.

Scythe men, although lumbered with a backbreaking job, cutting the grass every three or four days, could achieve a 'bowling green' finish, a skill that we've lost nowadays, as we have the privilege of many different types of grass-cutting machines available to do the work for us. But back then, if a higher cut was required, the scythe men would add an

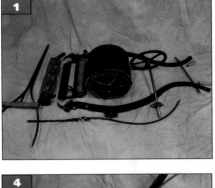

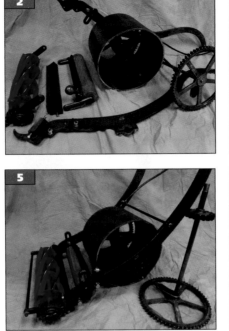

▲ Step by step assembly of Budding's lawnmower. This unique machine can be assembled in less than ten minutes from scratch with nothing more than a small adjustable spanner, enabling servicing and maintenance to be carried out easily and quickly.

extra leather sole to the soles of their boots so that they could achieve the desired grass height.

Despite their exhausting work they managed to entertain themselves by competing at picking a cigarette paper up by the blade without cutting any grass! They also balanced the tip of the scythe handle on their chin, with a 24in, razor-sharp, pointed blade balancing precariously 4ft above their heads – not something to try at home without at least 12 months' experience of using a scythe for eight hours a day, which must have earned the scythe-men of yore the confidence to handle a scythe, plus abs to die for.

Edwin Budding did not originally set out to make a lawnmower. He was working in a textile mill when its owner received an order for guardsmen's uniforms which specified that the cloth must be smooth and free from tufts and bobbles, and the mill owner asked Budding to design a machine that would trim the nap of the cloth. The mechanism that he invented was of a cylindrical blade spinning over a stationary fixed blade. Whilst testing the machine with John Farabee, the engineer next door who paid the development costs, he found that it also cut grass very efficiently, so they set about making their strange new machine. Working in secrecy, 35-year-old Budding had to test his machine at night

for fear of people thinking him a lunatic and madman for making such a strange contraption. Eventually, when he brought it on to the market, he advertised it with the phrase 'Country Gentlemen may find in using my machine, an amusing and healthy exercise plus do the work of eight men with scythes and brooms!', adding 'The eye will never be offended by those common circular scars and bare places which continue to be visible for several days.'

In 1831 one of the first lawnmowers was already being used at the Zoological Gardens at Regent's Park, and over the next six years Edwin Budding and John Farabee constructed 600 more. All the lawnmowers at this time were man-powered – it would be nearly another ten years before donkey, pony and horse-drawn mowers evolved, and over 50 years would pass before the first powered lawnmower entered the market, driven by steam (the internal combustion engine and electricity not yet being commercially viable).

In 1832, Ipswich-based Ransomes – the largest agricultural company in Europe – began to make Edwin Budding's machines under licence. The Ransome engineers modified Budding's original design by repositioning the wooden roller (initially placed between the rear roller and cutting cylinder) in front of the cutter, thus giving it more stability and balance

on uneven surfaces. This configuration is still the conventional roller/cutter layout on modern lawnmowers. They also covered and protected the heavy gears with ornate cast iron guards. Although this didn't stop the ingress of dirt and debris, it made the machines safer, protecting the users' feet and fingers whilst reducing maintenance. They named their new

▼ Edwin Budding replica, 2013. It weighs in at a hefty 176lb (80kg).

▲ Camel-powered lawnmower. With their unique load-spreading, splay-toed feet, camels were ideally suited for lawnmowing, since they left no hoof prints when they walked across a lawn.

▲ A 6in Greens 'Multum in Parvo', Latin for 'with little much'.

▼ Ransome Chain Automaton, with the newly invented 'chain drive' and a double-helix cutting cylinder designed to throw the grass evenly and directly to the centre of the grassbox.

models 'The Ransome New Automaton', and made it in several cutting widths from 6in to 36in.

1842 saw a pony-drawn lawnmower manufactured, by Alexander Shanks of Arbroath in Scotland. Cutting widths were 27in to 42in, which enabled an acre of grass to be cut in just one hour (the word 'acre' means the area one man could scythe in one day). At this time the Shanks design still used the small roller behind the cutting cylinder, but as the machine's main power was by 'pulling' rather than 'pushing' it didn't have the tendency to scalp or dig into the ground. One of their models was called the 'Shanks' Pony' – whence, some believe, this popular term for walking derived (but in fact the term 'shanks' nag' was already in use in the 1770s). Such pony and horse-drawn lawnmowers became very popular, especially with the owners of stately homes, sports fields, parks and other large grassed areas, and they continued to be manufactured until 1939.

Such lawnmowers cost from £4 10s to 20 guineas (£22, a fortune in those days). Leather boots for their ponies and horses (so as not to leave hoof prints in the grass) were custom hand-made by professionals. The fact that First and Second quality boots were available shows just how important lawnmowers and lawnmowing were, with the emphasis always on quality, as you wouldn't want the embarrassment of your neighbour knowing your pony was shod with Second quality leather boots, would you? This was the time when Great Britain was the envy of the world, and in the 19th and 20th centuries it dominated the world's lawnmower manufacturing industry.

Greens lawnmowers were classed in 'man' sizes, starting with a 'one man mower' and progressing through a

▼ Ransome Gear Automaton of 1897 with cast iron gears; 10in to 18in widths were available, costing £3 10s to £7 10s.

▶ Early 20th-century advertisement for the very popular 10in and 12in Ransome Leo and Cub side-wheel mowers.

▼ The Greens of Leeds and London 'Silens Messor'.

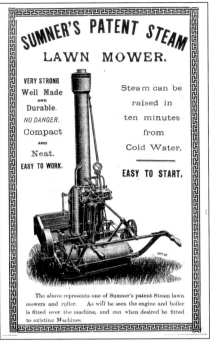

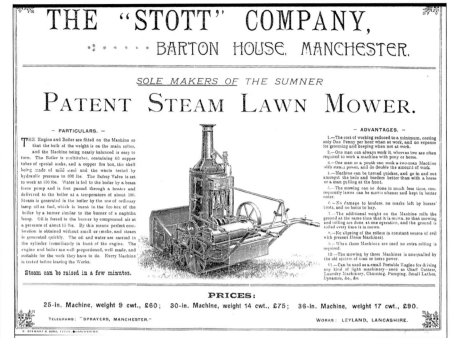

▲ The Sumner Steam Lawnmower was invented in the 1890s. It was a breakthrough in engineering design and convenience.

▲ The Stott Steam Lawnmower was made by British Leyland, later more famous for building motor cars.

'man and boy mower' to a 'two man mower'. Larger machines were classified as 'donkey mowers', 'pony mowers' and 'horse mowers'. Other animal mowers were powered by camels and even elephants, both of which had the advantage of not requiring leather boots.

The 'Greens Silens Messor' (Latin for 'silent cutter') of Leeds and London, manufactured in 1859, was the very first model to use the new 'block chain' rather than heavy cast iron gears. It made the machines quieter and lighter, which was important, as at that time many gardeners weren't allowed to use the 'noisy' geared lawnmowers early in the morning before people had awoken. The Silens Messor eventually found itself in the *Guinness Book of Records* in consequence of its model design not changing for seventy years. Another advantage of this model and its new featured chain design was that it allowed the cutting cylinder to be easily removed and turned around when the leading cutting edge became blunt, enabling the reverse cutting edge to be used without regrinding. Before welding had been invented, the cylinder cutter

blades were originally fixed in place by crimped wire, split pins or rivets.

Various other types of drive mechanisms were tried, including India rubber covered wheels by Barnard Bishop. Although this had the advantage of making the machines very quiet, they had a tendency to slide in wet conditions.

The origin of the steam lawnmower occurred in Leyland, Lancashire, where the Sumner Steam Lawnmower was invented in 1893 by Elias Sumner and his two sons, James and William, of whom James had already been fined a shilling (5p) for speeding on a steam tricycle. Their engine was powered by paraffin or petroleum, whereas steam engines at that time were normally coal-fired. It required just one man and 15 minutes' preparation to be ready to cut, and cost one old penny an hour to run, compared to the cost of two men tending and feeding a horse 24 hours a day.

By 1895 the Sumners had renamed their company the Leyland Steam Motor Company. They produced three lawnmowers, their 25in model being the lightest, weighing in at 9cwt (457kg) and costing £60. A 30in model weighing 14cwt (711kg) cost £75, and their monster 36in cost £90 and weighed 17cwt

(864kg) unladen. To this another 100kg could be added for water, fuel and a large grassbox – especially when full – bringing it up to nearly a ton. At that weight there wouldn't be a bump in sight, with the lawn rolled as flat as a snooker table! The average wage in England at the time was less than £2 per week, so these machines cost a comparative fortune (about the cost of a small house) compared to current values. Today a powered mower can easily be purchased for less than a few days' salary.

By 1900 the internal combustion engine was becoming established. Early in his reign King Edward VII ordered a demonstration of the new Ransome Petrol lawnmower in the grounds of Buckingham Palace, to great success, which marked the end of the steam lawnmower era. 1904 saw Ransome develop the first ride-on lawnmower, destined for Cadbury's Chocolates and Bourneville House for their workers' sports field. Such machines not only cut the grass, but, because of their heavy weight, doubled as a roller – especially important for bowling greens and the wicket on cricket pitches.

On the other side of the Atlantic, in 1907 in the US an electrical engineer

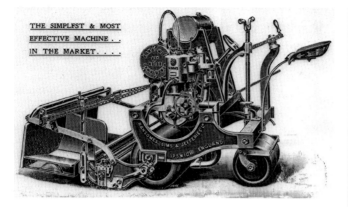

▲ The first ride-on machine by Ransome saw the introduction of the term 'horse power'.

▶ The Ransome ride-on lawnmower bought by Bourneville House (pictured) for the Cadbury's chocolate factory, photographed mowing the workers' sports field in 1904.

▼ Briggs & Stratton motor wheel engine of the early 1900s.

▼ Briggs & Stratton model 6B horizontal crank engine.

▼ Briggs & Stratton model 6H vertical crank engine.

Motorwheel

Model 6B

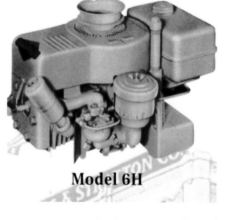

Model 6H

named Stephen Briggs was designing a small gasoline engine with Harold Stratton. Together they founded the Outboard Marine Corporation. Unbeknown to them, within a few years their motor was destined to become the world's most popular small mower engine, several varieties being covered in this book.

Among early lawnmower manufacturers were several prestige companies that would not normally be associated with the garden machine industry, such as Royal Enfield, famous for their motorbikes and guns. Some of their lawnmowers were used to achieve the velvet turf finish of the Wimbledon

Tennis Club. They featured precision gears and motorbike kick-type starting, popular on many models in the 1950s, and were advertised with the slogan 'Built Like a Gun', depicting a cannon. Another manufacturer with a similar heritage is the Swedish company Husqvarna, also famous for their motorbikes, sewing machines, chainsaws and guns, hence their gunsight logo. In due course Husqvarna would become pioneers of the first hovercraft and robot mowers.

In the early 1900s the Atlas Chain Company – aptly abbreviated to Atco so that the small, catchy name could be conveniently stamped on every chain link and side casing – specialised

▲ The Royal Enfield logo advertised its products as 'made like a gun'.

▼ The Husqvarna lawnmower logo represented a gun sight.

▲ Dennis 24in mower. Precision manufacturers Dennis Brothers of Guildford produced lawnmowers from the 1920s but are probably more famous for making fire engines and refuse wagons. They still make top-quality commercial lawnmowers today, having purchased the tooling and designs from the J.P. Engineering Company, which they have developed and improved.

▲ British Anzani and Hawker Siddeley 18in and 24in models with one or two front drive rollers. These unique ride-on lawnmowers were manufactured in cast aluminium.

▼ 22in Atco Standard and Aerator, 1921, with a powered aerator driven via the cutter shaft and sold as an accessory.

in manufacturing cycle chains and carburettors, an Atco carburettor being used in the first bomber to fly across the Atlantic. This famous company became involved in lawnmower production when the donkey that pulled the mower around the factory's grounds died of overwork. Charles H. Pugh the manager said, 'Is there not another way of cutting the grass without getting another poor horse?' So in 1919 they set about designing the first mass-production lightweight lawnmower featuring an open cast iron chassis. This had a traditional dark green chassis and post-office red cutters and

▶ A 12in Atco Standard of 1921, the first mass-produced petrol lawnmower. It was manufactured by Charles H. Pugh at a breakthrough price of 19 guineas.

▲ 22in Atco Standard and grassbox.

▶ Ladies advertising the new 24in Atco in 1922.

drive gears, powered by a Villiers 98cc propeller-fan-cooled two-stroke engine. Once the hand-crank was turned and the ungoverned throttle opened, the engine would roar into life, taking off with a huge amount of power that made the hairs on the arms stand on end! Since it was most likely the only piece of petrol-powered equipment most gardeners had ever encountered, first-time operators would have found it equivalent to a Ferrari.

It was never in any doubt that Atco intended to change the lawnmower market place. In the past the powered lawnmower had been the unique preserve of the privileged and the wealthy, but Atco set about shaking things up. They made their chassis design light enough to handle easily (175lb – still three times heavier than current models), and small enough to fit on their salesmen's motorbike sidecars. Consequently 1921 saw their first lawnmower, 'The Atco Standard', become an instant success. Consisting of a unique open cast-iron frame, built-in toolbox and crank-handle starter, it was launched at a breakthrough price-tag of just 19 guineas – a lot less expensive than the competition, and affordable to more humble homeowners. They also set up a service network of workshops throughout the country so that lawnmowers could be serviced every winter while they weren't in use, guaranteeing that they'd be ready for the next spring season. Sadly Charles H. Pugh himself never saw his lawnmower built, as he passed away before the first one came off the production line, but his legacy and the Atco brand name live on to this day.

Atco lawnmower production continued to increase rapidly through the 1920s and '30s and the company received four Royal Warrants, from King George VI in 1930 and 1940, Queen Elizabeth II in 1955 and Prince Charles in 1986.

1939 saw the development of a small car designed to change British motoring history. Called the 'Atco Safety Trainer', and based on the company's 1939 lawnmower chassis with the rollers and cutter removed, it was powered by a 98cc Villiers two-stroke engine, boasting a top speed of 10mph and claimed to achieve a 70mpg economy. It was fitted with a drum brake on the back axle,

and a cone clutch with forward, reverse and neutral gears. Starting the engine was via a unique crank-handle located between the seats: by pulling the crank handle upward the engine could be started whilst the driver sat in the driving seat. The three foot-control pedals were arranged with the throttle pedal placed in the centre, the brake on the right and the clutch on the left, typical of many cars during the 1920s and '30s. A dual choke and throttle lever was placed on the steering column, while a handbrake and manual air horn were mounted on the right-hand side.

The inspired idea was for one Atco car eventually to be placed in every school in Great Britain, to assist in educating children about the importance of road safety. Some were even used at Lancashire Police Headquarters. The car came complete with a service manual and was designed so a young person could learn to drive, service, repair, and maintain a vehicle before they were allowed on the road. What a different place the roads would have

been with this type of education and skill! Unfortunately, after making only 200 vehicles production was stopped in 1939 due to the outbreak of World War Two, when the company's attention was diverted to the war effort, including designing the carriage for the famous bouncing bomb and manufacturing a boat engine. Ironically, 56 years later Atco – along with Qualcast, Suffolk and Webb – would be acquired by the German company Bosch. Atco had meanwhile amalgamated with Qualcast (Quality Castings) in 1961. In 2011 the Home Retail Group (Argos/Homebase) licensed the Qualcast brand name, while the Atco and Suffolk brand names went to Global Garden Products. Later the same year Allett UK purchased the Atco, Qualcast and Suffolk machine tooling.

Among those privileged to drive or own an Atco car were some young men who became Grand Prix and Le Mans racing drivers in the 1960s, and today classic car enthusiasts from all over the world seek out these cars, which command thousands of pounds. There's

▲ The original 1939 Atco Safety Training Car, displayed at the British Lawnmower Museum.

▲ Atco Trainer showing its basic 1939 lawnmower chassis at the rear.

▼ Atco car drive transmission layout.

▲ On the Queen's highway the Atco car boasted an economical 70mpg.

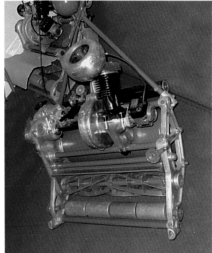

▲ Water-cooled aluminium JP 24in.

even an Atco Car Owners' Club for those lucky enough to own an example, dedicated to keeping this small part of British motoring history alive. (Replicas have been attempted, but they can easily be spotted, as they can't compete with the quality of engineering of the originals.) Atco also produced outboard boat engines in the 1950s, some being advertised in action passing the Statue of Liberty in New York, with a similar example being used in the James Bond film *Moonraker*.

In the early 1900s Jerram and Pearson Precision Engineering of Leicester were making the castings for Rolls-Royce motor cars, and after World War One they were, uniquely, manufacturing lawnmowers in aluminium rather than cast iron. Reputed to be the best and made to the highest engineering standards, their lawnmowers were some of the most expensive in the world and were promoted as the 'Rolls-Royce' of lawnmowers, their engineering so exceptional that their advertisements guaranteed them for 'life'. British engineering at its best. Their drive mechanisms ran in oil, kept dust- and dirt-free in enclosed aluminium (not prone to corrosion) castings. Later models from the 1960s had a cassette cutting system, which, without tools, allowed removal of the cutter in seconds via a thumb-turn knob, for resharpening and servicing. The company eventually ceased production in the 1970s, but similar cutting cassette systems are still being used to this day on domestic petrol and electric machines covered in this book.

Ransome also developed a double-helix cutting cylinder, with blades set in

◀ The Jerram and Pearson 12in and 16in JP Super, circa 1926, advertised as 'The Rolls-Royce of Mowers', and a snip at only one guinea an inch.

▼ The 'New' Ransome Chain Automaton, with double-helix cutter designed to throw grass evenly to the centre of the grassbox circa 1890.

▼ The British Flexa Lawnmower Company originated in Norway in 1947. The machines were subsequently produced in Woking in the UK, and the company was eventually bought by Wilkinson Sword and became Fiscars.

▲ One-wheeled side-wheel mower, uniquely designed to cut virtually right up to a wall. Other models could be fitted with longer handles to mow steep banks, but it would be another hundred years before the next 'bank mower' would come on to the market in the form of the Flymo.

▲ Early 1950s cast aluminium Rotoscythe with rear roller by Shay of Basingstoke.

▶ The Shay Rotoscythe was one of the first rotaries. Note the large wheels that made it easier to tackle undulating ground.

opposing directions designed to allow the grass to be thrown to the centre of the grassbox rather than just to one side. Although the design was costly it provided the best grass collection.

One of the first side-wheel mowers was introduced in the 1860s by Follows and Bate of Manchester. The side-wheel is now the most commonly found hand mower all round the world, being the least expensive way to cut grass because of its minimal use of materials, which makes them lighter and cheaper. Some of the original models cost less than a guinea (21 shillings, £1.05p), and even today a new side-wheel mower can be purchased for around £30, albeit of a lower quality (superior side-wheel machines costiing three to four times as much).

Because of their simple design, side-wheel mowers are more suited to a wider variety of grass than other types, giving them a world-wide appeal, especially in America and in places where grass is sparse. One tip to note, however, is that side-wheels don't cope well with grass border edges – they lose traction if one wheel drops off the edge, and will dig into the turf. (Over the years there have been accessories to tackle this problem, but none have been very successful.) The drive is via simple internal independent ratchet gears in

each wheel, giving it a differential effect when manoeuvred, ensuring that the cutter is always engaged in whatever direction the machine is mowing. An advantage of side-wheel mowers is that their design enables the grassbox to be fitted at the rear of the machine, allowing it to cut closer to flower beds or into corners. Many original grassboxes were made of wood (which woodworm loved) and tin, with cast-iron handles. Some were fitted instead with a canvas bag. Side-wheel mower grassboxes were often sold as an optional extra.

None of the above lawnmowers should be confused with the rotary grasscutter, which didn't start to become popular on the British domestic market until the 1960s. Although the rotary had first appeared in small numbers in the 1930s, vertical crankshaft engine technology wasn't yet developed, as it requires about three times more power to turn a rotary blade than a cylinder blade. Consequently early rotary mowers were only purchased for rough, overgrown or meadow areas where lawnmowers weren't suitable.

One of the very first rotary mowers was built by Shay of Basingstoke. Called the 'Autoscythe', it consisted of a strong, non-rusting aluminium chassis, with slick rubber tyres fitted on large, 9in diameter front-wheel rims, and a steel rear roller that was covered over with a heavy steel grassbox. It was powered by Shay's own two-stroke engine with a 16:1 ratio of

'petroil' mixture. Engine starting was accomplished by repeatedly wrapping a 36in-long rope with round wooden hand-pull knob around an aluminium pulley, bolted to the top of the engine flywheel. Three circular 1.5in multi position blades were fitted to the outer rim of a heavy steel circular disc. The unique blades could be adjusted several times to the next sharp radius when the edge became blunt, without the need to resharpen or rebalance. Shay also produced four-wheeled versions distinctively painted in red and yellow, incorporating a cleverly designed handle that doubled as a fuel tank housing the petrol and oil mixture.

Velocette motorbikes also produced quality mowers with their smooth-running twin-cylinder engines. Likewise, Hawker Siddeley – more famous for their aeroplanes – produced unique cast aluminium ride-on mowers with British Anzani. Another early manufacturer was the American company John Deere, whose slogan is 'Nothing Runs like a Deere' and whose machines are identified by their distinctive shade of green and yellow livery. They celebrated half-century of manufacturing lawn and turf equipment in 2013, their first garden tractor, powered by a 7hp engine, having entered the market in 1963. In 1972 they introduced the first electric garden tractor, powered by three car batteries, by 1984 had built a million of them, and in 2013 celebrated their five-

▲ Motorbike manufacturers and land speed record holders Vincent produced this superb and unique mower design in the 1960s. It featured all-aluminium construction, a one-hand wheel micro-set capable of infinitely variable height adjustment and their own Rapier two-stroke engine. The handle, which was bolted directly onto the cylinder head, doubled as the fuel tank and integral toolbox.

▲ One of the original Flymo advert logo used in 1965.

millionth plus their first robot mower. The company commanded a net income of $3.874 billion, with $43.267 billion of assets, and had 55,700 employees.

In 1964 Karl Dahlman travelled to a Brussels inventors' fair destined to make a fortune with a new lawnmower based on the hovercraft concept of Sir Christopher Cockrell (who, sadly, died penniless). His basic design consisted of an engine fitted on top of a bin lid. His Hovercraft Lawnmower Company was launched the following year, when its 'Flymo' product met with almost instant success, becoming one of the most famous garden machine names on the planet. Since just about everybody later aspired to own a Flymo, .you could say 'and the rest is history' – except that initially it wasn't plain sailing for the Hovercraft Lawnmower Company. Just as Edwin Budding found 135 years earlier, people were unexpectedly wary of the strange new contraption, and were reluctant to purchase it. It didn't look like a mower, and it was the first mower to be made of plastic, deemed a very flimsy material in the 1960s (the fact it was actually stronger than a police riot shield seemed to be beside the point).

So Flymo initiated several marketing strategies. Firstly they surveyed thousands of women, and asked the question: 'Given a choice, what colour would you like your lawnmower?' The overwhelming answer was orange,

which is still the prominent colour today. They then hired many company representatives, issued each one with a Flymo and instructed them to go knocking on doors, speak to the lady of the house and say, 'Would you like to have a go with a nice light mower?' – a very brave approach, especially when mowing was still very much the man's domain. But the strategy worked, and the product's brand name has now become synonymous with mowers, with many people saying they have a 'Flymo'

when they actually have another type or brand of lawnmower, in much the same way as they say 'Hoover' when they mean a vacuum cleaner.

We suspect that the robot mower may go through similar problems to those that Flymo experienced in 1965, and that Edwin Budding had experienced almost 200 years ago in 1830: the robot doesn't look like a mower, it doesn't make a mower noise (well, it hardly makes any noise at all). Who'd want one of these strange new contraptions? Nevertheless, perhaps before long everyone will aspire to own a robot hovering laser mower. Time will tell!

▼ The first Hovercraft petrol mower manufactured by Flymo in 1964 was constructed of glass fibre with a metal fuel tank and twin exhaust silencers.

▼ Rare dark blue 1960s electric E38 Flymo featuring geared-up pinion and drive gear to the blade.

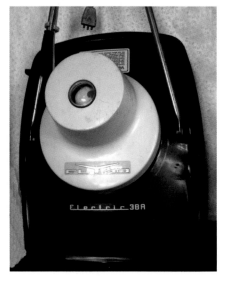

Chapter 2

Choosing and buying lawnmowers and lawn-care equipment

Garden and lawn sizes are measured and compared to the area of a full-size tennis court, which is 543m^2 (650yd^2 or 5,850ft^2). That's 78ft long – slightly longer than a cricket square or slightly shorter than a blue whale – and 31.5ft wide. A small lawn would equate to about half a tennis court, a medium lawn up to a tennis court and a large lawn would be one to two tennis courts. References to right hand and left hand are all viewed from the position of operating the machine. All references hereafter to 'lawnmowers' equate to cylinder machines; references to 'mowers' equate to rotary machines or grasscutters.

Mowers are different to other household products. They can and often are easily abused and neglected. Even the most house-proud of us think of it as 'that dirty, rusty old thing that lives outside under a plastic sheet or in the shed'. They're borrowed by neighbours to cut overgrown jungles wherein lurk hidden bits of rockeries, dogs' bones, tree roots, children's toys and the odd

forgotten tent peg. The same neighbour wouldn't ask to borrow your TV or fridge when theirs broke, but if they did you can be sure they wouldn't dare to abuse it like they would your lawnmower.

Nowadays it's worth considering saying to yourself, before you purchase a mower, 'Can I afford to buy cheap?' This option may well work out more costly in the long run, through premature repairs and replacement, plus the extra work and time it may entail during use. A term not often heard nowadays is, 'Buy a good quality one and it'll last!' But it's becoming especially pertinent today when purchasing products via the Internet

without spares or a service warranty backup. It may be worth mentioning the Greens Silens Messor lawnmower again, famous for the company never changing its design for 70 years. It cost £1 15s to buy – very expensive at the time – but they made their lawnmowers so perfectly that they lasted more than a lifetime, so that over 50 years their price equated to less than 9d (4p) a year. Compare that to replacing some modern machines every five or six years! Unlike, say, a camera or computer, where constant advances in technology mean models changing several times a year, the basic lawnmower design has remained virtually unchanged since the day it was invented.

◀ **24in Allett Ride-on, ideal for the larger lawn and for a perfect traditional finish. It has an articulated seat for tight cornering.**

▶ **17in Kensington cylinder petrol lawnmower.**

CHOOSING A MOWER

The bright and glossy new mowers in the dealer's showrooms make an impressive but confusing sight. Choosing the one most suited to your needs is based, however, on very logical considerations.

Advances in the design of lawnmowers using rotary (ie horizontal cutter blade) action mean that these designs have overtaken the traditional cylinder mower in the market. The great majority of mower sales are now of the rotary type due to the added versatility that they offer.

CYLINDER MOWERS

Cylinder mowers cut grass by a scissor technique. A rotating cylinder with five or more spiral-set blades cuts the grass against a cutter bar. A fine finish results and the heavy rear roller both levels the ground and applies a 'striped' appearance to the grass as the grass stems lie in opposing directions. The drivetrain for the cutting cylinder and drivetrain for the heavy rear roller is complex, and generally the whole unit will be extremely sturdy. The lawn best suited to a cylinder mower will be flat and without any steep inclines. Cylinder mowers are prone to damage of the cylinder and cutter bar by small stones or even cricket boot studs, and professional help will be needed to regrind the cutting bar and cylinder blades.

Perhaps the greatest disadvantages of a cylinder mower are its inability to cut long grass, and inevitable clogging when cutting wet grass. For those of us with the time to cut the lawn twice a week, or at least every five days, a cylinder mower certainly gives the finest results.

Cylinder mowers are available with different numbers of blades on the cylinder, from 5 to 12, giving from 52 cuts per metre up to 146 cuts per metre. For domestic use, cutting widths range from 30cm to 60cm, at an average speed of between 2 and 4mph. The narrowest cut width would suit an area half the size of a tennis court while the widest will cope comfortably with three times this area.

An innovation on cylinder mowers is a cassette system, enabling the cutter cylinder to be exchanged with a scarifier, the latter being used to remove matted, dead grass as well as moss and other weeds. A further feature to look for is a cylinder disengagement facility that enables just the rear roller to be driven, while the blades aren't engaged.

ROTARY LAWNMOWERS

The cutting action of a rotary lawnmower is by a rotating cutter blade set at right angles to the vertical axis of the engine. There are three basic types.

Hover mowers need no wheels, as they're supported on a cushion of air created by the spinning impeller. Petrol-powered hover mowers are all of the mulching type, ie the grass isn't collected. Cutting widths range from 38 to 50cm and cutting heights range from 10 to 34mm.

Wheeled rotary lawnmowers are either of the 'push' or 'self-propelled' kind. For the smaller garden, or where there are few slopes, the lower price of a push mower should be considered. Where there are slopes or rougher areas of the garden, and if cutting may involve long or wet grass, a self-propelled mower would be preferable. Wheeled rotary mowers have a wheel at each corner and the cutting width is approximately the same as the track width. If a garden includes flower beds, the wheels may drop over the grass verge and the edges will end up scalped. In this case, a better choice might be a rotary mower with a rear roller.

Rear roller type rotary lawnmowers have two important advantages. They overcome the problem of scalping the lawn edges and they also provide the 'striped' appearance that was once the province of the cylinder mower.

Features to look out for on rotary mowers are:

- Simple height-of-cut adjustment.
- Simple removal of the grass collection bag or box.
- Easy switching between collection, mulching and side discharge.
- Disengagable cutter drive.
- Disengagable traction drive.

Rotary versus cylinder mowers: advantages and disadvantages

Rotary
- Relatively few moving parts, hence cheaper for given width of cut.
- Engine must operate near full throttle, hence greater wear, more noise (especially blade noise) and greater fuel consumption.
- Cutters are cheap to replace and easy to sharpen and maintain.
- Will cut longer, wetter, rougher grass than cylinder mower.
- Perform better than cylinder mowers on inclines, subject to any lubrication limitations.
- Cutting height easily adjusted.
- Can be used to clean up autumn leaves and debris.
- Stones and hard objects do less damage to cutters, which are more easily repaired.
- Out-of-balance cutter causes serious engine damage.
- Noisy.

Cylinder
- Complicated drive arrangements, hence greater expense.
- Engine can operate at any speed desired and the mower still cuts. Smaller engine can cope with given width of cut.
- Cutter system more complicated, adjustment much more critical, maintenance of cutting edges needs professional attention. Properly adjusted they have a longer life than rotary cutters.
- Will cut to a better finish, but will only cope with much shorter grass than rotary mowers.
- May be fitted with scarifier cartridge in place of cutter cylinder (models from Allett, Atco, Qualcast).
- Not good on slopes due to roller skidding, higher risk of tipping over.
- Cutting height adjustment on Allett, Kensington, and the classic Atco Commodore, have easy knob-type adjuster.
- Stones, etc trapped between cylinder and stationary blade easily ruin cutter system. Regrinding is professional job.
- More all-round maintenance because of chains and drives.
- Quiet.

HINTS AND TIPS ON PURCHASING A USED MOWER

All sorts of second-hand lawnmowers and grasscutters are available everywhere, from the local garden machinery specialist to the boot fair and the Internet. Many of these will be bargains and quite usable, costing a fraction of the price of a new one. Used machines from garden machinery dealers would normally come with a warranty and service backup unless they specify otherwise, just like buying a second-hand car from a dealership. Private sales can be more 'Buyer Beware', so there are a few basic things to look out for. Checking these will only take a minute, but can save you time and loads of money.

PETROL ROTARY MOWERS

■ Before starting the engine, check the condition of the oil. It should be up to the 'full' level, and shouldn't be jet-black muddy or watery consistency. Put some of the engine oil on your finger – it should be almost clear. If it isn't, be wary, since this means the oil hasn't been changed regularly, or the machine may have been overworked. If the oil level is low, there's a good chance overheating may have taken place. Check the oil doesn't have a streaky silvery metallic colour; this could mean internal metal parts are worn. Ask what oil has been used – the engine manufacturer's oil will last the longest. Virtually all Briggs & Stratton, Suffolk, Qualcast and Villiers engines should only use straight SAE30 grade oil; this grade is very heat efficient. Mountfield and Honda use a multigrade. Most modern domestic mower engines' oil capacity is one pint (0.6 litre). Some older four-stroke lawnmower engine sumps only hold half a pint when full, including Suffolk cast iron 75cc and 98cc engines, Qualcast 98cc and 114cc aluminium engines, and Villiers 50cc and 75cc engines. If the oil is low in these types of engine lubrication may have been seriously compromised; the engine will have had premature wear and will consequently have a much shorter life, however new it may look. This may also be coupled with bad starting, low power and dark smoke.

■ Remove the spark plug lead, tip the mower backward with the handle downward, and take a look underneath at the rotary blade. Check if the blade tips are damaged, chipped or blunt. Check if the blade is bent. The blade tips should be at the same height from the deck on each side. CAUTION – tipping a mower engine the wrong way can have an adverse effect. Check that the engine is cool and the fuel tank is less than half full. If unsure of the correct direction, tip with the spark plug facing uppermost. On many modern rotaries this is when the handles are tipped downward.

■ Check that the engine starts easily.

■ Check if the engine emits smoke.

■ Check if there's black carbon discolouration on the chassis around the exhaust area.

■ Check if the machine vibrates excessively.

■ Check that the drive wheels or rollers run smoothly, with and without the engine running.

■ Check the chassis for corrosion or cracks, especially fatigue cracks where the handles join the chassis; this indicates the machine has been run with excessive vibration. If there are indentations in the deck pointing outwards, this indicates the blade has impacted objects. (Cracks in aluminium chassis may be uneconomical to repair.)

■ Check all the control cables aren't kinked. (Some control cables come complete with levers as an assembly, which can be a costly unit if replacement is required.)

■ If there's no tread on the tyres it's done a lot of miles.

NOTE: *Be cautious when tipping cylinder lawnmowers, since there can be exceptions to the guidelines set out above; especially on post-2008 Balmoral, Kensington, Suffolk Punch, Qualcast and Webb machines fitted with the Kawasaki sloping cylinder engine. So check the spark plug position. Before tipping, pull the recoil slowly till the rope meets resistance; in this position both the inlet and exhaust valves are in the closed position, minimising oil ingress into the cylinder head, air filter, carburettor and silencer.*

▲ **Tipping a rotary. If you're unsure which direction to tip a rotary for inspection underneath, remove the spark plug lead. Check that the engine is cool, the fuel tank is less than half-full and the spark plug is facing upwards. On many modern rotaries this is when the handles are tipped downwards.**

CYLINDER LAWNMOWERS

■ Regarding oil, see the section on petrol rotary lawnmowers (left).

■ Firmly grip the top blade of the cutting cylinder at one end and rock it up and down by pulling and pushing. Turn the cylinder 90° and rock again. Then repeat the procedure on the other end. If you detect any slight movement, play or sound, this may indicate that the cylinder bearings or cutter shaft are worn, only remedied by removing the cylinder and replacing the bearings or a costly new cutting cylinder. If there's any play it won't cut correctly.

■ Turn the cutter slowly and check each cutter blade edge carefully for damage or wear. Check how much 'meat' is left on the cutter (by 'meat' I mean the distance between the edge of the blade and the central spiders).

■ Check the bottom blade for straightness.

■ Check if there's any play in the rear roller shaft by slightly lifting the handles up and down.

■ Check the machine pushes smoothly forward and backward without the engine running. Any grinding noise could be from worn rear roller gears.

■ Test the clutch by running the engine, engaging the drive and momentarily holding the handles back. If the

▲ **Test the cutter bearings on a cylinder lawnmower by firmly pulling and pushing the cutter up and down.**

roller doesn't have positive drive and stalls or slips, adjustment or clutch attention may be required.

■ Check for any excessive noise, or vibration from the handles.

■ Once the engine has started, listen carefully for any knocking-type sounds, especially noticeable when the engine revs are quickly increased from tick-over. Several things could cause this type of noise. Check very carefully if the knocking sound comes directly from inside the engine (the sound often disappears once the engine isn't under load), as the knocking noise can come from outside the engine. If you're

convinced the noise comes from directly inside the engine be wary, as this could mean the crankshaft, con rod or big end could be worn, meaning the engine may only have a short life remaining, and will be guaranteed to require major parts and repair in the near future.

TRACTORS

■ Before starting the engine, check the condition of the oil. It should be up to the 'full' level, and preferably not of a jet-black muddy or watery consistency. Put some of the engine oil on your finger – it should be almost clear. If it isn't, be wary, since this means the oil hasn't been changed regularly, or the machine may have been overworked. If the oil level is low as well, there's a good chance overheating may have taken place. Ask what oil has been used – the engine manufacturer's oil will give the longest running hours.

■ Ask if there's a dealer's service history.

■ Steering: Check the free play in the steering wheel. Steering column gears can be costly and awkward to replace. Check there isn't excessive play in the track rod ends. The steering on most domestic garden tractors, even from new, isn't the same precise quality as a car, so always expect a certain amount of play.

■ Tyres: Check the sidewalls aren't cracked. Garden tractor tyres can be costly to replace (£30+).

■ Manual gears: Test each gear individually, including reverse. A replacement gearbox for a used tractor can often be an uneconomical repair (£400+).

■ Hydrostatic gears: Check forward and reverse drive under load (a slope is ideal). A replacement hydrostatic gearbox for a used tractor can often be an uneconomical repair (£400+).

■ Rear-axle: Check if there's up and down play on the rear wheel axles. (This test can only be carried out if the rear wheels are off the ground.)

■ Serial numbers: Check the serial numbers normally situated under the seat or bonnet. If there are no serial numbers there's normally a reason – possibly it's been nicked. (Ordering spare tractor parts without a serial number can be easier said than done.)

■ Starting: The engine should fire up quickly, without smoking or making any knocking or clanking sound, especially as it revs or when it's under load.

■ Check the cutter drive under load, cutting grass.

■ Check the cutter and drive belts for cracks and wear, as some can be costly to replace.

▼ **Rear-wheel steering gear on a Husqvarna front-deck Rider.**

▼ **Testing the rear drive axles for shaft wear on a domestic garden tractor. Jack up the wheel and pull the wheel up and down. If excessive play is present the axle shaft or gearbox housing may be worn.**

A CROSS-SECTION OF POPULAR MODERN LAWNMOWERS AND GRASSCUTTERS

▲ 1960 ten-blade Ransome Certese, made in 14in and 16in widths. One of the best hand-push lawnmowers ever made, with all-aluminium chassis and gear drive. It is favoured by top golf putting greens throughout the world.

▲ AL-KO 380HM Side-wheel, made in 10in and 15in contactless cylinder cutting widths.

▼ Promotional AL-KO image for their latest rotary mower.

▲ Hayter Envoy 14in with rear roller, electric induction motor, plastic deck and chassis.

▼ Aerodynamics of air and grass flow collection on AL-KO rotary.

▼ Countax C600H 50in V-twin cylinder ride-on tractor.

▶ Husqvarna front-deck ride-on with rear-wheel steering.

▼ John Deere E5 robot.

Chapter 3

The lawncare calendar and using a mower

LAWNS, GRASS AND TURF

Is there a difference between 'grass' and 'turf'? Yes. Turf is the surface layer of grass and its root system, commonly supplied in narrow carpet-like rolls for that fast-track instant lawn; it's also the term used to describe a horse racetrack. Grass, however, is often taken for granted.

◀▼▶ **Direction of mowing with a petrol, cordless or hand-push mower. First cut around the outside perimeter, then in parallel lines for a traditional pattern. Experiment with diagonal cutting, which can be quite eye-catching when viewed from different angles. Try circles, which can be novel if sufficient space allows (it's a myth that you need an area the size of an American prairie or a football ground to achieve this). It's also beneficial to mow in a different direction on each cut.**

It's nevertheless one of Nature's most remarkable and versatile plants. This hardy and amazing family of tall, narrow plants with jointed stems can be grown as pasture or as a lawn simply by preparing the ground and sowing grass seed. A few weeks later you'll be rewarded with an expanse of Nature's carpet.

The lawn's finish will be determined by the type of grass, which is a whole subject by itself. Whatever type of

lawnmower you have, the type of grass will seriously affect the finish, as the wrong type of grass won't provide the finish required for your needs, and your mower will end up taking the blame. So if you know a bit about the mechanics of grass, and how to make it flourish, it makes it easier to understand why a problem occurs and how to cure it.

Grass is one of the wonders of Nature. It can look and feel as soft as a velvet

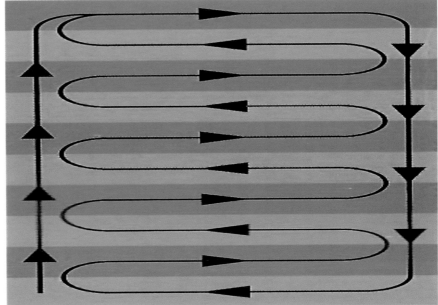

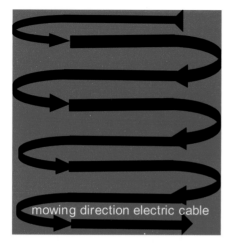

mowing direction electric cable

▲ **Direction of mowing with an electric. This configuration is especially handy if used by a mains-powered machine with a trailing cable.**

carpet, and we are privileged that Mother Nature has given us such an amazing plant. It can survive being churned up by cars, bikes, animals and children. It can be stomped on by thousands of people at a rock concert, and yet look as pristine as a sports pitch when 22 studded footballers play on it the next day.

However, if you want a perfect bowling green finish to your grass then it's no good starting with a ploughed field; conversely, if you want a football pitch for the kids to play on it's pointless trying to match the pristine turf of Wimbledon's Centre Court, which is looked after daily by a dozen groundsmen and only stepped on for tournaments. Either way, if you're happy with your lawnmower but not satisfied with the finish of your lawn, it's worth having a look at the type of grass you have.

MONTHLY MOWING CALENDAR

Weather conditions can change and vary enormously – in the UK a record temperature of -12°C was recorded in April 2013 and 20°C on the same date in 2012 – so use the following calendar as a guide only, and don't worry about the month too much. Follow it only when you consider the temperature and weather conditions are dry or warm enough.

JANUARY
Probably the least active month of the year lawn-wise, apart from removing leaves. If the weather is mild and dry the grass can be cut, but ensure the mower height is set above 1in (25mm). Avoid walking on the grass if the ground is frozen or waterlogged. If you don't want to service your machine yourself this is the ideal month to check in your machine for a dealer service. January's the time when they aren't too busy with repairs, and getting your mower serviced this month has the advantage of guaranteeing that it'll be ready for the first cut of the spring season. Often dealers have a winter or early season service discount available, and there's no harm in asking what deals are going this month – you also might get last year's price on a new mower.

FEBRUARY
Rake the grass and aerate the ground by slitting or spiking – hollow tine aerating is the best, as this method removes a plug of soil without compacting the ground around it; however, hollow tine aerators are also the most expensive, and using a manual hollow tine is also the most labour intensive. Aerating encourages grass growth by allowing nutrients, air and water to reach its roots. It also discourages moss. An application of lawn sand also helps encourage grass growth and strength.

MARCH
This is normally when all the fun starts: 11°C is the magic figure when grass will start to grow. March is also when ground conditions are usually suitable for the first cut. Set the mower on a higher cut to only trim the top of the grass. Check for any stones, bones, twigs or objects that may have appeared over the winter, then recheck that your mower is set above 1in (25mm), or browning or yellowing could result. The first warm, sunny weekend of the season is when every dealer will be suddenly inundated with machinery brought in for servicing. So ensure yours is ready to use prior to this, or you could be in for a longer wait than you envisaged.

APRIL
Mow once or twice a week, weather permitting, and if preferred on a slightly lower cut. To prevent grass damage, don't cut more than a third of the grass height in one mow. Reseed any bare patches; apply a lawn fertiliser or moss killer if needed.

MAY
Keep mowing – increase the frequency if desired. The famous mowing proverb 'little and often' is the secret to achieving that perfect groomed swathe. (Ask a top professional greenkeeper how often he mows – he'll usually answer 'At least three times a week.') An application of weed and feed could be applied if you missed out in April.

JUNE
In summer, mowing around twice a week is ideal (three times for the lawnmowerist connoisseur). A quick rake before cutting will keep runners of clover under control. Water as necessary and soak well after the sun has gone down.

JULY
Carry on mowing as in June. As a general rule collect the grass clippings, but if the weather situation is hot and dry and the lawn is free of weeds, the grass can be left on. If so, mulching is by far the

▲ 'The joy of mowing', Allett Kensington.

LAWN TREATMENT

There are many different types of lawn chemicals available on the market, from fertilisers to selective lawn weed killers. Lawn Sand is one of the most popular, but as all lawns are different, because of diverse soil types and climate conditions, we suggest that you consult a reputable garden centre for the right product for your particular turf type. They'll be able to provide helpful advice regarding the application of the right amount of the right product at the right time to meet your specific needs.

Lawn Sand is a tried and trusted remedy for the control of moss (which thrives in the damp British climate). It hardens the grass against disease and encourages finer grasses that green-up the turf. It can be applied from late spring to autumn. Lawn Sand contains iron sulphate, which reduces the ph level in the soil, which helps deter worms from casting. Leave the mower grassbox off for two to three days to allow granules to settle into the turf. In order to ensure that you use chemical applications safely, always read and follow the instructions carefully.

Ideally you should apply Lawn Sand just before it rains – this saves you the job of watering it in, and protects the turf from scorching. Although it can be applied by hand this may not give an even spread, so we recommend you use a lawn spreader, of which there are two main types: the drop spreader and the rotary spreader. These are manufactured with a plastic or stainless steel hopper in various capacity sizes. The drop spreader works via a revolving paddle that turns when the wheels revolve. It drops the chemical directly under the spreader. It's available in 12in to 24in widths and is ideal for precise spreading, especially useful when applying weed killer alongside flower beds or a pond. Rotary spreaders work by dropping the chemical on to a spinning fan, which distributes the granules over an area up to 6ft in diameter. This makes it ideal for larger areas.

When choosing a spreader ensure that it has a variable flow adjustment, so that a variety of chemicals or seeds can be spread at different flow rates. Some models can also be used for spreading salt on paths to melt ice or snow. Lawn chemicals and salt can both be very corrosive to machinery, so always hose off the spreader or mower with water after use.

favourite option, as the mulched grass will preserve about a third of the ground moisture, besides releasing nutrients. Also, the mulching method won't leave any brown or yellow unsightly grass, and reduces mowing time by about a third. Rotary models with aerodynamically designed decks that can collect and/ or mulch via a simple mulch plug, easily fitted in seconds without tools, are a good compromise. A dedicated mulch mower will give a much finer mulch, but will have the disadvantage of being unable to collect – but if used frequently (once or more than once a week) the need to collect grass would be an extremely rare occurrence anyway.

AUGUST

Carry on mowing regularly, water as necessary. If any cracks appear in drought conditions – especially likely in clay-type soil – fill with soil and sharp sand. Precious moisture can be preserved if the grass can be cut slightly longer or mulched.

SEPTEMBER

Start leaving the grass slightly longer and apply an autumn feed. This will allow the grass to thicken and protect the roots from the oncoming winter snow and frost. Traditionally most mower manufacturers renew their prices around September, so if you're looking for a bargain September to December is the best time to buy. A new mower therefore makes a sensible Christmas gift, and will save you the trouble of buying one just a couple of months later amid the spring rush.

OCTOBER

Rake and remove any thatch, aerate the lawn by spiking and apply an autumn fertiliser if you've not already done so the previous month.

NOVEMBER

Remove fallen leaves and any worm casts with a stiff broom. If the grass is wet don't mow, as this will compact the ground, with the adverse effect of poor drainage.

DECEMBER

Time to service the mower – preferably not on the wet or frozen lawn, where the grass can become a black-hole phenomenon of the disappearing screwdriver, nut and bolt, which miraculously rematerialise with a thump during the first cut the next year! In the past virtually all lawnmower dealer service work was done in the winter months, well in advance of the spring, whilst the mowers lay dormant. Nowadays the same work is often left right to the last minute.

LAWNMOWER SAFETY FIRST

Mowers can be dangerous, and accidents do happen – though you're unlikely to be as unlucky as a man in Ohio who shot himself when he mowed over a bullet! Always take all the following precautions:

■ Before using a mower, always read the operation and instruction booklets supplied with the machine.

■ Familiarise yourself with the operating controls, especially the 'Operator Presence Controls'.

■ Never run an engine in an enclosed space.

■ Check the engine oil level each time before starting the engine from cold.

■ Switch off the engine before refilling the petrol tank. Do not refuel indoors.

■ Store petrol in a cool and dry place, away from sparks, open flame or pilot light.

■ Avoid transporting machines with fuel in the tank. Check fuel caps are secure.

■ Do not overfill the fuel tank – allow space for expansion. Wipe up any fuel spillage or let it evaporate.

■ Check fuel pipes and joints for leaks. Empty fuel by running the engine dry.

■ Check which way the machine can be tipped before turning it on its side.

■ Wear trousers and hard shoes when operating any type of mower. Never mow barefoot.

■ Remove stones, objects and all debris from the area before mowing.

■ Do not use a mower with a four-stroke engine on slopes greater than 15°.

■ Never tilt a rotary mower when the engine is running. The body cannot give protection from the rotating blades. The high rotational speed of the cutter blade means that the blade may continues to rotate after the engine is switched off.

■ Never use a rotary mower with a damaged body or guards.

■ If a rotary mower is used without the grass collector, make sure that the grass deflector plate is in the down position to protect the operator from stones, dust and other debris.

■ Remove any build-up of grass, leaves or other combustible material from the silencer/exhaust area.

■ Check whether the silencer has a spark arrestor, especially if you're operating in an area where a fire could be started.

■ For petrol rotary mower under-deck inspection, tilt the front wheels upwards, dropping the handles to the ground. Do not tip the mower sideways, as this can contaminate and flood the air filter. (Check the spark plug is facing upward.)

■ For electric rotary or cylinder lawnmower underside inspection, always remove the mains plug.

■ Use an RCD (mains circuit breaker) on mains electric machines. This protects you against electric shocks.

■ Never use a mains electric mower when the grass is wet or in the rain.

■ Avoid running over the cable. Replace the cable if it is cut or damaged.

■ If a rotary mower starts vibrating or changes normal sound, stop the engine immediately and investigate.

■ Regularly check that the cutter blade bolts and all other nuts and bolts are secure.

■ Before working on any petrol mower, disconnect the spark plug lead and tie it back so that it cannot touch the sparking plug.

■ Always renew complete blade sets on rotary mowers to retain the balance. Use new bolts and fittings.

■ Check for bent, worn or damaged blades.

■ Do not use unbalanced rotary blades.

■ Check that any part of the engine is cool before touching it.

■ Keep feet and hands away from the blades.

■ Never leave a mower unattended with the engine running, especially if children are present.

■ Children can be inquisitive – beware they do not put water or soil in the fuel tank. Keep under lock and key.

MOWING

PREPARING TO MOW

■ Damage to blades should be avoided. On cylinder mowers damaged blades affect the cutting. On rotaries they may affect the balance as well, and cause vibration and engine wear.

■ It's good practice to rake or brush the area before mowing to remove harmful objects such as stones, hard twigs and parts of toys.

■ Grass is best not cut while wet. It won't cut well, and wet grass cuttings and mud are even worse for mowers than dry grass cuttings and earth.

■ Check for loose parts, including the cutter bar fixing bolts and blade fixing bolts on rotaries.

■ If necessary, lightly lubricate the external parts of the clutch and throttle control cables, to ensure free movement.

■ On cylinder mowers, lubricate the bearings of the cutting cylinder and roller. If there's no oiling hole, tilt the mower to get oil to run in.

■ Top up the sump (four-stroke). Remember that oil is essential not only for avoiding undue engine wear, but it also helps cool a hard-working engine.

■ Top up the petrol tank with petrol (four-strokes) or petrol-oil mixture in the recommended proportions (two-strokes).

NOTE: *If it's necessary to turn the mower over, remember to turn off the petrol and remove the tank or empty it. Drain the oil or tip the mower backwards. If the mower is electric start, remove the battery.*

SETTING THE MOWER HEIGHT

Coarse grass is best for wear, fine grass for appearance. Longer grass of about 13–20mm (½–¾in) will better withstand the attacks of feet, children, pets and bicycles. Closer-cut grass of, say, 7–10mm (¼–²/₅in) is better for appearance. Closer cutting is suitable only for dense, close-growing grass, otherwise it will look sparse and lack colour when short, because of too much earth showing.

If your grass is appreciably longer, the general opinion is that it's best to cut it in two goes three to four days apart; the mower gives a better finish if used this way. Also, as a general rule you shouldn't cut more than a third of its length in one go. However, there's an advantage to cutting heavily and cutting short if the grass in an area is getting coarse. Cutting short favours the finer grasses (if present, of course) that don't grow well when shaded by long, broader grasses. It may be worthwhile keeping the area short for a month or so to see if the ratio of fine to coarse improves and gives a more pleasing appearance.

MOWING ANGLES

Rotary mowers will cut grass sticking-up in all directions, whereas cylinder mowers sometimes miss small clumps growing at an awkward angle.

It can pay to use a different pattern at alternate mowings, going crossways and diagonally and finishing up by going over it again in the usual directions and sequence to give a uniform finish. This can deal with the thicker tufts better as well.

Cylinder mowers sometimes miss clumps because the bottom blade needs resetting. Without the 'scissors' action against the blades of the cylinder, clean, uniform and complete cutting cannot take place.

FREQUENCY OF MOWING

It's advisable not to mow too frequently in dry weather. If the box is left off a cylinder mower the cuttings help the dryness by forming a mulch. Remember also that dry weather means dust, and dust means more wear. If you live in a dry area, check the air and fuel filters on your mower more frequently.

At the first spring cut, set the blades high. Later, cut every week while the grass grows, and cut twice a week during the peak growing period if weather permits.

STARTING A MOWER

- If a self-propelled type, ensure clutch is disengaged.
- Set choke (unless automatic). Use carburettor tickler or priming button.
- Set control to start position, or set throttle about one-third open.
- Pull starter.

AFTER MOWING

- Clean grass cuttings and dirt from cooling fins and other parts of engine.
- Rotary mowers: scrub out the under-deck with water and a stiff brush until down to metal.
- Cylinder mowers: brush off all cuttings and dirt. Use a wet brush for the more awkward areas.

Cleaning takes very little time if done after every cutting – the juice from grass and other green-stuff is corrosive, and difficult to remove when left to dry.

END OF SEASON STORAGE

- Turn petrol off and run the engine until it stops, to clear the petrol line.
- Remove, drain and dry out the petrol tank thoroughly. In steel tanks, put in about a tablespoon of light oil, replace the petrol cap and turn the tank in all directions to spread the oil. Empty out the excess and replace the cap. This light coating of oil will discourage rust formation. Trying to use last season's petrol is the cause of many mowers failing to start in the spring!
- Four-strokes: drain the oil sump thoroughly and refill with fresh oil to the normal level.

- Remove the spark plug, pour in one tablespoon of light oil (two-strokes) or engine oil (four-strokes). Use the starter to turn over the engine five or six times to circulate the oil, then replace the spark plug.
- Thoroughly clean the complete mower. Remove all covers and clean out all grass and dirt. Lubricate all external moving parts and turn them to circulate the lubricant thoroughly to help prevent rust.
- Wipe over all metal parts of the mower with an oily rag to reduce rusting.
- Remove or fold the handles and raise the mower off the floor to let air circulate, using bricks or pieces of wood. Choose a spot as dry and well ventilated as possible.
- Cover with an old sheet or similar fabric. Do not use plastic bags or sheets as they cause condensation with changes of temperature.
- Four-strokes: turn the engine so that it's left on compression (both valves closed). Sticking valves cause failure to start in the spring.

If the above all seems rather arduous, remember that a very well-known and long-established mower manufacturer says failure to prepare for storage in the winter will cause more damage to the mower than an entire season's hard use.

HEIGHT OF CUT, THE VITAL STATISTICS

Often neglected or regarded as unimportant, the height of cut of your grass can be critical for a number of reasons. Take a football pitch: if the height of cut is more than 28mm the game is slowed down; if lower than 25mm, the turf can be under pressure and tear, causing players to slip and sustain injury. Without getting too technical, and without the aid of a stimpmeter, if a putting-green surface has more than 3mm the golf ball will have a speed and mind of its own; slightly shorter and your handicap may well be out the window. It's a similar story at the bowling green – ever wondered why the ball keeps going out of play? And at the tennis court too – the Centre Court at Wimbledon is a perfect 8mm, which will suit some professional players more than others who favour a faster or a slower game; it determines how high the ball will bounce, travel or spin. Cricket connoisseurs always comment on the state of the wicket. If the wicket square is spot on, top players can work their magic with a perfect googly. It's a far cry from the era before the invention of the lawnmower, when cricket ground grass was kept short with sheep, especially on the outfield, where the sheep naturally did their little deposits and the players used to slip in it, hence the cricket term 'in the slips'.

Chapter 4

Carburettor, fuel, lubricants and filters

THE CARBURETTOR

The earliest carburettor dates from the 1880s, when Karl Benz (who coincidently started working on lawnmowers as a young engineer) worked on an internal combustion engine intended for a car. But why do we need carburettors? What does this small, ingenious piece of engineering work do? In a nutshell, it mixes petrol and air in an exact and precise ratio. It's designed to start, run and accelerate an engine's speed without hesitation; it stops the engine from stalling under load, lets it idle on tickover and lets it rev to mindboggling speeds (12,000 rpm on chainsaws), whilst at the same time ensuring that it runs smoothly and economically.

When the piston moves down on the induction stroke, air is drawn into

◄ **A selection of air filters, oil filters and manufacturers' basic service kits, ideal to keep the engine economically maintained. When purchasing replacement filters it can be handy to take your old filter to a service dealer so that he can match the shape, as nowadays there are many similar but subtly different shapes.**

the engine combustion chamber, creating a partial vacuum. The volume of air drawn in is determined by the engine speed, normally controlled by the position of the throttle.

On most mower engines, petrol supplied from the fuel tank can either be fed downward by gravity, or sucked upward via a diaphragm. Fuel introduced by gravity is fed into a reservoir called the float chamber. The amount of fuel is constantly regulated by a float and needle valve. The petrol then mixes with air in a narrow-throated passage called the venturi, the principle here being that when air speed increases the pressure drops. When the throttle is opened by a valve called a butterfly, air flows in the narrow part of the venturi as the air speed increases, and petrol is either sucked into the airstream from the float chamber through a fine jet, or pumped via a diaphragm.

Petrol and air have different properties. Petrol remains at the same density whatever the flow rate. However, air becomes less dense the faster the flow. Fuel is mixed by weight, at approximately one part petrol and fifteen parts air. The carburettor constantly regulates

and alters the petrol–air mixture in proportion, preventing the mix becoming so rich that it won't burn in the cylinder, or making the engine run uneconomically.

However, to start an engine from cold a far higher mix of petrol is needed, approximately three parts petrol to one part air. This is simply attained by restricting the airflow by means of a choke (called a 'strangler' in the US). Note that if the choke is controlled manually it's important to turn the choke off as soon as the engine warms (in some cases, depending on the engine, this can be less than a second), otherwise premature engine wear can be caused by neat fuel running down the cylinder bore walls. Many modern mower engines are fitted with an automatic choke, which automatically regulates the fuel mix according to the air temperature via a bi-metal strip or electronics.

The latest mower engines are now much more fuel-efficient, providing cleaner running with far less emissions deposited into the atmosphere. Many have no fuel mix adjustment, since if it could be altered it wouldn't comply with current emissions regulations.

FUEL

If you don't read any other section in this book, read this one!

SOME THINGS YOU DIDN'T KNOW ABOUT PETROL

Fuel varies enormously from petrol station to petrol station, with different companies blending different fuel from all over the world. With current fuel emission standards, petrol from the pump will start to deteriorate after storing for only one month. The benefit of this is less pollution, but the drawback is that fuel now has a very short life. Petrol from the pump has been subtly changing over the years and is now prepared predominantly for cars, which besides having larger jets are less likely to 'gum up', having sophisticated electronic fuel management systems. Many mowers, on the other hand, have smaller jets (finer still on hand-held garden machines such as grass trimmers, chainsaws, hedge trimmers, etc), are often made with 'serious economic restraint' and are regularly designed to the lowest cost. Consequently they require a little more consideration.

Regular 98, 95, 95E5 and E10 unleaded petrol is currently OK in all lawnmowers. E5 and E10 contain 5–10% ethanol. More than 10% ethanol will cause corrosion damage to components in the fuel system, and you'll have no idea why your engine isn't running smoothly or starting properly. Currently the government is discussing raising ethanol content to around this higher percentage, which may cause

problems in the garden machine market. Ethanol content of 5% or more attracts water moisture, and when fuel is stale will turn to a gum-like gel, blocking the jets, which then turns to a white powder that corrodes carburettor parts.

These very common engine problems caused by stale or contaminated fuel can be easily avoided and rectified by following these few simple tips:

Fuel additives

Add fuel stabiliser preservative to your petrol, or use ethanol-free fuel if you're keeping your fuel for more than four weeks. This is especially important in machines not used regularly, such as in generators, cultivators, blo-vacs, garden tractors, ATVs, snow blowers, boat engines, older classic cars and motorbikes etc – and is all the more important when mixing oil in the fuel for two-stroke engines: once oil is mixed with petrol, besides diluting the fuel it can increase deterioration to just a few weeks.

Adding a fuel stabiliser will ensure easier starting. There are now many brands on the market, including Briggs & Stratton Fuel Fit and Honda Pro Fuel Stabiliser. All ensure better starting, cleaner running and less maintenance attention. If stabiliser isn't used during the cutting season, at least add it to the fuel for the last cut of the season so that the carburettor and jets won't 'gum up' over the winter period. With stabiliser currently costing a similar price to one litre of petrol it's extremely cost effective, and more than covers the cost of not having to drain and dispose of any fuel from the mower tank or fuel can.

NOTE: *Fuel stabiliser won't bolster or revive stale fuel, it will only keep it stable at its current octane and condition; so only add it to* fresh *petrol. Some pump fuel may already be a few weeks old before you purchase it.*

Pump fuel, which degrades after six weeks, can gum up the carburettor, blocking the fine jets with a varnish-like substance. In many cases this can only be rectified by immersing the carburettor in an ultrasonic bath.

Fuel containers

Only use an approved fuel container designed specifically to store or carry petrol. Look inside for debris or water. Ensure it's clean and that the cap seals.

Keep petrol in a cool place away from direct sunlight. Ensure the temperature is less than 30°C or 86°F.

Steel fuel containers and tanks can rust and corrode, so check the inside for rust, debris and water. Most pump fuel is stored in underground metal tanks where moisture droplets can accumulate by condensation, which form on the tank sides and contaminate the fuel, especially if it contains ethanol, which naturally attracts moisture. A build-up of dirt in fuel is a common cause of engine problems.

Water contamination of fuel

Have you ever taken your mower to be repaired because the engine wouldn't start, or runs unevenly, and the service agent has said, 'You've got water in the tank, mate'?

This may often be followed by a small

◄ **Fuel Fit 250ml fuel stabiliser for either two- or four-stroke engines. These preservative can extend fuel life by more than 20 times. The latest Briggs & Stratton Fuel Fit 100ml is enough for 10 litres (2 gallons), part number 992380; the 250ml is enough for 25 litres (5 gallons), part number 992381. These will keep fuel stable at the octane level you received it for up to two years.**

▶ **Typical corrosion in a carburettor caused by water in the fuel. Even if this carb is cleaned in an ultrasonic bath it probably won't recover, and most likely it'll need to be replaced.**

◀ As well as maximising engine life, alkylate fuel will make your machine one of the best-starting, least-polluting and cleanest-running, with the least amount of maintenance. It's available in one-, five- and twenty-litre containers, for two-stroke, four-stroke or four-mix engines with or without catalytic converters. It's also suitable for older classic cars, motorbikes and boat engines. Alkylate fuel for two-stroke and four-mix engines is already pre-mixed and it isn't necessary to add any oil or fuel additive.

argument, especially in cases where you've just spent your hard-earned cash on a brand new machine (possibly because your old one had similar symptoms), or you've recently picked it up from a service – in neither of which circumstances will it be covered under a service or a manufacturer's warranty. This can be especially awkward if you purchased your machine via the Internet and it's still within the warranty period, since it will necessitate you having to return it to the original supplier (which will entail removing the fuel and oil, finding a cardboard box, dismantling, repacking and posting) or taking it to the local service agent, and possibly having to rely on the goodwill of the supplier or else be faced with a bill for a carburettor and fuel-system clean. (In some cases, if water has been left in the engine for a longer period, corrosion of aluminium parts can be terminal to carburettors.)

As far as you're concerned you didn't put water in the tank, you've kept it in

a locked shed and you've always used a clean fuel can with a filtered funnel; and the shop, manufacturer or service dealer won't have put water in it either. But the service engineer has seen it all before – numerous times.

If you're still unsure about where water in the fuel came from, read the 'Fuel containers' paragraph (opposite) again. It will help to keep your blood pressure down, and save you pulling the recoil rope over and over till it snaps.

ALKYLATE FUEL

There are already a few countries where petrol from the pump isn't allowed in garden machinery, and 2013 saw this restriction commence in the UK with the introduction of fuel caps embossed with '10% max ethanol' – if pump fuel is used the engine warranty could be void. The remedy is alkylate fuel, which we can all use. It's better for you, the mower and the environment.

A few facts. Alkylate fuel was originally introduced for professional

users decades ago for medical reasons, when people became aware that their headaches and other health problems were being caused by breathing in engines fumes. It's now recognised as the benchmark for protecting users, people nearby and the environment throughout the world. With its years of shelf life without loss of quality, the fire and rescue, marine and military services and zoological gardens found it more reliable for engine-starting than pump fuel – which is especially important in emergency life-or-death situations. It's also the preferred fuel for many racing cars and motorbikes. In the future it may well become the only fuel allowed in small engines, which is already the case in some countries.

Other advantages over petrol from the pump are that alkylate fuel eliminates spark-plug sooting up and hot engine-starting problems, and stops the build-up of carbon deposits on pistons and valves. Engines consequently run smoother and start easier.

▶ Pump petrol fumes have many adverse effects, such as headaches etc, but getting the message across is comparable to the medical profession trying to convince people that smoking cigarettes 'may' be bad for their health!

▼ Aspen plugs.

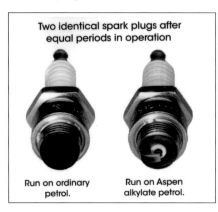

Two identical spark plugs after
equal periods in operation

Run on ordinary
petrol.

Run on Aspen
alkylate petrol.

Although alkylate fuel is more costly, this is compensated by longer engine life, less repair trips to the workshop, smoother running and longer service intervals. It prevents the need to dispose of pump petrol that's gone 'stale'. It saves time in not having to drain fuel from your mower at the end of the season and enables you to store the machine for long periods. It can clean deposits left in the engine by pump petrol (in which situation a short phase of smoking may be noted), and you don't need to purchase or mix oil with fuel for two-stroke engines; this eliminates the risk of mixing an incorrect oil-fuel ratio, which is a lot more important nowadays. (Older two-stroke engines would run without trouble if a drop more oil was mixed in the fuel, albeit it may have smoked more and sooted the spark plug prematurely, but modern two-stroke engines may be damaged if more than the recommended oil-mix is used, caused by the oil residue burning on the cylinder wall. Too little oil in any engine will result in premature wear.)

With reduced fumes and less unburnt fuel mixture from the exhaust, your clothes won't 'smell', especially from older less efficient engines, and particularly whilst using hand-held machines like grass trimmers, chainsaws, blowers, hedge and brush cutters etc, where the exhaust gases are much nearer to the user. Accidental fuel spillage will evaporate, unlike pump fuel. The oil is biodegradable, and even the polyethylene plastic container can be recycled. Once incinerated, carbon dioxide and water are the only substances formed. Plant life will benefit by less ground ozone from reduced carbon monoxide emissions.

Still sceptical? Then try these experiments. (NB: No responsibility is taken by the author or publisher for any adverse problems arising from these experiments, which must only be carried out by a competent person.) (1) Carefully pour a small amount of petrol from your can into a jar and take a sniff. Then go down to your local service dealer and ask for a sniff from his alkylate can. The alkylate has virtually no smell, and is clear like water. The petrol stinks and varies in yellowish hue depending on its quality – the paler, the fresher (like urine). (2) Carefully pour a small amount of petrol into a jar. Carefully pour a small amount of alkylate fuel into another jar. Place a piece of polystyrene in each jar (polystyrene packing chips or similar). The polystyrene in the petrol jar will completely dissolve almost immediately, as it's full of solvents that are harmful if breathed in. The polystyrene in the alkylate jar is unaffected, because alkylate fuel contains virtually no harmful solvents and substances such as sulphur, benzene, lead and aromatics.

Alkylate fuel can also be used in Coleman dual-fuel-type stoves, for fishing and camping, making them far less expensive to run (currently about half the cost).

OILS AND LUBRICANTS

RECOMMENDED OIL GRADES FOR DOMESTIC FOUR-STROKE ENGINES

Capacities and grades may vary, so always check the owners' handbook for your specific engine. Remember, with lawnmowers there can always be exceptions.

Use the manufacturer's recommended oil grade, specifically designed to match the engine's running temperature. Always recheck the oil level after filling and before starting,

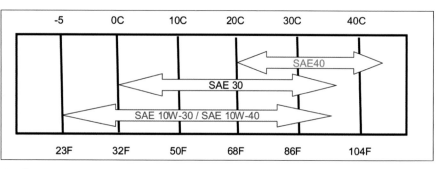

▲ Oil viscosity temperatures chart. Using multigrade oil 5W-20, 10W-30 or 10W-40 will increase oil consumption, so check the level regularly. If overheating occurs additives in multigrade oil and viscosity will deteriorate. With straight 30-grade oil the viscosity can be less affected.

◤▼ A selection of lubricants.

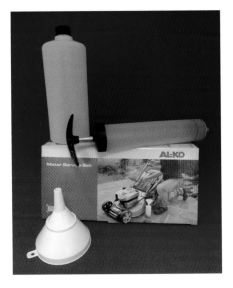

◄ The oil-changing kit by AL-KO removes old oil or fuel without spilling or the need to tip the machine on to its side.

◥ Briggs & Stratton two-litre capacity oil change kit, part number 992423. It siphons oil directly out of the engine sump, without the need to tip the engine. Empty sump oil when the engine is 'warm' – do NOT change oil when the engine is hot.

and top up if necessary. Change the oil every 25 hours of running time. NB: Too much oil or too little oil can damage the engine.

TOP TIP: *Drain the oil when the engine is warm.*

Ever wondered what the 'SAE viscosity rating' on your mower oil means?

Viscosity physics is extremely complex. It's stated in kinematic viscosity (kv) and centistokes (cst), and ideally you need an honours degree in engineering science to understand it. But simply put, viscosity is the oil's flow speed, which is measured by a device called a viscometer. The thicker (higher viscosity) the oil, the slower it will flow; the thinner (lower viscosity) the oil, the faster it will flow.

Many oils are similar, running at a constant temperature such as in water-cooled engines, like cars. However, all domestic mower engines are air cooled, where the engine temperature can vary enormously depending on either a heavy or light workload, a hot or cold day, or summer or winter weather.

Multigrade oils have additives – good on a cold start-up, but will deteriorate if the engine overheats – whereas straight 30-grade oil is all oil and nothing but oil, which stays more constant. Having said this, modern mower oils are a marvel of chemistry.

Other terms that are useful to understand include:

- API: American Petroleum Institute, formed circa 1930.
- SAE: Society of Automotive Engineers.
- SJ/GF: An oil specification introduced in 1996 to meet fuel economy and emissions legislature. This increased performance from 0W-30 to 10W-50, meeting low-temperature operation, high temperature deposits foam control and phosphorus content (for valve protection) requirements.

- SL/GF: Specification introduced in 2001 to improve economy and viscosity retention, while reducing emissions and oil consumption.
- SF/CC: Designed for mono grade oil. Keeps the engine clean, prolongs engine life, combats acids, oxidation and foam. For horticulture and farm equipment.
- W: Winter grade – the oil is tested to lower temperatures, to lubricate on cold engine start-up.

Manufacturer	Oil specification	Sump capacity (0.6 litre =3–6.5hp engines; 1.4 litre = 7–20hp engines)
Aspera	SAE 30 API SF	0.6 litre (1 pint)
Briggs & Stratton	SAE 30 API SF/CC	0.6–1.4 litres
Briggs & Stratton	SAE 30 API SJ/CD	0.6–1.4 litres
Briggs V Twin	SAE 30 API SF/CC	2.0 litres (inc oil filter)
BSA	SAE 30 API SF	0.5–1 pint
GGP	SAE 30 SF CC	0.6–1.4 litres
Honda	10w/30w API/SJ	0.6 litres and upward
Husqvarna	SAE 30 API SG	0.6–1.4 litres
Kawasaki	10w/40w API SG	0.6 litres and upward
Kohler	SAE 30 API SF	1.4 litres and upward
Loncin	10w/30w API SG	0.6 litre (1 pint)
MAG	SAE 30 API SF	0.6 litres and upward
Mountfield	10w/40w API SG/CF	0.6–1.4 litres
Qualcast	SAE 30 API SF	0.5–1 pint
Suffolk	SAE 30 API SF	0.5 pint
Tecumseh	SAE 30 API SF	0.6 litre (1 pint)
Villiers	SAE 30 API SF	0.5–1 pint

NOTE: *Petrol evaporates, oil does not; we therefore recommend not to store two-stroke petrol mixture for long periods, as the mixture ratio may change.*

RECOMMENDED OIL MIXTURES FOR GARDEN EQUIPMENT WITH TWO-STROKE ENGINES

Aspera	25:1	Flymo/Husqvarna oil
Flymo Hover	25:1	Flymo/Husqvarna oil
Tecumseh Hover	25:1	Flymo/Husqvarna oil
Husqvarna	50:1	Husqvarna oil
Echo	50:1	
Kawasaki	50:1	
MacAllister	50:1	
McCulloch	40:1	McCulloch oil
Mittox	50:1	
Mountfield	50:1	Mountfield/GGP oil
Partner	50:1	Husqvarna oil
Ryobi	50:1	Ryobi oil
Stihl	50:1	Stihl oil
Zenoa	50:1	

NB: These are general grades, specifications and capacities; check your owners' handbook, as your engine model may be different. If you don't have a handbook ask your garden machinery dealer for one. There may be a small charge, but it'll be worth it.

WHICH DIRECTION CAN YOU TIP A MOWER?

Ideally remove oil and fuel, then the machine can be tipped. However, for a quick maintenance job here are some tips:

Before tipping a mower for any small job, whether inspecting underneath, checking the blade(s), changing the oil or just cleaning, check which direction it can be tipped. Many engines can be adversely affected if sump oil runs into the carburettor, which can damage the diaphragm and air filter. If a sponge filter is fitted this can be squeezed out and refitted. If a paper filter is fitted, once contaminated with oil just replace it. Oil

▼ **Tipping mower.**

can also fill the cylinder head, creating too much compression and fouling the spark plug, with no chance of start-up without removing and cleaning the plug. In this situation (on vertical crank engines) remove the spark plug, place a rag by the plug hole (to catch the spraying oil), and pull the recoil over and over till no more oil comes out. Clean the plug and refit.

As a general rule, ensure you have little fuel in the tank. Remove the plug cap (which avoids accidental ignition) and tip the machine with the spark plug uppermost. If this isn't practical or feasible, tip the machine with the carburettor uppermost. Avoid tipping with the spark plug or carburettor pointing downward.

NOTE: *Take extreme caution when tipping the machine if hot – fuel can ignite if near hot engine parts, so wait till it's cool. Most mower fuel caps are vented and fuel may drip. If fuel or oil leaks on to grass the consequence will be dead grass and soil on contact, which will take several weeks to recover.*

CHECKING THE OIL LEVEL

Before checking the oil level, clean around the oil cap and dipstick tube to ensure that debris doesn't enter the engine. To get the most accurate reading, ensure that the machine is standing on level ground. Remove the dipstick and wipe with a clean cloth. Screw or push the dipstick back to its normal position. The oil level is only correct when it's at the full mark on the dipstick. In cases where there's no dipstick, the oil level should be flush with the top of the filler tube. Ensure the engine sump isn't overfilled with oil, as this can be detrimental to the engine's running, by too much pressure forcing oil to pass through seals, gaskets and piston rings.

CAUTION: Hot oil and engine components can cause severe burns. Allow the engine temperature to drop from hot to a warm level, before draining or handling the oil.
CAUTION: Engine oil is a toxic substance and must be disposed of properly. Do not put oil down the grid, a drain or in the bin. Contact your local council or authority for guidance on recycling or disposal.

FILTERS

AIR FILTERS

The air filter is the quickest and easiest service part to change or clean on your mower. Although often neglected, it allows the correct amount of clean air through the carburettor to the engine. Many modern engine air filters can be changed in seconds with a screwdriver or even without tools. The smooth running of the engine and power depend on the filter being in good condition. Debris, clogged dust or damage will alter the air intake, which in turn will alter the engine's performance.

Check, change or clean the filter after at least every 25 hours of running – this is the average amount of time that a mower is normally used in one year. If it takes, say, four or five hours or more to cut your lawn every week, in effect your machine is doing the equivalent of one year's work every five to six weeks. In these cases change the oil and filter more often – or, we'd suggest – change the machine for a larger one. Check more often if the machine has been worked scarifying, aerating or in dry dusty conditions. Paper-type filters are made to an exact micron specification, letting in air but not dust. Never apply

▼ **Cleaning foam filter. We suggest you invest in plastic gloves for this job. A handy tip is to carry out the procedure with the foam element in a thin plastic freezer bag; this will remove the oil evenly without the mess.**

▲ These designs of filter aren't fitted to any of the mowers in this manual, but may be encountered.

▲ The air passing through a labyrinth, found on two-stroke hover mowers...

▲ ...and a domed section. The technique is pre-filtering, and a turbo action is imparted to the air, which throws dirt aside before the air is allowed to enter the carburettor.

▲ The second one has an oil bath; the correct level of oil is marked in the container...

▲ ...into which a metal or plastic stocking fits, the whole sealed off with a lid.

a liquid cleaner or an air blast to paper elements. However, paper filter elements can be tapped to remove large bits of garden debris and should be white and clean; if they're grey, grubby or dusty looking don't hesitate to change and replace them.

There are a few different air filter types. In many budget and older engines the commonest type is oiled polyurethane foam. The block of foam plastic should be cleaned in petrol (or alkylate fuel, with no smell), squeezed

dry, a tablespoon of engine oil placed over one face, and then gently squeezed to work the oil through it (place the filter in a thin polythene bag to avoid mess). Never run an engine with a foam filter that isn't oiled: one calculation shows that when oiled, its efficiency collecting particles is about 95%; without oil it's a meagre 25%. A similar type, especially in older engines, uses oiled aluminium foil.

In the case of mowers fitted with a snorkel filter on the handle, a good guide to the efficiency of the air filter is

whether there's dust in the tube. If there is, clean the pipe with a pressure washer and fit a new filter element – the old one is useless.

FUEL FILTERS

One of the commonest filters is a simple wire or plastic gauze, fitted in the petrol tap or the petrol line. Clean by washing in clean petrol; don't try to brush it, as it can easily be damaged. Larger mowers sometimes have an inline petrol filter with a paper type or replaceable element. They're inexpensive and can be replaced easily when necessary.

Inline-type filters must be fitted the correct way round; an arrow will indicate the direction of fuel flow. When refitting a used filter, double-check the direction, as an incorrect fitment would allow trapped sediment to pass to the carburettor.

Tapered filters (usually in sintered metal) should have the point of the taper towards the fuel flow – this presents the maximum surface area.

▼ When fitting an inline filter, always check that it's fitted the correct way round. Most have an arrow denoting direction of flow.

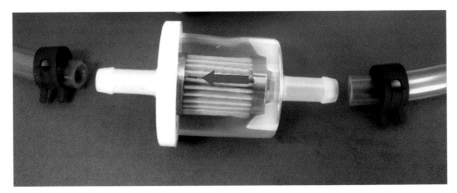

▼ Tank filters are often used in hand-held machinery where space is paramount, such as in grasscutters, hedge trimmers and chainsaws.

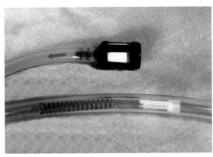

Chapter 5

Cylinder lawnmowers

Why use a cylinder lawnmower? Where are they used and who uses them?

There's something very spellbinding about the rhythmic sound of a cylinder lawnmower that makes it more enjoyable than a grass-cutting rotary. It's very much like a cherished classic car. The sound makes us smile, and evokes a certain atmosphere and emotion that's quintessentially very British and something to be proud of. Whether it's watching the hypnotic flow of the individual cut blades streaming into the grassbox, or listening to its unique sword-crossing sound as the blades physically cut the grass, something about the entire process feels *right*. Why? You'd have to ask the head

◤ **Landscape with mower.**

▶ **Practice green.**

◀ **A 1949 five-blade, iron chassis, 12in Qualcast Panther. The Panther was possibly the most popular lawnmower in the UK from the 1920s to the 1960s. This particular machine was owned by Jean Alexander, famous actress in *Last of the Summer Wine* and *Coronation Street*.**

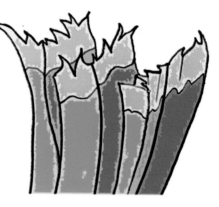

▲▶ The effect of cylinder and rotary cuts respectively on blades of grass.

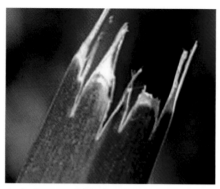

▲ A damaged blade of grass.

groundsmen and gardeners of the hallowed turfs of Wembley, Wimbledon, Lord's Cricket Ground, Buckingham Palace, Old Trafford, top football clubs, Royal golf courses, putting and bowling greens, the pristine lawns of the gentry in their stately residences, and, of course, the millions of budding lawn and garden enthusiasts throughout the world who want a perfect sward.

In a recent survey 21 out of 100 lawnmower purchasers considered the quality of cut to be the most important reason for preferring a cylinder mower. The secret of a good cut is twofold: the cylinder cutter's sharpness and the setting (or the keenness) of the cut – without either, the finish will be greatly compromised. But once the cylinder

principle is understood, both can be achieved with only a few seconds' adjustment to the mower.

When purchasing a new cylinder lawnmower, or when collecting or receiving delivery of your machine after a service, it's important to ask the specialist to demonstrate the machine, showing you how to set the cutter and how to adjust the height of cut – ideally on the lawn, where you can see the difference in cut, and they can advise you and adjust your machine to the best setting for your particular grass conditions.

The cylinder lawnmower is capable of giving the best finish by far of all grasscutters, and is unequalled in this sector compared to other grass-cutting machines available today. It's the only

machine that will give a perfect sward, and is often the single major factor in transforming a patch of grass into a lawn. Among the reasons for this phenomenon are:

- The front and rear rollers run close to the point at which the grass is cut, which allows very low heights of cut to be achieved accurately, without scalping the lawn surface.
- The rollers apply even downward pressure as the mower moves across the lawn surface, creating crisp light and dark stripes whilst minimising soil compaction, without wheel marks.
- The full-width rollers allow the cutter to overhang the lawn edge even where the lawn is landscaped in a contoured design, without gouging out chunks of turf or dropping off the edge.
- Cylinder lawnmowers always cut in one direction, throwing the grass directly into an open box where the clippings can be constantly checked visually, unlike rotary grasscutters, which cut in all directions and have an enclosed rear grassbox or grassbag.
- The cylinder cuts like scissors, giving a clean, straight cut without bruising the grass tips, and thus giving a greener sward. This provides the added benefit of a quicker recovery time, whereas the cut of a rotary grasscutter is more like a scythe or a machete, thrashing and bruising the grass, which can turn the grass tips brown after a few days.

The cylinder's crisp, clean cut is perhaps the single main reason why this 180-year-old tried and tested design has virtually not changed to this day,

▼ The 'cuts per yard' factor is the number of times the cylinder blades contact the fixed blade while the mower travels forward one yard. This factor controls the fineness of the cut – the more blades the cylinder has, the finer and smoother the finish will be, as demonstrated in this picture. A basic four- or five-blade cylinder cutter will give 30–40 cuts per yard. This equals one cut per inch, which may leave the lawn with an unattractive ribbing (ladder) effect. A six-blade cylinder will give 60–100 cuts, eight–ten blades will give 80–120 cuts per yard and a twelve-blade cutter will give 150 cuts per yard, ideal for a bowling/putting green finish. There are three ways of achieving more cuts per yard: (a) with more blades, (b) with more revolutions per foot, and (c) by a combination of the two, which will give the maximum number of cuts.

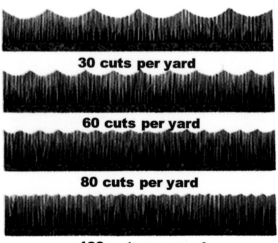

30 cuts per yard

60 cuts per yard

80 cuts per yard

100 cuts per yard

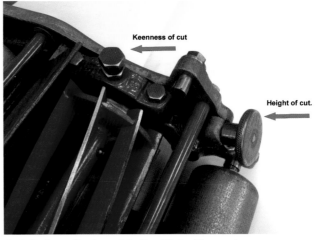

▲ Cylinder adjustment screw for altering the keenness of cut. These screws raise or lower the cylinder on to the bottom blade.

▲ Cylinder adjustment bolt with locking nut.

and why it's still the preferred machine throughout the world for cutting the most prestigious of lawns, capable of giving the traditional striped, low-cut, groomed finish for which all lawn and garden professionals strive.

The roller is the mechanism responsible for those spectacular shapes and patterns, whether circular, diamond, chequered or striped, which are envied all over the world, and are found on such famous grounds as Old Trafford, Anfield, Lord's, Wembley Stadium, Wimbledon and Buckingham Palace. It's no surprise that the dying wish of some people is to have their ashes scattered over such beautiful surfaces.

If the cylinder cutter is sharp but isn't adjusted correctly, or the blades are blunt, some of the grass stems will be left uncut, and you have to go over the lawn twice in consequence. The 'cutter set' is the single main reason for a poor cut on a cylinder lawnmower, leaving the grass with an effect called 'laddering' as a result of giving less cuts per yard. The laddering effect is caused by either (a) the cylinder cutters not touching the bottom blade, which is called 'off-set', or (b) only some of the cylinder cutters touching the bottom blade. This means the cylinder is eccentric and 'not true'. This in turn is caused by either faulty or worn cutter bearing(s), or by one or more of the cylinder blades being bent after having caught on an object. The cutter shaft (normally on the drive side) can bend by impact damage. In all these cases a

▼ Testing the cutter setting with paper. The paper is carefully fed into the cylinder to check that it cuts right along the length of the bottom blade. In the mid-1850s Ransome said they tested the cutter setting to 'the thickness of a gentleman's business card'. Today we'd test it to the thickness of the page you're reading.

▼ Height of cut adjustment is altered by moving the front roller(s) up or down via an elongated slot on the front roller bracket, often adjusted and fixed without tools by a hand wheel. Model shown is a Qualcast Superlight Panther.

▼ Height of cut adjustment and keenness adjustment on Webb Witch, Wasp and Whippet hand mowers. These models have a nut on an eccentric cam to adjust the cutter up or down. On some cylinder lawnmowers the cutter stays stationary and the bottom blade moves up or down.

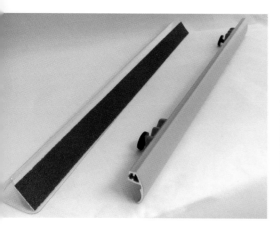

◀▲ **Cylinder sharpener by Multi-Sharp, consisting of an abrasive strip and clamp.**

▲ **A Multi-sharpener *in situ*. Adjust the cylinder as you would for the keenness of cut. Similar inexpensive clip-on sharpeners are available from ALM. These devices can easily be fitted to electric, petrol, cordless and hand lawnmowers without the need of tools; they can achieve a sharp edge without the need of a lathe. Suitable for 8in to 20in cutter widths.**

regrind would be the best solution to remedy the fault.

The other main setting fault is when the cutter is set 'too hard on'. This causes several problems, the principal of which are (a) the friction of the cylinder blades heating up on the bottom blade, which causes premature wear, and (b) considerable strain is conveyed to the drive, transmission gears, chains, belts and engine or motor, creating a noise that will drive you insane. Take extra care on setting the cutter on electric cylinder mowers, as a 'too hard on' set can cause the motor to overheat and burn out; couple this to long grass on a hot day, and, depending on your model, it could end with your imported budget mower taking a premature trip to the local landfill scrapyard. Ideally, on electrics you should set the cylinder blade to just very lightly 'kiss' the bottom blade. On the other hand if the cutter is 'off set' no detrimental damage will be done to the mower, other than it won't cut a blade of grass! These adjustments, working like a fast pair of automated scissors with two metal blades contacting all the time, haven't changed in principle over the best part of 200 years since the invention of the cylinder lawnmower in 1830.

A damaged cylinder blade that's slightly bent won't cut on that blade, as it won't be equidistant to the centre of the cylinder, and will give a poor cut or simply make a racket, and is normally only remedied by a regrind. In some cases, depending on the material, shape and angle where an object impacts the cutter, the bottom blade or blade carrier can be damaged or even broken. Small nicks can be rectified by carefully hand

filing the damaged blade, and if a blade is only slightly bent it can be tapped back carefully with a hammer to realign the cutter profile, by holding the cutter blade with a gloved hand and tapping the blade at the bend. (NB: Wear strong protective gloves, and remember that you're holding sharp blades and that your hammer skills might not be as accurate as you'd like). Depending on the quality of the blade, more than a tap may be necessary, but extreme caution must be taken not to hit the blade too hard; this can damage the cutter bearings, bearing housings or chassis parts. If you're not 100% confident in this course of action you'd best let a pro deal with it at a service dealer.

All this aside, if the cylinder cutter hasn't been sharpened for at least a season and the blade edges are dull, a vast improvement can be gained by simply taking it for a regrind on a lathe. If you remove the cylinder cutter and bottom blade you would save a good 50% of the service cost, but check with your local service dealer first.

If the blades aren't damaged the cylinder cutter can be sharpened by a few DIY methods without a lathe. One method is called 'back lapping'. An oil and grit grinding paste similar to valve grinding paste is applied to each blade. With the cutter lightly set on the bottom blade as on a regular setting, turn the blade in the 'opposite' direction to its normal rotation. Depending on the model, remove the cutter belt or chain, attach a hand-brace to the cylinder nut and turn. When finished ensure all the paste is removed, as abrasive compound can damage moving parts, especially if contaminated around cutter bearings.

These handy tools can be sourced from garden machinery and DIY shops. They consist of an aluminium oxide abrasive sharpening strip fitted to an aluminium or plastic plate, which clips on to the bottom blade. To install:

a Clean grass and debris off the bottom blade with a wire brush.
b Cut the sharpening tool to the width of the cutter.
c 'Back off' the cutting cylinder to an 'off set' position via the cutter adjustment screws, allowing enough gap to fit the abrasive plate.
d Reset the cylinder evenly so that the cutter is just 'kissing' the sharpening abrasive all along its length.
e Rotate the cylinder by switching on the machine and running the cutter for about one minute.
f Check all the blades are evenly sharp, and that whilst spinning the sound has an even tone. If not, repeat the procedure for another minute until the cylinder is sharp and has an even sound.
g Remove the sharpening tool and reset the cylinder to the bottom blade. Slowly turn the cylinder and test each blade with paper along the length of the bottom blade.

If a clean paper cut isn't achieved, remove the bottom blade and file a flat edge, or take the bottom blade to your

▲ Typical hand lawnmower adjustments for setting the keenness of cut. Look for the cutting cylinder adjustment screw, nut or bolt. On most modern lawnmowers they're situated just above each end of the cylinder cutter shaft. Some modern side-wheel mowers such as AL-KO, Brill and Husqvarna are designed to be adjusted a fraction 'off set', called 'contact free' cutting, which is frictionless, making these machines lighter to push and quieter. They're supplied with a wafer-thin, two-thousandths of an inch metal shim to test the setting.

local service dealer for an inexpensive regrind. If the blade is worn to a thin edge replace the blade. (Some bottom blades can be reground on the reverse side to extend their life.) Before working on or installing cutters, ensure that electric machines are disconnected from the mains supply, cordless machine batteries are disconnected, and remove the spark plug lead and fuel from petrol machines.

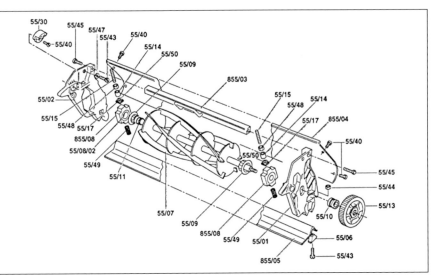

▲ Exploded view of cassette cylinder cutter assembly (covers Allett Kensington, Atco Balmoral, Classic, Windsor and Suffolk Punch models).

▲ Check the 'meat' left on the distance between the edge of the blade and the cylinder spider. This determines how many regrinds (or years) are left in the cutter.

▲ When refitting chain split-links, always check that the nose of the link faces in the direction of travel. This prevents the split-link coming off. Note that all lawnmower chains are a different size and pitch to bicycle chains.

▼ Adjust chain tension by turning the shaft a complete revolution. Tighten on the chain's tightest spot, which minimises any slack areas.

▼ Ensure the chains run in line – if they don't, there's a reason. Check bearings and shafts.

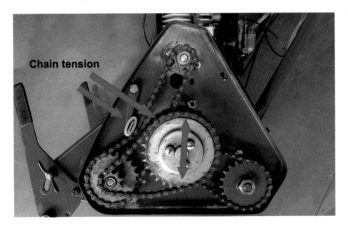

Chain tension

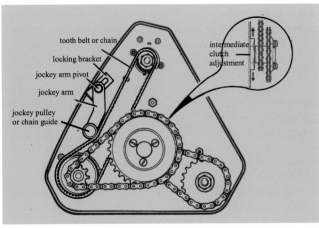

tooth belt or chain
locking bracket
jockey arm pivot
jockey arm
jockey pulley or chain guide
intermediate clutch adjustment

LUBRICATING POINTS

A few drops of light oil or general-purpose grease will keep your lawnmower free-running all year. If there's no oil cap or grease nipple at the cutter bearing it's most likely to have a 'sealed bearing', designed to keep out grass and debris – and, unfortunately, oil, and can only be lubricated on a strip-down. Some engineers would say, 'If you immersed a hand lawnmower in a bucket of oil it wouldn't do it any harm plus it would preserve it for an eternity', which may be true, although we don't recommend it, as a few too many drips of oil on a pristine lawn may just defeat the object you're trying to achieve! Plus the fact that grass will stick to anything that's oily or moist. Mind you, a quick wipe over for a few seconds with an oily rag when you've finished cutting wouldn't do it or the lawn any harm either, especially wiping over the blade tips, which keeps them knife-edge sharp, and keeps corrosion caused by moisture and grass juices at bay (especially whilst stored over the winter). This protection can be extremely beneficial if a fertiliser or chemicals have been used on a lawn, some of which can be exceptionally corrosive to most types of metal, including aluminium.

CYLINDER MOWERS OLD AND NEW

Various hand-push lawnmowers, past and present – especially older, pre-1960 machines – were designed to last more than a lifetime. They used heavier, more robust materials, which in turn gave the lawn a better 'roll', since if a machine is too light it loses its effectiveness to roll out surface bumps and undulations. Many of these vintage machines are still around today and are well worth the cost of restoration or an annual service.

If you're considering purchasing a vintage lawnmower, keep in mind that most of them are likely to have seen many years of use. But don't let that put you off – they may have 40 or 50 years on the clock, but there's a good chance they'll still have another two or three decades left in them, and may last a lot longer than a brand new one. However, check the life left in the cylinder cutter by measuring the distance between the blade spiders and the edge of the cutting blade.

However, most of the machines illustrated in this chapter are still currently made in the UK, and represent the most popular powered domestic cylinder lawnmowers currently on the market.

Many of the latest models have the added advantage of being more than just a lawnmower. Robot mowers, for instance, are a lifestyle product, changing the very way we live. Many modern cylinder mowers have the ability to change and upgrade into a complete lawn-care clinic, by transforming into a variety of garden machines via a quick-change cassette system. Besides

▶ 12in JP Maxees, named after a member of the company founder's family, Uncle Max. The Maxees was made in 10in, 12in and 14in sizes and had a superbly engineered steel chassis and a geared-up six-blade cut. It also featured a cutter cassette that was easily removed without tools. The unused machine pictured has been dry-stored since new in 1970 and was owned by the Jerram and Pearson family.

▼ Qualcast B1 five-blade cast-iron chassis, extremely popular in the 1970s, here customised with a pink furry handle and wheels and a 'leopard-skin' grass throw-plate. This particular model was owned by Lily Savage, otherwise known as Paul O'Grady.

▼ Jerram and Pearson 10in geared-up six-blade Mini Mo once owned by Albert Pierrepoint, Britain's most famous hangman. In the 1950s he was paid £15 per hanging – coincidentally the same price as his lawnmower.

▲ Bosch budget lightweight steel chassis, five-blade side-wheel, 2013.

▲ 12in Qualcast Superlight Panther, with five blades and lightweight alloy chassis. One of the most popular cylinder roller hand lawnmowers made in the UK from 1970–2000.

▶ The Ransome Certes was manufactured in the 1960s–80s: aluminium chassis, 14in and 16in geared-up ten-blade. This was probably the best hand lawnmower in the world for the finest finish, ideal for putting greens.

▼ The Greens Zephyr of 1960–70 came in 14in ten-blade and 12in eight-blade models, all transported and sold in individual wooden crates. This particular example was specially made in chrome as an exhibition piece.

◀ Ransome Ajax of 1975: aluminium chassis, 12in six-blade, geared drive.

▼ Eight-blade Webb Witch 12in with steel chassis, 1950–90. Also in the same range were the six-blade Webb Wasp and the 10in Webb Whippet.

▶ **Allett seven-cassette Lawn Care System, comprising a six-blade cutter, ten-blade cutter, verticutter, brush, scarifier, aerator and dethatcher.**

▶ **The six- and ten-blade cassettes of the Allett Lawn Care System. Five-, six- and ten-blade cutter cassettes fit 14in, 17in and 20in models.**

cutting grass, this new generation of machines is able to scarify, aerate, verticut, dethatch, brush and groom your lawn – facilities previously found only on expensive professional lawnmowers costing four times as much (approx £4,000 plus), which until now had made them prohibitive to lawn enthusiasts who don't own a stately home or golf course and haven't won the lottery!

These models aren't just domestic lawnmowers, they're able to convert into entire professional lawn-care systems:

- Allett 14in, 17in, 20in, Kensington
- Allett Kensington Electric 12E, 14E
- Allett Classic Petrol 14L, 17L
- Allett Classic 12E Electric
- Atco 14in, 17in, 20in, Balmoral
- Atco 12in, 14in, Windsor
- Qualcast Classic 14in, 17in
- Qualcast Classic 12in, 14in electric
- Suffolk Punch 14in, 17in
- Webb C12E, C14E, C14L, C14K, C17L, C20K
- Webb 14in, 17in, 20in

OPTIONAL ATTACHMENTS AND WHAT THEY DO

Note the differences between the gaps of the blades. The 5-blade cutter will tackle longer grass than the 10-blade; it's the distance between the blades and the front roller that determine the height of grass that the machine can tackle. To calculate the maximum height of grass your machine will cut, use this simple formula:

a Place the machine on a hard flat surface.
b Measure the distance between two of the cylinder blades.
c Alter the machine to the highest cut by adjusting the front roller downwards.
d Measure the distance between the fixed bottom blade and the ground and add them together, ie 2in + 1in = 3in grass stem height.

TOP MOWING TIP

Always cut grass in dry conditions, whatever type of mower you have. Wet grass will just stick to anything and clog the machine, especially the rollers, wheels, cutters, grass-chute and underneath the chassis. If wet grass is left on the machine to dry it can cling to metal parts and pull paintwork off when removed. Wet cut grass, if left uncollected, will lay in unsightly clumps and take longer to decompose, which can block out light and make the grass go yellow. Dry grass is dispersed more evenly, decomposes swiftly and is far less unsightly.

▼ **This illustration shows the difference between six- and ten-cylinder blade cuts.**

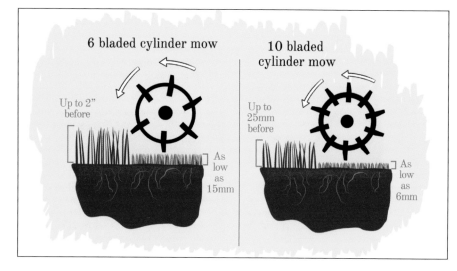

6 bladed cylinder mow

Up to 2" before

As low as 15mm

10 bladed cylinder mow

Up to 25mm before

As low as 6mm

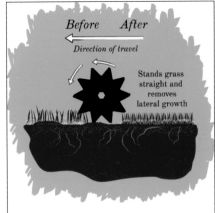

▲▶ **Verticutter cassette. The term 'verticutter' denotes 'vertical cutting'. This is designed to keep the grass upright whilst removing its lateral growth.**

If your grass is taller than 4in your lawnmower will more than likely just flatten it, as you have grass rather than a lawn and had best get a grasscutter to do the job. A 10- or 12-blade cutter will give a lot more cuts per yard, for a smoother, finer finish, but won't tackle as long a stem, *ie* 1in + ⅝in = 1⅝in maximum grass length. This type of lawnmower would be used at least three times a week on putting greens, bowling greens and pristine show lawns.

VERTICUTTING

The objective of verticutting is to prune the grasses to improve tillering and stolon formation, which increases the turf density and is important for all fine turf, especially on bowling and golf greens. The numerous blades are spaced 35mm apart and set to cut down to a maximum depth of zero mm.

Verticutting controls thatch by removing the dead and dying grass plants that will ultimately contribute to the thatch layer. The blades are designed to produce upright grass prior to mowing, which will give a cleaner and more consistent cut. It's also a method of controlling weeds and coarse grasses that lie flat in the sward, such as Yorkshire fog and annual meadow grass. Used regularly every one to two weeks in good growing conditions, from April to September, it'll help maintain a firm low thatch surface and healthier growth right through the season, make scarifying far easier, and will cause less damage.

WARNING: *Don't allow verticutter blades to contact the soil. Any bumps in the lawn need to be resolved before use, with a consequence of possibly damaging the lawn.*

Uses aggressive steel blades spaced 64mm apart and cuts down to 6mm deep into the soil and thatch. This allows air, water and nutrients to easily penetrate into the soil. It gives good seed and soil contact for premium germination when over-seeding the lawn. Such blades prune the grass plants (like pruning a bush), and this causes extra shoots to grow, thickening the turf by giving a higher plant density. The chopping action is a good way of controlling lawn and creeping weeds such as speedwell and trefoil (yellow sucking clover).

▶ **Annual meadow grass is wear-resistant, survives waterlogging, is shallow-rooted, seeds at low height and can be difficult to mow out.**

◀ **Common lawn weeds such as Yorkshire fog are yellowish in colour and unattractive in a lawn. They can thrive in poorly drained soil but are intolerant to verticutting.**

▶ **Damaging effect of lateral grass growth.**

▲ ▼ The dethatcher is the most aggressive cassette.

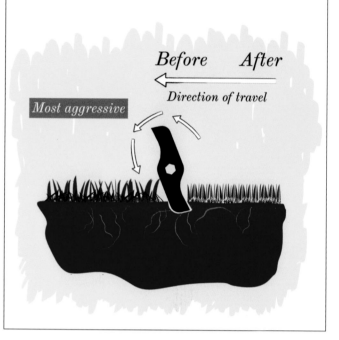

▲ Illustration showing before and after dethatching.

▼ Aerating makes for a healthy lawn as it eliminates soil compaction by making a slit that allows air, nutrients and water to penetrate the surface.

▲▼ Aerator cassette.

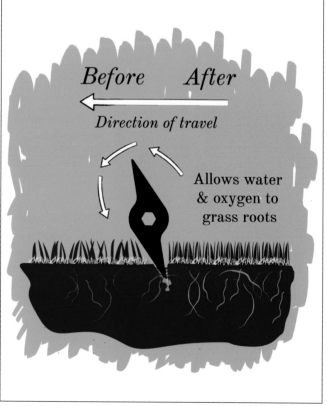

▲▼ Scarifier cassette.

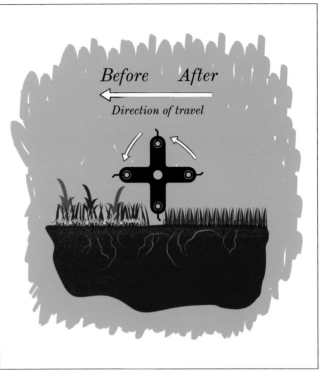

Before   After

Direction of travel

▲ Scarifying encourages grass growth whilst discouraging moss growth.

▼ Leaves can smother grass and kill it within weeks by excluding the light. Leaves also decrease grass vigour and encourage moss. In addition worms love leaves, and moles love worms, and they can even burrow through tarmac. The environment under leaves can also cause fungal lawn infections.

▲▼ Lawnbrush cassette.

Before   After

Direction of travel

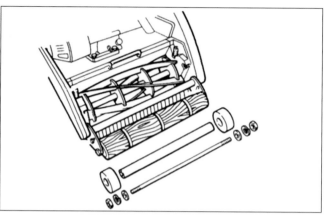

◄ Shows the different volumes of debris that can be raked out of a lawn by a scarifier, dethatcher and verticutter.

▲ Twin front rollers, designed for cutting longer grass with a cylinder lawnmower. The full-width front roller can be removed and replaced by two narrow, slightly larger-diameter rollers fitted one at either side. This allows grass stems to be cut without flattening, which allows the upright grass stems to pass straight between the cutters.

All the machines pictured here are fitted with a 5- or 6-blade cylinder cutter as standard (except 12in electric and push models), with the option of a 10-blade cylinder cassette for a finer finish.

There are many other makes and models with different types of drive mechanisms in a variety of different designs, utilising chains and belts with metal or plastic gears, but all follow the same basic principles.

REMOVING A BOTTOM BLADE WITH SEIZED OR TIGHT SCREWS

You're likely to come across this problem quite often, especially on machines that haven't been serviced regularly – especially if stored in a damp place – or on older machines (in other words about 90% of mowers). Here are several tried and tested methods of removal without destroying the machine, damaging the bottom blade or conveyor plate or throwing the mower through the shed window in frustration because one little screw just won't budge! Although many of these screws only have a very short thread – often less than ½in or 10mm – they can be extremely tight. They're machine tool factory-fitted to ensure they won't come loose, so it's

virtually impossible to make the initial turn with a screwdriver.

If you still have no success with obstinate screws the alternative is to heat the bottom plate around the screw (this expands the metal), then tap the screw anticlockwise with the punch. However, this exercise requires extreme caution. Firstly remove the fuel and oil if it's a petrol model, remove the

electric supply if it's mains-powered, and remove the battery if it's cordless. Check what type of material you're working on – aluminium alloys and plastics will melt at quite low temperatures, cast iron can crack, and steel can distort. If you're not 100% confident with using heat, or the proper equipment isn't available, we suggest you entrust this operation to your local professional service dealer.

▼ Cutter and drive adjustment. The belt drive should engage when the control levers are depressed at one third of travel. Ensure that when the drive clutch lever is disengaged the machine can be pushed freely forwards and backwards.

▼ Removing a tight bottom blade screw with an angled or centre punch. Note the angle of the punch, which needs to be as near to the blade as possible so as to minimise the risk of cracking the bottom plate by downward force. This plate is especially vulnerable on cast-iron types.

▶ Switch assembly.

TIPS FOR ELECTRIC CYLINDER MOWERS

There are various popular mains cable anti-pull holders (Allett, Atco, Hayter, Qualcast, Bosch, Flymo, Mountfield, Viking), designed to protect the cable and switch casing from fracture when the cable is pulled. These are overlooked by many users, but will more than double the life of the mains cable and switch if used, since they're designed to protect the cable and switch so that the trailing cable doesn't continually pull or strain at the switch housing. (Many people comment 'I always wondered what that bit was for...')

Look out for fatigue cracks on the switch trigger, and a damaged or fatigued mains cable near the casing. Many switch casings have been designed not to come apart. On these models inner switch spares often aren't available, and they can only be repaired by replacing the whole switch unit.

NB: Current electricity safety regulations suggest that in order to prevent possible electric shock, damaged or cut mains cables should be replaced, and not repaired by a join.

▼ Flymo inner switch.

▼ Qualcast inner switch.

Check for crack here

Check for mains cable fatigue here

Chapter 6

Rotary lawnmowers

The first and foremost tip to keep in mind when mowing with a rotary cutter is 'always cut the grass in dry conditions'; but any one of the following tips can save you more than the price of this book.

As has already been pointed out in the previous chapter, wet cut grass will stick to anything and clog machines up – especially rollers, the grass chute and around the underneath of the cutter deck. Once the grass chute is clogged the problem escalates, since the cut grass has no outlet, thus causing strain on all the mechanical parts. Each revolution of the blade creates yet more grass build-up. And because wet grass is more than twice the weight of dry grass, it makes the mower work harder, creating extra heat, which will shorten the life of the motor or engine.

As well as causing damage to the mower, if long wet grass is cut and left uncollected it can dry in unsightly matted clumps, which will take longer to decompose, blocking out light and making the grass go yellow. By contrast, when grass is cut in the dry your mower will give its best performance, the grass is dispersed more evenly, and recovery time is reduced for new grass growth.

◄ **Mountfield power drive aluminium chassis grasscutter.**

Once caked-on grass dries it can pull paint off, especially if removed when dry – not much of a problem on aluminium or plastic chassis machines, which have great resistance to corrosion, but in the case of steel chassis machines such deck corrosion will greatly shorten the mower's life by making it thinner and weaker, if not checked and protected with rust inhibiter.

Paint flaking off the 'outside' of a steel chassis, especially in a cracked star-like shape, will often indicate damage caused when the blade hit a small, solid object like a stone months

beforehand. The greater damage will lurk underneath. Before addressing such a rusted area, test it by poking a thin screwdriver in the metal to assess the extent of corrosion. If the screwdriver penetrates the steel there could easily be a 'situation' if the blade impacted an object – it could penetrate through the chassis at high velocity, causing injury to you or a hole straight through the kitchen window! In most cases steel chassis rotaries are less expensive than others, and chassis replacement would be classed as an uneconomical repair.

▶ **Hayter Harrier cutaway. This is one of the few machines fitted with a blade friction disc, for protection against impact damage to the engine crankshaft. Models fitted with this mechanism have an engine crankshaft lifetime warranty if the blade should accidentally impact on an object – a handy insurance saving you the price of a new engine.**

Replacement chassis come without any parts attached – every nut, bolt, wheel, gearbox and engine or motor needs to be removed and refitted on to the new chassis. You're also very likely to come across seized or other worn parts in the process.

NOTE: *Some rotary chassis are protected with a double skin protecting it against minor impacts. Some have engine crankshaft protection warranty against heavier impacts. When replacing the machine, it's worth checking which is best suited to your lawn.*

All this said, whatever type, make or model of grass-cutting mower you have, whatever's said, written or advertised on domestic, professional or heavy-duty machines, they've all been designed only to cut *grass*, and not a field of bricks!

GETTING THE BEST FROM A ROTARY MOWER

FOLDING HANDLES
Unlike vintage machines, which have fixed, solid handles, most modern petrol and mains electric rotary mowers have tubular fold-down handles, folding either halfway, two-thirds of the way or fully from the base of the chassis. You'd think this would provide a safe

and quick way to store the mower, or a handy way of transporting it, especially when loading it into the car boot, but BEWARE! A cable can very easily be kinked and damaged at one of the handle's folding points – an annoying clanger, especially when folding the handles on a new machine for the first time, since it can often be remedied only by a premature cable replacement. Extra care is required when folding the halfway-type handles which fold back

on themselves, especially if one of the cables carries 240V. On this type of handle the control cables bend at four pivot points simultaneously, and there can be three or four control cables including throttle, clutch, operator presence, mains, key/button start ignition cable and the recoil rope, and you need to keep an eye on all of these whilst folding the handles.

The secret is to fold the handles *very* slowly, keeping your eyes on each

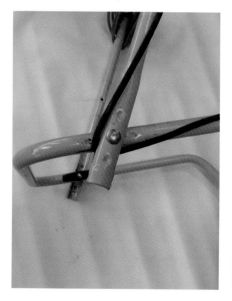

▲▼ **Incorrect cable position.**

▼ **Correct cable position. When folding mower handles, check that the control cables and the mains cable aren't going to be trapped and kinked between the handle pivot points, an easily neglected hazard. Even if you don't read anything else in this book, avoiding the risk of cable damage in this way will have saved you more than the price of buying it!**

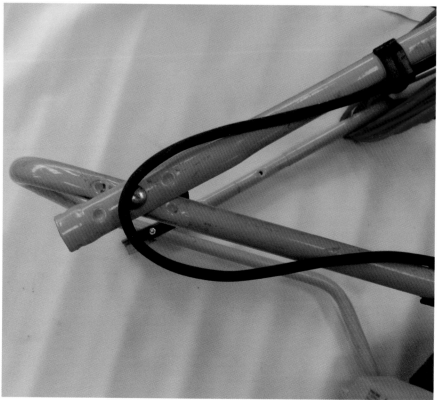

cable at each pivot point. Ensure the cables are free to bend on the inside or outside of the pivot points and not in between, where the cables can be caught, bent, kinked or cut. There aren't many things more frustrating than when your grass hasn't been cut for three weeks and you've just purchased a new mower, especially when it's just been demonstrated, only to find that when collapsing the handles the control cables have ended up being kinked, and the sticking controls can only be remedied by replacing them.

The most common way of folding such handles is via a nut and bolt, which in most cases are stronger than the handles. Most of us don't have a convenient torque wrench available to tighten these fixings if they loosen, but if they're *over*-tightened they'll crush and deform the handles so much that they'll never keep rigid again. So always ensure that the handle bolts are just hand-tightened or lightly nipped up, without distorting the tube.

BLADES

Although made from solid steel, mower blades have only been designed to cut grass, and one impact, or one object in its way, could easily spell disaster. A rotary blade spins at over 100mph, and if it momentarily stops dead from an obstruction, some sort of damage will occur. This affects various parts. Firstly the blade, which may bend, takes the initial impact, which if the mower has a petrol engine is then transmitted directly to the engine crankshaft. Depending on the position of the engine stroke, the impact may bend the crankshaft, or break the con-rod. The damage on the blades pictured overleaf would most likely be terminal for the mower. So before cutting, always take a quick look over the lawn first. Cutting too low, hitting a bump, digging into the ground or catching a tree root can do the same damage as hitting a hidden rock or an old bone.

There are several popular machines on the market that have impact protection. In one variety a cutter-blade tensioned by a centre bolt is attached to a friction disc; the blade moves on the disc if an impact occurs, which helps prevent damage to the engine crankshaft and cutting mechanism.

▲ In many cases the hand wing nuts and bolts on folding handles can be stronger than the tubular handles, so tension them only hand-tight. If they're over-tightened they'll distort the handle, causing it to move constantly. This can only be remedied by replacing the handles.

▼ Typical handle vibration fatigue will always occur at the weakest points, *ie* where there's a bend, join, bolt or crimping. Look for weakness cracks in handles caused by vibration from an unbalanced rotary blade or a rough-running engine.

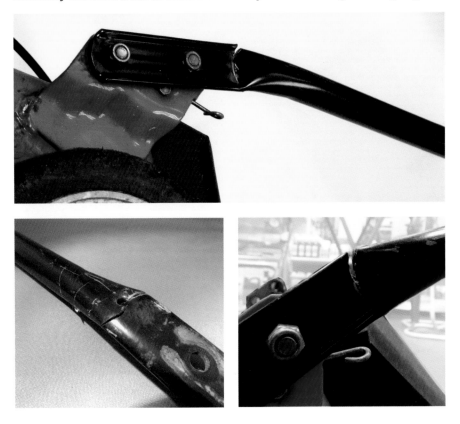

▲ DIY blade balancing. A simple and easy method to balance a rotary blade.

▼ Pro blade balancing. This professional equipment checks precisely the balance of the blade (just like balancing a car wheel) and whether the blade is distorted, bent or out of true, via the variable probe at the base of the balancer. Blade balancing and sharpening is probably the most cost-effective part of the servicing on a rotary mower (bar the engine oil), since it'll keep it running for the maximum hours with the least vibration fatigue whilst placing the least strain on the engine or motor.

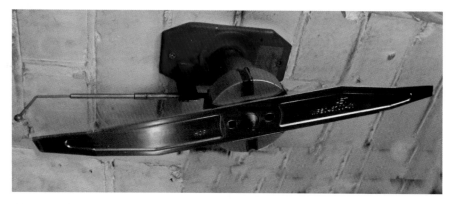

▼ Impact-damaged blades – RIP (now in lawnmower heaven!).

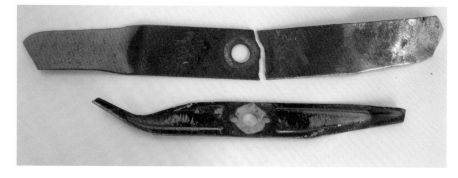

Some models fitted with this mechanism have a lifetime crankshaft warranty against accidental impact. In another variety two or four swing-tip blades are fixed by a single bolt on the outer circumference of the disc, and if an object is encountered the blade pivots backward, dissipating the impact.

GEARBOXES

There are two main types of clutch drive: friction-disc and direct engage. Both types work well and have very few issues. Worm and drive gears work in a synthetic oil bath – many domestic models are sealed for life and are virtually maintenance free. Consequently there are normally no internal service parts available for these types of gearbox if a fault develops, such as no drive, slipping drive or a drive that won't engage. Provided the clutch cable and drive-belt tension are adjusted correctly, the whole unit as an assembly would require replacement. However, some external parts are available, including drive shafts, axles, tension springs, drive pulleys and arms, depending on the model.

DRIVE/CLUTCH CABLES

Most drive/clutch cables should be adjusted to start engaging the drive when the lever is depressed to about a third of its travel. At this point the mechanism is at the point of take-up. When the lever is then fully depressed it engages the drive/clutch completely.

▲ Common 90° gearbox fitted to the rear wheels or roller on power-drive rotaries, showing belt tension springs.

▲ Rotary gearbox *in situ*.

▶ The gearbox is driven by a belt, which is taken directly off the engine crankshaft. Constant belt tension is achieved via a spring attached to the rear of the gearbox. If drive to the rear wheels is poor, check for a worn or glazed belt, damaged pulley or damaged tension spring.

▲ Typical self-propelled rotary gearbox.

▶ Checking and adjusting the correct belt tension on a Qualcast Concorde, Elan and Eclipse, 1970–2010. When replacing the drive belt, slacken the two large cross-point screws a half-turn anticlockwise, move the small motor pinion forward or backward to the correct belt tension, then retighten the screws. A broken/snapped belt on Concorde models is normally caused by either impact damage to the cutter or a blunt cutter.

Chapter 7

The ride-on garden tractor

The tractors covered in this chapter are primarily petrol-powered for large domestic gardens, and not designed for the rolling prairies of America. Larger commercial models have twin-cylinder engines or are diesel-powered. New tractors coming on to the market will be more environmentally friendly, quieter and fuel-efficient, and will possibly be electric-powered via a battery.

ANATOMY OF A GARDEN TRACTOR

▲ Countax C600H tractor showing transaxle drive and powered take-off (PTO) pulleys to the sweeper brushes.

◀ Typical garden tractor with its component parts. This model is an AL-KO Powerline.

◀ Countax tractor triple-blade belt configuration and jockey pulleys, showing counter-rotating blades and the direction of flow of the cut grass. *(Courtesy Countax Tractors)*

► **Turning circle geometry on Husqvarna rear-wheel-steering rider. Rear wheel steering gives the tightest turn and is ideal for awkward areas around trees and obstacles.**

► **Transmission layout of rear-mounted engine on Husqvarna rear-wheel-steering rider.**

◄ **Husqvarna cutter deck. An aerodynamic bio-deck and blades cut grass finely into mulch, eliminating the need for grass collection.**

BUYING A GARDEN TRACTOR

There are thousands of different ride-on mowers on the market, but each has different and unique characteristics. So if you're thinking of a new tractor, try sitting on several different makes and models. Check out the controls as you would on a new car. The pedals, seat position and steering come in diverse forms – some will be easy to operate, some will be more complex, like having to pat your head and rub your tummy at the same time. One may be uncomfortable, another will be snug. Some controls will favour the left hand or foot, others the right. In other words, always ensure you have a demonstration before you buy.

When purchasing a new tractor for the first time, choosing the right one – whether new or used, large or small – is important. Making the right choice first time could possibly save you thousands of pounds, and hours of time. It should be a machine that, once bought, should put a smile on your face, give the finish you want, and be a pleasurable experience to operate, rather than giving you an annoying 'pain in the grass' every time you use it!

It's also worth checking out the after-sales service from your supplier. You might not think that your brand spanking new tractor will ever break down, but garden tractors are complex machines with mechanical moving parts. Some are made with 'serious economic restraint', and will eventually require maintenance and parts, just like a car. An authorised servicing dealer will give advice, maintain and repair the machine on site if necessary, or collect and deliver it for a service, ideally in the winter when you're not using it – which can be extremely handy, especially if on an extended warranty period. Bear in mind that many tractor manufacturers don't make engines or gearboxes and, unlike cars, have their chassis, engines and gearboxes made by different companies, and are covered under different manufacturers' warranties.

Don't be put off by the size of a tractor when viewing one for the first time in a showroom. They look deceivingly large, but once in the garden will look a lot smaller. In most cases purchase the biggest you can afford

without going overboard (remember, you don't need a Rolls-Royce to go to the corner shop), as this may well be the most cost-effective in the long term. Generally the larger the machine, the quicker you'll get the job done, the less times you'll go up and down and the less wear and tear there'll be, as you'll mow for less hours and consequently less miles. As a result the machine will last much longer, plus you'll have a comfier ride. Any cost you may have saved purchasing a smaller or less expensive model will most likely get eaten up by more replacement parts, additional repair bills and perhaps a shorter machine life. Also, a wider cut – besides travelling fewer miles with consequently longer service intervals – will allow you to cut closer up to trees and under bushes or obstacles, as the cutter protrudes farther outside the wheelbase. You'll also find it easier to cut over the lawn edge without the wheels plummeting off the border, especially on contoured, shaped areas.

You could well be surprised by the manoeuvrability and turning circle on a large tractor, which may well have the same or a tighter turn than some smaller tractors. The turning circle is important: the tighter it is, the more manoeuvrable and the more convenient it will be (ever wanted to do a U-turn in the road, but ended up doing a frustrating five-point turn?) – especially if the garden area is landscaped with trees, bushes, corners, a pond, fence posts, greenhouse, winding paths and the odd trampoline, or even just for manoeuvring it in and out of the shed. So always check on the turning circle, which might be quoted with different measurements: the actual width of the turning circle is what you need to know, *ie* the amount of grass that's left uncut.

The other important consideration for ease of manoeuvrability is the sort of gearbox it has. There are three main types: manual, hydrostatic and variamatic.

The manual type is similar to that in a car, with from three to six forward gears plus reverse. Modern manual gearboxes are reliable and require little maintenance, other than checking their oil level. Manual gearboxes use up very little oil or grease. The clutch pedal needs to be depressed each time you need to alter your speed or direction. However, unlike a car it isn't necessary to move up the gears one at a time, as there's sufficient torque in the engine to set off in any gear. Normally you select the gear for the speed you wish to travel and just set off: the higher the gear, the quicker the speed. Manual gearbox tractors are normally less expensive to purchase than hydrostatic.

NOTE: *If the gears in a manual gearbox are hard to select or disengage, ensure that the drive belt isn't binding or turning the top pulley on the transaxle gearbox.*

Hydrostatic gearboxes are similar to those of an automatic car, and are the easiest and most convenient to use. They're virtually maintenance-free and have proved very reliable. They generate less belt-wear than a manual gearbox, as the belt has a constant tension and doesn't need to slip on the pulleys to engage or disengage. Forward or reverse and speed control is either by foot-pedal or a hand-lever, with no need to clutch, which has the added advantage of switching the tractor from a snail's pace to quickly in either forward or reverse direction. In the past these gearboxes were only fitted on the more expensive tractors, but with recent technology and mass production there's now only a small difference in cost, and it's worth the extra. Once you've driven with a hydrostatic gearbox you won't want to go back to a manual.

The variamatic gear/belt-type system uses pulleys that, by pressing a foot pedal or moving a hand-operated lever, vary the diameter of the drive pulley by widening or narrowing discs to a larger or smaller diameter, which in turn alters the gear ratio, varying the speed to the drive wheels.

Other general considerations regarding the size of lawnmower tractors are that larger tractors will be comfier, and, being fitted with a hydrostatic gearbox, will have the advantage of not having to change gear. This makes them less fatiguing and more user-friendly, especially if fitted with a V-twin engine, which has less vibration, and is consequently quieter and smoother. Also, larger engines inherently work with less effort. (As in cars, a Ford Fiesta and a 3-litre BMW may both do 70mph, but the BMW, with its larger engine and wheels, will do it more smoothly and with less effort). Tractor seats also vary in comfort just like a car, so check the height of the back support of the seat. Some even have armrests. Larger wheels and seats also render undulations and bumps less jarring, making the entire experience and ride much more pleasant.

TYPES OF GARDEN TRACTOR

The five main types of domestic ride-on garden tractor currently available on the market are capable of cutting and either collecting or mulching the grass from small to large areas in five different ways:

a Direct-collect. This is the most efficient and economical way to collect grass, which is thrown the shortest distance via a rear chute directly into a rear pivot-mounted grassbox. After reversing up to the compost heap, pulling a lever or pressing a button discharges the grass whilst the driver stays in his seat. A mulch plug can block off the grass-chute opening (many can be fitted in seconds without tools); this retains the clippings to be cut and re-cut into fine shreddings via the aerodynamic shape of the deck and blades. When the clippings are small enough they drop to the ground as mulch.

b Powered (or towed) sweeper, often with integral roller for a groomed effect. Achieves excellent collection even when damp, and applies a more groomed finish than the direct-collect system, although more costly and bulky and requires additional maintenance. The groomed effect is achieved by a revolving brush bolted to the chassis, powered either by a belt via a powered take-off (PTO) from the gearbox, or an independent towed brush sweeper powered whilst in forward motion by the sweeper's own wheels.

c Side/rear discharge and mulch. Cut grass is directly ejected from a side or rear duct straight on to the ground, or a mulch plug is fitted and the clippings are transformed into mulch within the cutter deck by being cut and re-cut by the blade.

d Side eject, vac collect and mulch. Grass is side-ejected up a chute via aerodynamic blades that create a draught into one, two or three independent rear boxes. The cuttings are emptied by removing each box by hand, with the advantage of being able to empty cuttings manually into a recycle bin or directly on top of a compost heap.

e Dedicated mulch. The cutter deck and blades are aerodynamically designed purely to mulch. As this isn't a compromise between mulching and collecting, the mulching process is superior to the systems described above.

▲ Hayter 10/30 10.5hp 30in rider. This long-established popular tractor features hydrostatic drive, mulch, collect or side discharge and a very tight turning circle leaving only 600mm of uncut grass.

THE RIDER

A small, compact lightweight chassis with a mid- or rear-mounted engine and no front bonnet. Normally the least expensive type, riders mainly have just a single blade with a small cutting width on a centrally mounted cutting deck. Riders allow the operator to easily see to the front and sides without obstruction. They often have a walk-through design, allowing easy access to the seat. Grass collection can vary between direct-collect, mulch, side and rear discharge. Smaller versions are the only type of tractor capable of fitting through gaps narrower than a 29in doorway. Ideal for large domestic gardens of less than half an acre, made from 21in to 36in cuts, with rope-pull or key-start engines of 5hp to 12hp, with a choice of a manual, variable automatic or hydrostatic gearbox.

GARDEN TRACTOR

Conventional chassis configuration with engine and bonnet at the front, and a central cutting mechanism with single, twin or triple cutters. Grass collection can vary from either a separate bag/box, a direct-collect system or powered or towed sweeper, which can be emptied without leaving the seat. (Non-collect models have either side discharge, rear discharge or mulch options.) Ideal for larger grass areas and available from 30in to 54in cut, all have key-start engines from 10hp to 23hp, with a choice of a manual, variable automatic or hydrostatic gearbox.

Most tractors now have the convenience of electric key start, instead of a recoil engine pull, and many have a button to engage the cutter via an electric clutch (an alternative to a manual cutter engage lever). These have the advantage of having constant belt tension, unlike lever- or pedal-operation engaging the cutter via a slipping belt. The secret on electric cutter clutches is to let the engine warm up from cold for a few minutes before engaging the cutter. Raise the height of the cutter deck or start the cutters on an area with low grass. On many models, when the clutch is engaged this places a momentary direct load on the engine, with the consequence of the engine possibly stalling if cold.

FRONT DECK RIDER

These tractors are designed for awkward areas and tight spaces, having rear-wheel steering that allows a very tight turning circle, similar to a forklift truck. Most are designed as dedicated mulchers, with no need to collect the grass. The cutter is mounted in front of the wheels, having the advantage of allowing it to reach into corners and under trees, bushes and benches etc.

ZERO TURN TRACTOR

Probably the sexiest and most macho of ride-ons, and often nicknamed 'The Beast'. Large and medium-sized models with rear or side grass discharge are used on

▼ Husqvarna all-wheel drive with articulated rear-wheel steering.

▲ An underside view of the Husqvarna all-wheel drive with articulated rear-wheel steering – ideal for intricate areas.

USING A GARDEN TRACTOR

Whenever you mow your lawn, always remember the seven golden tractor rules:

1 Always cut in the dry.
2 The slower the forward speed, the better the cut and the better the grass collection.
3 The higher the cut, the less the strain on the cutter belt.
4 Use maximum engine revs when cutting.
5 Look out for tree roots and undulating ground.
6 Keep the blades balanced.
7 For best results cut little and often.

▲ Zero-turn in action.

large, rough and awkward terrain. Rather than a steering wheel, two levers, placed one each side of the operator, are moved backward or forward and control the two rear wheels to revolve at different forward and reverse speeds. The front heavy-duty wheels work independently and spin in any direction (like a shopping trolley). Although these machine are often manufactured in bigger sizes, the design allows them to be manoeuvred in tight postage-stamp spaces in any direction effortlessly – they're easily capable of turning on a sixpence. Sizes vary from 36in to 60in-width cuts, powered by 15hp to 30hp engines.

RIDE-ON CYLINDER LAWNMOWER

Ride-on cylinder lawnmowers are designed for the serious home gardener or professional requiring a traditional rolled and striped formal lawn where the finish is paramount. They're available in 20in to 36in widths, with five to twelve cutting blades, 73 to 145 cuts per metre, micro-cutting height adjustment from $3/32$in to $1\frac{3}{8}$in (2.4mm–35mm), and 5hp to 8hp engines. Some models are fitted

▼ Husqvarna zero-turn P-ZT 48 with grass collector.

▼ Allett Buckingham 24in six-blade 5hp cylinder ride-on.

with an adjustable rake directly behind the front roller, which stands the grass stems upright before they're mown.

All cylinder mowers supported by full-width front and rear rollers allow the cutter to overlap the grass border without the machine dropping off the edge of the lawn. Some models have a trailing auto-steer seat, which ensures that the seat follows the mower precisely when turning around curved borders or pathways. They can also be used without the seat as a pedestrian lawnmower, which can be convenient for more intricate areas where a ride-on may not be practical. Cylinder lawnmower engines are generally smaller than tractor engines, as cylinder blades require less power to cut and consequently are more fuel-efficient.

TROUBLESHOOTING AND MAINTENANCE

Some irritating problems that can occasionally crop up on tractors include non-starting, poor grass collection, uneven cut, vibration, brake seizing and punctures. Most can be remedied quickly and easily.

TRACTOR STARTING PROBLEMS
Before starting, check:

a The engine fuel and oil level. Check the fuel tank is at least half-full (with fresh fuel) and that the oil is at the 'full' mark (but not above) on the dipstick. (Some engines have automatic ignition cut-out when they're low on oil.)
b The gear lever or pedal is in the neutral position. Move it backward and forward and reposition to neutral.
c The choke lever is in the 'on choke' position. Follow the throttle cable to the engine; check that the control lever on the carburettor travels all the way to a full stop, and the cable adjustment holder is tight.
d The brake pedal or lever is depressed. Some models require more foot pressure (adjusting the seat forward may help). Depress the pedal several

times to dislodge any trapped debris, or release a jammed or stiff cut-out switch.
e The parking brake is engaged. Depress several times as above.
f The cutter lever or switch is disengaged.
g The grassbox is seated in position and fitted properly. Check it's fitted evenly all the way round and hasn't been dislodged, doesn't show a gap and isn't lopsided. If the box has been caught or strained (especially after emptying), the safety cut-out contact may not be activated.
h You're sitting on the seat! Some seat contacts are sensitive (especially if they're operated by a lightweight person), and some only work when you sit fully back in the seat. Try adjusting the seat forward, especially if the engine tends to misfire when travelling at speed or over bumpy ground.
i The fuel tap is turned on. If an inline tap, the lever should be in line with the fuel pipe when on. (Switch off the fuel when storing.)
j The fuel filter (if fitted) isn't blocked.
k The battery is charged. Have it tested if you're unsure or if it's over three years old. If it's over five years old

we'd suggest you replace it, as the power will be compromised.
l If the engine turns over but doesn't fire, ensure the fuel is 'fresh' (less than six weeks old if bought from the pump). We'd suggest you use fuel stabiliser or alkylate fuel (see Chapter 4).

There are a few more complex reasons why a tractor or the cutters won't start, but before we get highly technical we can remedy 80% of common no-start faults for the 95% of people who don't have an honours degree in engineering and may have overlooked a straightforward solution such as one of the following:

There have been many frustrated customers who've demand a service engineer call-out only to be embarrassed when the engineer points out that the fuel tap is turned off, there's insufficient or no fuel in the tank, or the battery charge is low! So check the battery has a full charge (a tractor battery and charging system have far less power than a car battery and charge system). If a rapid or loud clicking sound is heard when the ignition key's turned, and the engine doesn't turn or turns over slowly, this is a sure sign that battery power is low and will normally be rectified by recharging. If after charging the same fault occurs, it's either a defective battery (three years is an average battery life) or a faulty solenoid. Either will be easy to replace as a quick DIY job.

The solenoid consists of a heavy strip of metal activated by an electro magnet. The metal strip connects to two contact points and 'makes' or 'breaks' the electric circuit. Because the strip is heavier than most switch contacts it doesn't pit or burn away as a lighter switch would. To test a grounded solenoid, connect positive (+) solenoid terminal to positive (+) battery terminal. Quickly touch the negative ground (-)

▼ **Typical garden tractor solenoid, which is a heavy-duty switching mechanism used to handle the large amounts of current necessary to start the engine.**

▲ Chassis-mounted seat safety cut-out switch.

▲ Tractor seat safety cut-out switches are either fitted in the seat (as in the picture) or in the chassis under the seat.

▲ Various tractor safety cut-out switches as fitted on foot brake, cutter drive, seat and direct collect grassboxes. These won't allow the engine to start or the cutters to engage unless the foot or park brake is engaged, the operator is sat on the seat and the grassbox is fitted correctly.

solenoid terminal to the negative (-) battery terminal. If the solenoid is in good condition the plunger will 'snap', making a clicking-type noise, which closes the main contacts.

A common non-start problem is often a simple electrical contact fault. On modern garden tractors there are four or five safety cut-out switches. If any one of these develops a fault the engine starter motor will automatically be disabled. The problem may simply be caused by dirt or debris contaminating the contact, or the wire to a terminal may have been dislodged, possibly from vibration. Check the control pedal or lever, as it may be out of adjustment. The purpose of the safety cut-out switches is to avoid a potential accident by ensuring the operator is in full control before starting the engine (as with an automatic car) or moving, and to prevent the operator not being in control whilst mowing.

This electric circuitry ensures that when the ignition key is turned the tractor won't lurch forward or backward and the cutter(s) won't revolve. The cutter also

won't be allowed to start or revolve if a direct-collect grassbox is fitted incorrectly, ensuring that the tractor won't throw cut grass or an object 40 feet in the direction of an unsuspecting onlooker, or through the neighbour's greenhouse. Depending on the tractor model, check the grassbox switch first, which may simply not have actuated if the back of the grassbox has been caught on a bush, tree trunk or the compost heap whilst emptying or manoeuvring.

The various safety switches are located as follows:

■ On the rear of the machine where the grassbox contacts the framework, and is the most likely place to check first, especially if you've dislodged the box on an object and it's moved out of alignment. The tractor grassbox cut-out safety switch won't allow the cutters to engage if the grassbox isn't fitted correctly.
■ On the parking brake pedal, lever or linkage.
■ On the cutter engage lever or switch.

■ On the reverse position of the gear lever, or on the ignition switch.
■ Under or inside the seat. This is wired to stop the engine if the operator leaves the seat without first disengaging the cutter and engaging the parking brake. If the engine misfires whilst the tractor's being used on a bumpy surface, check there's enough weight on the rear of the seat by adjusting it forward.

Check each switch and wire connection individually, ensuring they activate when the appropriate operation is engaged. Some models have been designed not to cut whilst reversing; others require a reversing switch to be activated before the cutters will engage.

A faulty or worn ignition switch may also be the problem. Replacing one is a relatively easy and straightforward job,

▼ Four-switch position plastic ignition terminals are marked with symbols for stop, lights (or reverse), on and start.

▼ Selection of popular garden tractor and mower ignition keys.

▼ A popular type of gnition switch.

▲ Inexpensive transparent paper inline fuel filter showing direction of fuel flow, ideal for garden tractors, riders and walk-behind garden machinery. Debris is caught on the outer side of the element.

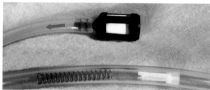

▲ Fuel filter for hand-held machinery such as grass-trimmers, chainsaws and hedge-cutters. Inline tank pickup filters are designed to drop via gravity to the lowest part of the fuel tank, whatever angle the tank is at.

▲ Air and oil filters. Check air filters every 25 hours, or more often if used in dusty conditions (25 hours equates to one year's work).

but be aware that there are different five-pin ignition switches, all of which look alike. If replaced with an incorrect switch this can cause the wiring to short and burn out. Before fitting, ensure that the wiring configuration on the terminal pins exactly matches the terminal formation on the original, even when ordered as a genuine spare part.

Besides fuel being stale or carburettor 'gumming up' occurring (see page 32), there are other fuel issues that will stop an engine from starting up or running smoothly, namely substances that find their way into the fuel tank such as grass, water, twigs, dirt and debris. These can be picked up in many different ways, such as from the huge fuel petrol station tanks or in the form of dust and particles from the top of your fuel can and funnel.

So check your tractor has a fuel filter fitted, and if it has check that it isn't blocked. Inline fuel filters are inexpensive and are simple to fit in seconds. Many have a transparent outer casing that's ideal to see the fuel filter condition; it also enables you to confirm that fuel's in the fuel line. There are several types with variable filtration efficiency, ranging from micro to a coarse filtration that will stop larger debris. Paper-types filter out finer particles. Fibre types are ideal for fine filtration on small engines. Most inline filters can't be cleaned if the filter is partially blocked, so don't mess about, just change it.

Many engines over 15hp are fitted with an oil filter, which you should replace every time you change the oil. Unscrew anticlockwise to remove. If the

filter is too tight to turn or is seized on there are oil filter strap-type removers to assist turning, available from your service dealer or a motor accessory shop. Before fitting a new oil filter, smear a thin film of oil around the filter oil seal and then screw up to finger-tightness only.

BELTS

The most common wearing parts of a domestic garden tractor are the cutter belt and the cutter blade, especially if the blade has had an impact, which will cause the machine to vibrate. If the blade momentarily stops on an impact, the engine won't. It can cause the belt to slip, resulting in a flat spot, just like an F1 car tyre requiring a premature pit stop due to excessive vibration.

Heat is the greatest enemy of a drive belt, and can shorten the life of a brand new belt to just a few minutes. There are several causes of heat generation on a tractor. The most common cause is cutting the grass too low and/or too quick. If the blade is labouring, the energy from the engine will cause heat and friction in the belt and pulleys, causing the belt to distort. The second most common cause is the belt tension. If the belt is over-tensioned the pulleys will transfer heat to it; if under-tensioned it will slip and cause friction on the belt, causing it to 'burn' and melt on the pulleys. If the cutter belt is vibrating, slipping or showing any signs of wear, such as cracks, burns or an uneven wall, *replace it*.

When ordering a replacement belt, note that genuine tractor belts are made to an exact size and shape, and are

▼ Briggs internal filter. This five-stage cyclonic air cleaner chops up debris into manageable-sized pieces and disposes of them via a primary discharge and duckbill chute, minimising debris build-up in the cooling fins and air cleaner and thereby giving the filter a longer life.

specifically manufactured to a complex blend of materials, including the space-age product Kevlar, which is lighter and five times stronger than steel. Although genuine belts are pricier, they can be more cost effective, as they're designed to cope with slipping and diverse operating temperatures to last the maximum amount of hours, thereby saving on service and breakdown time. Exact equivalent belts are rarely available, and a non-genuine belt won't perform or last as long. (If it's half the price there's normally a reason.) There are thousands of belt sizes, and it's extremely rare for different tractors to use a common or universal belt (surprise surprise). Also, ensure you ask for the correct belt type: be very specific. For instance, if you rang a supplier and ordered a 'drive belt' for your XYZ-model tractor without giving a part number, unless the dealer queries the order he'd naturally order a belt for the drive, which would be to the wheels. It would therefore be unfortunate for you if you actually wanted a drive belt for the cutter! (There's always more than one belt on every tractor.)

BLADES

Cutter blades can be reground and balanced easily and economically, or replaced when worn or damaged. Balancing the blades is just as or more important than their sharpness. When your car or steering wheel is shaking due to a wheel being out of balance, you almost immediately take it to the garage for a simple rebalancing job. When their tractor is shaking, however, many operators just carry on until the machine shakes itself to bits, even when a similarly simple, inexpensive rebalance job would quickly put it right. An out-of-balance or damaged tractor blade will prematurely wear every part of the tractor if not attended to without delay, and will literally knock years off the machine's life.

Like any type of mower, garden tractors have only been designed to cut grass. Consequently if the spinning blade impacts anything else, such as the ground, tree roots, the odd toy or stone etc, some damage will inevitably occur, and will either cause the blade to vibrate or the belt to burn, which in turn will cause the drive to vibrate. On machines with more than one blade, check that they're level and meet together on the same plane. When cutting around bushes and trees check that no twigs enter above the cutting deck and obstruct the belts, which can easily throw a belt off if caught between the belt and a pulley.

POOR GRASS COLLECTION

The blades on garden tractors need to be checked regularly, and should be reground and balanced every season. In the case of a blade having been impacted, get it reground and balanced straight away. To inspect the cutters and shafts properly it's best to remove the cutter deck assembly. This may not be as daunting as it looks. It will generally take only a few minutes.

There are many different designs of cutter deck but on most domestic tractor models its removal follows the same basic principles. Nevertheless, these instructions can only be a general guide – your model may differ, so always consult your handbook. Many cutter decks are easily removed within a few minutes without tools or needing to jack the tractor up. Consequently after every 25 hours' running time (normally one year's work) it's worth taking a good, close, unobstructed look at all the component parts that are difficult to see from above or underneath the cutter deck. To remove the cutter deck unit:

a Ensure the cutter is disengaged.
b On side-discharge decks, remove the grassbox chute (if fitted).
c Move the height lever to the lowest cutting position.
d Remove any belt guard (if fitted).
e Disconnect or unhook any control cable or tension spring, unplug any wiring connectors attached to the top of the deck (if fitted).
f Gently ease the cutter belt off the engine pulley.
g Depending on the width of the cutter, decks are fixed by either one or two bars with an R-clip or bolt at the front, between the front wheels.
h Remove the R-clip(s) or bolt(s) from the front of the cutter deck bars/ bracket.
i Remove the rear of the deck, which

▼ **Checking the blade bearings by rocking and pulling the blades. Any play or grinding noise detected indicates that bearing replacement is required.**

▶ **Check the cutter belt for splits, flat spots or damage. Check the deck for corrosion, pulley and bearing wear. Ensure the belt configuration is correct before refitting the deck. On some complex belt configurations, draw the belt layout or take a snapshot before removing the cutter belts.**

rests on a bar on either side or is fixed with clips or bolts.

j The cutter deck should now be resting on the floor. If not, check what's still holding it up and disconnect it. (There may be a deck hanger.)

k Pull the cutter deck out by sliding it from underneath the tractor. It isn't necessary to remove the cutter belt off the deck, as it'll come out attached. If you find the deck snags on something when sliding, remove it from the opposite side or turn the deck at an angle.

To refit the cutter deck reverse the procedure, checking the cutter belt configuration is correct.

Once the deck is removed, clean off any grass or debris from the top of the deck with a stiff hand-brush or garden hose. (Some tractor decks have a wash port, allowing a hose to be fitted directly on to the deck; when the cutters are engaged water pressure cleans the whole of the underneath, including the grass chute.) Inspect the cutter belt carefully for any wear or cracks. Check the belt pulleys for any distortion or wear, and check that they spin true without a grinding noise. Check the pulleys aren't loose by checking the pulley shaft and nut. Check for any play in the cutter shaft or bearings by giving it a good tug in all directions. Check the wear on the pulley brake pad, if fitted. Normally the cutter belt would be changed each season, or after 25–30 hours of work. Before removing the belt from the pulleys, make a note of its configuration around the pulleys.

Once everything has been checked on top of the deck, carefully turn it upside down. Check underneath the metal deck for corrosion or cracks, especially around the blade shaft mountings. Most tractor cutter blades bolt on to a central blade-mounting boss with one or two fixing bolts. The bolt(s) are attached to a drive shaft, which is mounted on to an aluminium or steel housing often called a 'quill housing', which is bolted on to the tractor cutting deck. The important thing here is to check the quill housing and shaft to see if the bearings are in good order. *Wear gloves* – these blades can be sharp.

▲ **Quill housing and blade shaft.**

a Check the blades for any damage or wear.

b Spin the blade and check if it runs smoothly without any grinding or uneven movement. (Blade pulleys may be 'braked' – you may need to disconnect or move the brake pad if one is fitted.)

c Take a strong, firm grip on the central cutter shaft and give it a positive side to side, up and down, pull and push in various directions. Turn the blade 90° then test it again.

d Firmly grip the tip of the blade and rock it up and down. If there's any movement or play in the shaft the bearings require replacement. (On many models the bearings, drive shaft and housing may come as one complete unit.)

▼ **Check cutter blades are aligned at the centre for an even cut.**

e Check that each of the blade tips are level and not bent – turn the blade 360° to see if the opposite tip is at the same height and on the same plane.

f On triple- and four-blade decks check that all the blades are at the same height when they meet at the tips.

Most central blade bolts are a right-hand thread, but on some twin contra-rotating blades one blade may have a left-hand thread. It's very important to regrind and balance each blade – an unbalanced, bent or damaged blade will create uncomfortable mowing, give an uneven cut, have a louder sound, and will promote premature wear via vibration on the whole of the tractor. Blades are inexpensive to regrind and balance (and far cheaper than replacing the blade), and we suggest you take them to a specialist with a professional blade balancer, since some blades aren't flat and some have a shaped centre hole that makes finding the exact centre more tricky – which makes DIY balancing more problematic. Some blades may also be wider and longer, with specially shaped aerodynamics designed to assist grass collection or create mulch, all of which further complicate finding a perfect balance.

After the blades have been checked, ensure that when you refit them you have the blade wing tips facing upwards toward the tractor. Ensure that the blade bolts are tight, and that the cutter belt is fitted the correct way around the

▼ **This picture shows the same cutter turned 180° and out of alignment at the centre. This will produce an unattractive, uneven cut (as well as vibration). In this instance new blades are required.**

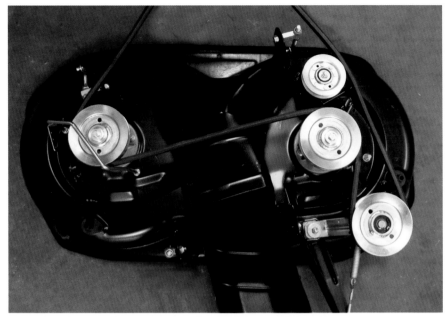

▲ Deck underside. Check the blade wing tips are not damaged or worn. They generate air flow to convey cut grass to the box.

▲ Plan view of a popular 36in twin cutter deck showing belt configuration and grass chute.

jockey pulleys before engine start-up. Pay especial attention to ensuring that the belt's on the correct side of any belt guides. (If the cutters are engaged with an incorrectly fitted belt the belt can be damaged, rendering it useless within seconds.)

BRAKES

The brake systems on garden tractors are, in the main, quite reliable. They're situated on the side of the gearbox, whether manual or hydrostatic. Depending on the model, some can be awkward to inspect as they can be partially obscured by the rear wheels, chassis or brake linkage. Removing a rear wheel or jacking up the tractor is normally sufficient to inspect the brake pad and disc. Brake discs are 2–3in in diameter, and spin all the time the rear wheels are in motion, thus ensuring the brake will work whether the engine is running or not.

Nevertheless, they can cause problems that can fool you by demonstrating the wrong symptoms. If the tractor has been working fine but won't drive, don't automatically assume it's a drive fault, as a seized brake could cause the same symptom. A common cause can occur if the tractor is left with the parking brake on – moisture will cause the disc and brake pad to oxidise and seize together. When not in use, and provided the tractor

isn't left on a slope, we suggest you store it with the brake disengaged. To unseize a brake put the tractor in neutral or, if a hydrostatic gearbox, pull/push/slide the gearbox dump valve, normally situated at the rear of the tractor near the tow bracket, or in front of or behind one of the rear wheels. Rock the tractor back and forth till the disc moves. If this doesn't work follow the brake linkage from the brake pedal to the brake disc and move the brake rod manually back toward the pedal, then try rocking again. Failing this, remove the rear wheel nearest to the brake and tap around the brake. (You may find the wheel is seized to the axle, especially if the machine hasn't been serviced regularly; always put a slither of grease – copper slip is ideal – on the rear axle before replacing the wheel.) DO NOT force or hammer the wheel off sideways. The gearbox drive axles haven't been designed to take sideways strain, and are only held in place by a circlip inside the gearbox; if forced outwards the fixing can easily be dislodged, which is only remedied by removing and dismantling the gearbox to refit the circlip. If you still have no joy with the brake, the brake pad can be removed by its two fixing bolts. On some tractors these can be awkward to access, and the axle/gearbox will have to be removed first.

The most common causes for the

brake not working are because the brake linkage requires adjustment or the brake pad is worn out. Rectifying these problems is a straightforward job as domestic garden tractor brakes are just manually operated by a simple pushrod, there are no hydraulics involved; the only problem on some models is the accessibility of the brake disc. The brake consists of a small oblong brake pad, which sits in a recess in the casing. Clean around the brake area, replace the pad and check the brake pushrod is clean and free to move. Apply a small smear of grease without getting any of it near the brake pad.

NOTE: *Whenever you overlubricate garden machinery grass and debris will always stick to it.*

BATTERIES

There are two main types of battery: a starting battery as found on garden tractors, designed to cope with high amp loads over a short period; and a deep-cycle battery, designed to provide low to medium amp loads over a continuous period. Just like cars, virtually all modern domestic garden tractors run on a 12V system. The battery is either a lead acid or non-spill (dry) lead acid.

In the main a tractor battery requires

▲ Typical domestic dry tractor 12V 18AH (amp hour) lead acid battery.

▲ Typical tractor 12V 24AH lead acid battery.

little maintenance, but because of the tractor's smaller capacity it may need to be charged more frequently than a car. If the engine doesn't start after half a dozen attempts the battery could be drained, especially if used in cold temperatures, which can decrease battery power by half, especially after being dormant for three months. Added to this, a battery more than two or three years old won't have as much power as it had when it was new.

During the winter charge the battery every couple of months. Run the engine for ten minutes to lubricate the engine and dispel moisture. This prevents internal parts from corroding. If a lead acid battery is fitted, a normal car battery charger can be used. If a dry sealed battery is fitted (these are normally a flat type), check the owners' manual or consult a service agent for the correct type of charger. Some tractors include a trickle charger for dry battery models.

On average the life of a tractor

▼ Typical 12V 5AH battery for key-start walk-behind mowers.

battery is about three years. After this period, even if holding a charge it'll have less power than when new, especially in cold temperatures, which can decrease the power by 50%. Remember, a fully charged battery is a good battery and will have the longest life.

On liquid batteries the liquid electrolyte level of each cell can be seen at a glance via the transparent casing, eliminating the need to remove the battery top to check them. If any of the six cells are low they can be topped up with distilled water. Sealed-for-life non-spill lead acid batteries need no maintenance other than charging. The more amps, the greater the power capacity of the battery. Amp hours are typically quoted for a 20-hour cycle, *ie* a 50AH battery will supply a 2.5A load for 20 hours (50 ÷ 20 = 2.5).

NOTE: *When purchasing a replacement tractor battery, choose the highest AH rating that can be accommodated on the machine. Ensure the battery positive and negative terminals are the same way round as the original; this will make certain that your terminal wires will reach. Tractor batteries are made with the positive on the right or the left.*

PUNCTURES
Getting a puncture is always a pain in the gr-ass, wherever you are, and the fact that it's only flat at the bottom doesn't help either. Your tractor will be awkward to steer, and the costly tyre can be damaged if driven on. Most common domestic tractor tyres are tubeless, so if you have anything

resembling a thorn hedge in the vicinity of the tractor there's a good chance that sooner or later you're going to get a flat. Thorns are exceptionally sharp and strong; they'll go straight through a garden tractor tyre and an inner tube too, if one is fitted. (One advantage of an inner tube is that the tyre can be run at a lower pressure, easily down to 10lb/in^2, for a good firm grip on damp grass if required, whereas a tubeless tyre requires pumping to a higher pressure).

There are several ways to sort this problem. The quickest and least expensive solution is tyre sealant, which will cure puncture problems permanently. Even if you get several more perforations from thorns or nails thereafter, the tyre still won't deflate.

Several brands of tyre sealant are available, consisting of a syrupy liquid that coats the inside of the tyre as it spins, instantly resealing any perforations of the tyre wall. To fit tyre sealant:

1 Lift the tractor so the wheel is off the ground.
2 Allow the tyre to deflate by removing the centre of the valve, achieved by unscrewing the internal valve stem anticlockwise. (A valve core removal tool is normally supplied with the sealant.)
3 Check the correct amount of sealant required by comparing the tyre size embossed on the outside of the tyre to the quantity of sealant stated on the bottle.
4 Position the wheel with the valve at the four or eight o'clock position.
5 Fit the plastic tube provided with the sealant on to the outside of the valve and squeeze the sealant slowly into the tyre.
6 Refit the valve stem by carefully screwing it clockwise.
7 Spin the wheel several times to ensure the sealant has covered the entire inside of the tyre.
8 Inflate the tyre to the correct pressure; no more punctures in that tyre! If you pick up another thorn or puncture the sealant will automatically reseal the hole as it turns.

A rough guide of how much sealant you'll need, depending on the tyre size (so check it), is that approximately one litre of sealant will protect two front tyres or one rear on a domestic garden

◀▲ One-litre container of tyre sealant. It normally comes with a valve removal tool and filler tube.

▲ Fitting tyre sealant will eliminate and prevent punctures and flat or damaged tyres, saving you time and money. If you have anything resembling thorn hedging it's advisable to add tyre sealant during your mower's annual service; even better, ask for tyre sealant to be fitted before you take delivery of a new or used tractor.

▼ This tyre valve removal tool also doubles as a valve cap, so is always to hand.

tractor. Larger tyres require more sealant to give adequate protection. Don't use less than the quoted amount, otherwise the whole of the internal tyre wall won't be covered. However, no harm will occur if slightly more sealant is inserted. Tyre sealant can be fitted in inner tubes or tubeless tyres.

NOTE: *Tyre sealant won't cure a puncture problem if the air valve is damaged, the tyre wall is cracked or the tyre has a gash large enough to sink the Titanic!*

Tyre sealant is also ideal for use in wheelbarrows, golf karts, garden trailers, sack trucks and mobility scooters etc.

Another quick and easy option is a tyre inflation canister. These convenient compressed air canisters, although only providing a temporary repair, will re-inflate the tyre without removing the wheel – ideal if the tyre has deflated and you've no access to a pump. They're also very handy in awkward situations, like when you've only half-finished mowing or the grass is a foot tall because it's rained for the last fortnight and you're going on holiday in the morning!

The alternative – probably the most time-consuming, more expensive and, possibly, less effective – is jacking the

tractor up, removing the wheel, taking it to a car tyre dealer and having the puncture repaired or waiting for an inner tube to be ordered (it's guaranteed to be a non-stock 'odd size'), then return home and refit the wheel, only to pick up another thorn on the way back to the shed.

NOTE: *If a rear tyre is punctured the wheel may be seized on the axle if it hasn't been regularly serviced or axle-greased, and if the wheel is forced off it can dislodge the axle retaining clip. This can only be remedied by removing the gearbox and stripping to refit the dislodged clip.*

THE SOD'S LAW OF GARDEN TRACTOR PUNCTURES

1 A puncture will always occur on a slope or in an awkward place.
2 It will be muddy, facing the wrong way, and situated where it will be hard or impossible to push.
3 It will be as far away from the garden shed as possible.
4 It will rain as soon as you get a flat.
5 It will be in the evening, at the weekend or whatever other times the repair shops are shut.
6 The grass won't have been cut for three weeks, tigers will be wandering about and you'll be going on holiday for a fortnight the very next day.

◄ **Internal gear configuration on typical manual transaxle five-speed gearbox. Tractor manufacturers use various different gearbox companies; the make and model of the gearbox will be stamped on the casing for spare part ordering.**

▼ **Tecumseh and Peerless 920 series transaxle. Note the external brake assembly can be fitted on the left or right side, depending on the manufacturers' model. Permanent lubrication is 30oz (887ml) of Bentonite grease, part number 788067C. Note this view is a guide only – yours may differ.**

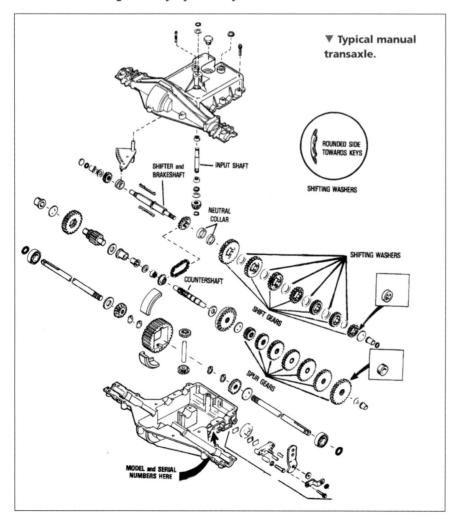

▼ **Typical manual transaxle.**

SHIFTER and BRAKESHAFT

INPUT SHAFT

ROUNDED SIDE TOWARDS KEYS

SHIFTING WASHERS

NEUTRAL COLLAR

SHIFTING WASHERS

COUNTERSHAFT

SHIFT GEARS

SPUR GEARS

MODEL and SERIAL NUMBERS HERE

TRACTOR TRANSAXLE GEARBOXES

Tecumseh and Peerless gearboxes can be quite complex and we don't recommend attempting internal repairs, especially where a failure has occurred on a hydrostatic drive, which frequently results in a whole unit replacement. Below are some guidelines to assist you in making an accurate evaluation of a power loss problem on a hydrostatic drive, to eliminate any unnecessary replacement and hence cost.

External gearbox functions need to be checked first to determine if the hydro is the fault:

1 Check the drive belt for wear. If slipping, reset to the correct tension. Incorrect running symptoms are the belt jumping or chattering on the pulleys, making the drive pulsate and uneven. Check the pulleys for wear or damage and replace the belt.
2 Check if the gearbox is overheating – if the oil is too hot its viscosity will reduce pressure. Ensure the cooling fins aren't damaged and the housing isn't clogged with debris or grass.
3 Check for oil or grease leakage. If there is any, it could be seal or axle shaft wear. It's worth checking with a pro.

1 Ensure the gearbox is cool.
2 Place the gear lever halfway between forward and neutral positions.
3 Position the tractor on a 17° incline. (If you don't have an inclinometer, a phone app is available.)
4 Drive the tractor up the slope with the cutter disengaged. Normally there should only be up to a 20% loss of power. Excessive power loss would be classed at 50%.
5 Move the drive lever slowly to avoid front-wheel lift, return to neutral and shift forward. Note the forward response.

▲ Hydrostatic transaxle gearbox brake.

▲▶ Hydrostatic gearbox cutaway showing internal mechanics. Hydrostatic gearbox parts aren't normally serviceable, and the complete unit would need to be replaced. Debris or a twig can damage a fin, so check the cooling fan isn't damaged. Also, remove any grass build-up on top of the gearbox to prevent overheating.

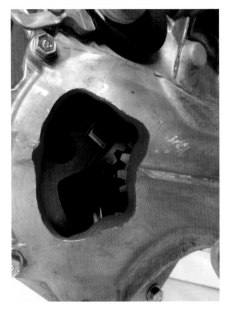

On average a garden machinery dealer will spend more time servicing a garden tractor than a garage will on a standard car service.

◀ Transaxle gearbox.

▼ Hydro gearbox.

CHECKING GEARBOX OIL LEVEL

a Ensure the tractor is on a level surface and engage the parking brake.

b Locate the filler plug, normally near the gearshift rod situated on top of the gearbox (in general at the rear of a tractor by the tow hitch, but yours may differ). Use needle pliers under the filler plug, applying a rocking action until it's removed.

c Use a dipstick at 45° (Tecumseh part no 35942). Half an inch of oil will show when fully inserted. The gearbox takes 16oz of EP90 gearbox oil, which can be fitted via a gooseneck oilcan.

d Refit the filler plug with silicone lubricant spray. Note that some tractor oil filler plugs may be awkward to access.

Filler Plug

The illustration here is a general assembly guide. Your model may be different depending on the manufacturer's specifications.

Chapter 8

The robot mower and future developments

TO BOLDLY MOW WHERE NO MAN HAS MOWN BEFORE!

In the future, perhaps, discreet, completely soundless laser mowers with no moving parts will groom lawns by disintegrating the grass into moisture and nutrients and automatically recycling it into the ground as natural fertiliser, with GPS satellites informing it if it's missed a bit. But until then we have the robot mower – a pretty good substitute.

Since before the invention of the landmark labour-saving lawnmowing contraption of 1830, man has always strived to save himself yet more work and time – not an easy task in this case, as the original basic design was so good. In fact it took another 120 years to achieve the next generation of grass-cutting machine, with the innovative technology of a

◀ 'To boldly mow where no man has mown before!' The Ransome Spyder II remote control 4x4 25HP all-terrain robot, price £33,000.

▼ The evolution of mowing. In the beginning man invented the scythe, but it took 2,000 years to invent the robot mower.

▲ The world's first robot mower, produced in 1995 by the Swedish company Husqvarna. Almost silent, and powered by environmentally friendly daylight via solar panels similar to those fitted on the Space Shuttle, its development cost was a million pounds, and they were sold in the shops at £2,000.

▲ A radio-controlled lawnmower was developed by Webb in the 1950s, but it took another 40 years for a fully robotic mower to be developed.

▲ Robot rainbow.

▼▶ Solar energy and battery powered hybrid robot.

remote radio-controlled lawnmower in the 1950s.

Unfortunately the safety technology of the time wasn't good enough, and it was quite possible for the hapless operator to loose control and watch his machine plough through the flower beds and disappear through his neighbour's garden fence. It took the world's engineering experts another 40 years, up to 1995, before Husqvarna came up with a robot machine that would cut the grass safely and reliably – albeit at a cost of a million pounds to develop and £2,000 each to purchase; and it took virtually another 20 years for them to be mass-produced in sufficient volume to be affordable without the purchaser needing to take out a second mortgage.

2013 machine sales statistics indicated the robot-type mower to be one of the fastest growing categories of grass-cutting machines on the market for years. Already popular in Europe and around the world, they're now becoming more desirable in the UK. Currently the robot mower is seen more as a lifestyle choice than 'a machine for cutting grass'. Since its invention the fully robotic mower has mainly been the choice of busy techno-thinking people who can see its advantages – for one thing, buying them precious free time to spend elsewhere by getting the lawn cut by doing nothing. It's hard to put a price on that. Many people are content as long as the grass is cut, and would

rather be playing golf or watching TV whilst the robot cuts the grass. Robots don't go on holiday, so you can!

Nowadays things are changing. When we used to be sleeping at night we can now go shopping, and there's no reason why a robot mower can't cut in the dark into the early hours – they're virtually silent from only a few yards away (unless they're stolen, when an ear-splitting anti-theft alarm is sounded; many robots also have a pin code for extra security). Robots can operate in the rain; they're fitted with rain sensors that automatically command it to return to base, or it will skip mowing altogether if wet conditions continue. And when the robot senses it's low on power it'll automatically return to its docking station to recharge itself. Any robot that wanders outside its designated area (which in most cases means its been stolen) can be automatically alerted to a mobile phone or the police (or service dealer if it senses a fault) and can be tracked via satellite and recovered at its final destination, to the great satisfaction of the owner and the local constabulary.

Robot mowers are extremely fuel-efficient, with very low energy consumption. They produce no harmful emissions or exhaust fumes, and operate at a fraction of the running cost of conventional grasscutters. Various models have electronic sensors on the blades, which transmit low current to the motor when the grass is short, conserving battery power, and providing more power when the grass is longer. Some models have a 'spiral mode' pattern to clear an area where the grass is longer, ensuring the lawn gets cut evenly.

Domestic robot mowers cut the grass with two to six cutting blade tips, which can tackle areas up to 400m^2, while larger machines can cope with 4,000m^2. They can deal with slopes up to around 25°, and if the robot is tipped or lifted sensors will automatically cut the power to the blades and drive. On encountering an object, person or animal the robot will stop and redirect itself without causing damage; its sensors enable it to work around flower beds, bushes and trees.

Powered by lithium-ion batteries, most robot mowers have a built-in backlit LED control panel for easy and intuitive programming, with different settings and timings for different gardens. Height of cut is easily adjusted as desired. Robot mowers can find separate garden areas using inbuilt search systems, and when a recharge is required, or if it rains, they'll automatically return to their docking station by following a guide or boundary wire via a homing signal. Once recharged, or when the rain stops, they'll automatically return to complete their programmed cutting duties.

2013 saw an unprecedented growth in robot mowers as many major brands competed in the market for the first time, including AL-KO, Bosch, Etisia, Flymo, Honda, John Deere, Ransome, Stiga and Viking, plus a few Far East contenders joining the already established Husqvarna, Brill and Friendly Robotics Robo Mo machines. Some are now available from supermarkets and mail order companies for the first time, whereas in the past robot mowers were the domain of specialist dealers. However, careful consideration should be given regarding where you buy your robot. Sometimes specialist equipment is needed for servicing them, while most current models need setting up and require a perimeter wire to be installed at the owner's premises. Though robot installation is quite simple to do yourself, it may be worth looking for a local specialist that offers set-up installation and a demonstration, including back-up service during the warranty and after it has lapsed.

▼ The first Bosch Indigo robot mower.

▲ The first Flymo robot with docking station.

▶ **Ransome Spider II commercial robot four-wheel drive and four-wheel steering all-terrain 48in cut, powered by remote control via a 23hp Kawasaki engine costing £33,000. It's to be found on golf courses and rough terrain areas, making it much safer for the operator to oversee the grass-cutting from a distance, especially where steep, slippery gradients are found. A 6.5hp 190cc Spider Mini with 22in cut was also available with a smaller but hardly mini price tag of around £9,000 in 2014.**

▲ Under the cover of a Robomow RM400. On this robot the body conveniently hinges up like a car bonnet, showing the single rotary blade and motor layout.

Who knows what the future might hold in these garden industry-changing times? 2013 saw the world-famous Chelsea Flower Show lift its very stringent 'Garden Gnome' ban for the first time (gnome mean feat in its centenary year). Perhaps we'll see synthetic plastic grass allowed next, and

▼ Robomow RM400 showing the clip-on single blade and height adjustment wheel. The Robomow comes in semi and fully robotic models.

▲ Robot electronic circuitry board – each robot has its own system. When a fault occurs, a fault diagnosis code will show on the LCD display screen. The fault code can then be checked in the Robot manual or on the Internet to find the specific procedure required to rectify the problem.

instead of saying the lawn wants mowing we might say 'I'm just going to give the lawn a brush and vac', or 'I'm off to scratch and sniff the artificial flowers whilst I give them a quick dusting', or 'that robot's keeping our garden neat and tidy'.

As has been mentioned, most domestic robot mowers are governed by installing a perimeter wire around whatever area you wish it to work. The thin single-strand wire, carrying a safe 12V, is installed around the edge of the lawn for it to work fully robotically (if the cable is severed or no signal detected the robot will automatically stop). This wire is initially pegged down on the grass surface, where the grass will eventually grow over it, or it can be buried approximately an inch (25mm) deep in the turf by using a half-moon edging iron. Note that it's worth pegging the wire on the surface for the initial set-up period, so that it can be fine-tuned to the exact shape required once you're happy with the proportions of the area the robot needs to mow. No special skill is required for this process. Ponds, trees, posts, flower beds etc can be avoided if the wire is placed around them. A one-time program set-up follows this process. The robot's recharging station is then put in the circuit, ideally near an electricity outlet.

Some robot models can be used without a perimeter wire fitted, with sensors redirecting the machine when no grass is detected beneath it. These models are ultra-easy to set up, virtually needing only to be taken out of the box, placed on the grass and have their start button pressed. If a heavy overload is sensed the cutter will stop, and direction is automatically altered. However, such models are only classed as semi-robotic, since when the battery power runs low the mower doesn't automatically know (on pre-2014 models) its way back to a recharging docking station. There may also be slight issues if your lawn area isn't defined exactly by a border or path.

Before purchasing a robot mower it's worth drawing a simple sketch of your area and taking it to a local specialist for them to determine the most efficient wire layout.

▲ Robomow RM500 triple-blade. This robot can be used in fully robotic mode or can be remote-controlled via an integral control panel for guidance in awkward areas. Access to its components is a more involved process on this model, involving snap-on chassis clips.

▶ Underneath a Robomow 500. Triple clip-on blades and grass-height adjustment wheel.

▼ Three basic robot installation steps. (1) Lay out the perimeter wire on top of the grass; (2) preset the day and times for mowing; (3) after the robot has cut, the perimeter wire can be finely adjusted and positioned to the edge if necessary, where the grass will grow over it, or preferably sunk an inch (25mm) below the turf.

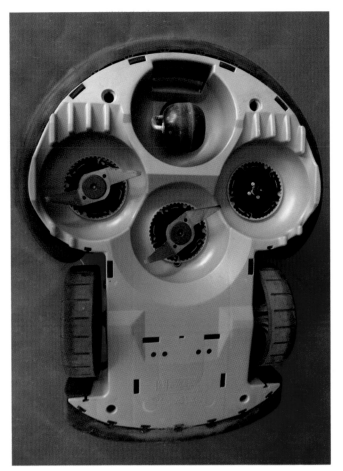

Chapter 9

Servicing and maintenance

THE SERVICE SCHEDULE

EVERY MONTH OR EVERY 12 HOURS OF OPERATION

NB: New four-stroke mowers should have the sump drained and refilled with fresh oil after the first two to three hours of operation.

- Remove the spark plug and clean the electrodes with a wire brush. Reset gap to 0.76mm (0.030in), or as recommended by manufacturer.
- Check condition and tightness of electrical leads.
- Rotary mowers: check cutting edges of cutter bar or disc blades. File down small nicks only. If large nicks are evident, remove cutter assembly and check balance.
- Check the security of all nuts and bolts.
- Cylinder mowers: check the setting of the bottom blade to ensure it has the correct 'scissors' action with the blades of the cutting cylinder.
- If necessary, lubricate the moving parts of the height adjusters and controls.

◀ Blocked air intake.

EVERY TWO MONTHS OR EVERY 25 HOURS OF OPERATION

- Service the air filter.
- Clean the contact breaker points (unless electronic ignition). Turn the engine to give the widest gap and reset this to correct figure.
- Four-strokes: drain and refill the oil sump.
- Check the fuel filter (if fitted). If a filter isn't fitted, remove top of carburettor and check for dirt.
- Run the engine for three to five minutes until it's thoroughly warmed through. Check the idling and speeding up response and adjust the carburettor if necessary.
- Remove cutter bar or disc and check the balance.
- Adjust the hand-control settings if necessary, including clutches on cylinder mowers and self-propelled mowers.
- Adjust the chains or belts on cylinder mowers and self-propelled mowers if necessary.
- Lubricate all mower parts as appropriate, including the height adjustment.
- Cylinder mowers: check the blades aren't bent.
- Cylinder mowers: check the condition of the blade edges. If necessary, lap

the edges by turning the cylinder backwards (with a handbrace on the shaft or by other means), having lapping compound on the bottom blade, which is set close. When the edges have improved, clean off all compound very thoroughly and reset the bottom blade.
- Grease the chains (if fitted). Inspect the condition of any drive belts to check for cracking.

NB: In dusty operating conditions, more frequent servicing of the air and fuel filters and changing of the engine oil will be needed.

END OF SEASON OR EVERY 75 HOURS OF OPERATION

- Check engine compression (use a screw-in compression tester). If not very satisfactory, consider overhaul.
- Remove cylinder head (obtain new gasket). Remove carbon deposits. Inspect valves and consider regrinding; adjust tappet clearance (four-strokes).
- Two-strokes: clean out ports with a wooden tool and blow out all carbon. Wipe clean carefully.
- Check the starter mechanism and renew the cord, if necessary. On

models that have sharp pawls gripping a cup (without recesses, the non-ratchet type), sharpen up the pawls with a file to improve the grip.

■ Four-strokes: drain oil sump very thoroughly. Refill with fresh oil of recommended viscosity.
■ Dismantle and clean out the carburettor, fitting new gaskets when reassembling.
■ Dismantle and clean out the fuel tap. Clean the fuel filter, if fitted.
■ Check and clear the vent hole in the petrol tank cap.

■ If there's a valve on the crankcase breather in the valve chest, check whether it works freely. If not, dismantle, clean, and renew parts if necessary, and refit using a new gasket set.
■ Air filter: fit a new paper cartridge, or, if polyurethane foam or stocking and dry element type, wash and if still looking dirty consider obtaining a replacement.
■ Check the condition of the cutting blades on rotary mowers and consider fitting a new set (with new

bolts and fittings, never the old set), or consider dismantling cylinder mower to send the cutting cylinder away for regrinding.
■ Check the wear of all bearings in the mower and consider what action needs to be taken. New bearings can be fitted, and plain bushes can usually be reamed out and fitted with new insert bushes. If the hole in the bush has worn oval or the wear is offset, fit a new bush, as hand-reaming a new hole concentrically is extremely difficult.

BUYING SPARE PARTS

As we've said before, all lawnmowers and grasscutters are different, so most manufacturers' parts won't fit on other machines. There isn't a standard belt, chain, bearing, blade, cable, sprocket, roller, gasket or thread etc. Consequently be wary when ordering spare parts without a part number: different models can be called the same name, and there can be many models within a range –

for example there are about 20 different models of Suffolk Punch!

A handy thing to have is the owners' handbook. Many have exploded views of the parts with part numbers, which is extremely handy when ordering spare parts. Without it the 'common ordinary standard thingamajig' that you want is hard to explain to a computer that calls it a 'nylotron washer' (an actual part). Some

specific manufacturers' handbooks are available, including the owners' handbook, the spare parts handbook, the workshop manual and the technical and engineer manuals. All may possibly be sourced from your local garden machinery agent. Many manufacturers didn't make in-depth service manuals, but many older, vintage out-of-print handbooks can be sourced from the British Lawnmower Museum.

SPARK PLUGS

The condition of the spark plug will give you an indication of the state of the engine and how it is running.

Spark plugs need replacing or cleaning more often in lawnmower engines than cars, which have sophisticated engine management

◄ **Champion spark plug. A trademark of the Federal-Mogul Corporation.**

► **Anatomy of a spark plug. Champion spark plugs have been fitted as original equipment to millions of garden machine engines all over the world. (Courtesy of Federal-Mogul Corporation)**

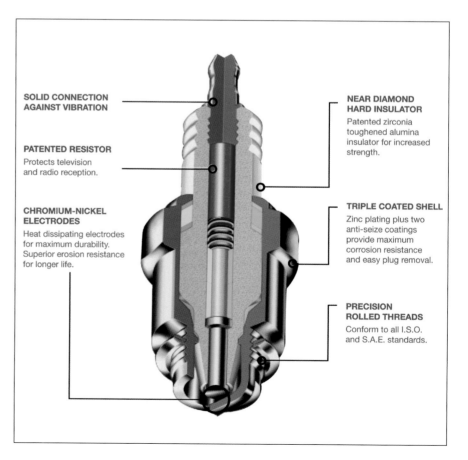

SOLID CONNECTION AGAINST VIBRATION

PATENTED RESISTOR
Protects television and radio reception.

CHROMIUM-NICKEL ELECTRODES
Heat dissipating electrodes for maximum durability. Superior erosion resistance for longer life.

NEAR DIAMOND HARD INSULATOR
Patented zirconia toughened alumina insulator for increased strength.

TRIPLE COATED SHELL
Zinc plating plus two anti-seize coatings provide maximum corrosion resistance and easy plug removal.

PRECISION ROLLED THREADS
Conform to all I.S.O. and S.A.E. standards.

▲ Spark plug in good condition, showing that the engine is running correctly. The centre insulator should have a light brown or grey deposit.

▲ Carbon-fouled spark plug.

▲ Oil-fouled spark plug.

systems. Carbon will build up on the electrode insulation of a mower, which can cause the engine to misfire or become hard to start. The spark plug is one of the first things to change. It can be quickly and cheaply replaced and fitted, and eliminates a faulty plug being the cause of an engine-starting or running problem.

FLOODED ENGINE/WET SPARK PLUGS

An engine won't start when it's flooded (*ie* when the combustion chamber is overfilled with fuel). This is normally caused by an incorrect fuel and air mix or because the spark plug, having been unable to spark for a number of reasons on a cold start-up, has drawn more fuel into the combustion chamber each time the engine is turned over. Remove the spark plug, pull the cord a few times to let the fuel evaporate, clean and dry the spark plug and then refit it. Alternatively go for a cup of tea and return in ten minutes and give it another try, without the choke or throttle turned on.

CLEANING

Regularly check and remove any accumulated grass and debris build-up from air vents and filters, especially on electric machines. A blocked air intake will starve the motor of vital cool air and if continually left unchecked can overheat the motor, causing excessive wear and premature, costly replacement. In the case of budget

imports a motor replacement may even be a non-economical repair, or the part might not be available. Check more often when cutting in dry, dusty conditions, particularly when scarifying, which creates large amounts of dust and debris that can block an air intake

within minutes. On some models the air intake filter element may be covered with a shroud and hidden from view underneath. Check these filters regularly depending on cutting conditions – this will ensure maximum motor-running hours.

▶ Blocked air intake on electric models.

SHARPENING BLADES

ROTARY CUTTERS

Examine cutting edges regularly. This will enable you not only to check their condition but also to look for corrosion of the cutting area, as well as nicks or more serious damage to the blades themselves. Small nicks can be filed away, but resharpening larger ones isn't really practical as so much of the metal has to be removed right along the blade edge. More seriously the mower's balance will be affected, and the other side must also be attended to, both for safety and for the sake of avoiding engine damage through vibration.

Rotary cutters take many forms. Some cutter bars have an integral sharpened edge at each end; others have cutting blades bolted on. Cutting discs may have two blades, three blades or two blades plus two grass deflectors. In all cases, these are bolted on. Some blades are triangular, giving three cutting edges that can be used in turn as they blunt.

It's very important for safety to inspect all bolts and fittings very carefully. Any looseness must be investigated: is the locknut losing its grip? Is the shake-free washer (if fitted) too flattened or blunted to do its job? Is there any sign of the bolt-hole becoming enlarged? If the enlargement is unmistakable then it's likely that the bolts will work loose again, despite the use of locknuts or other locking devices: a new disc is the only safe step here.

It goes without saying that the central fixing bolt holding the bar or disc to the end of the engine crankshaft must always be checked. Most of them are tightened down on a Belleville washer, with the domed surface always on the bolt-head side. These washers aren't merely washers, they're also springs, because of their shape, and the important advantage of this is that when parts settle down while the mower's running the Belleville washer still retains its pressure on the bolt and prevents it from loosening any further. Another advantage is that if the cutter strikes a heavy object it's free to give and spin round under the washer, which still retains its grip and continues to hold the cutter and make it turn again once the obstruction's been cleared.

Sharpening

Sharpen to an angle of 30°, and keep the angle even all along the cutting edge. Note that the back of the blade is turned up to form a grass deflector. Don't sharpen to a point, as this will quickly burr over and give a poor cutting edge. Leave a slight shoulder of about 0.4mm (0.16in) . This will wear back to give a good, long-lasting edge.

Balancing

Whatever the type of cutter, the general procedure is the same. You need a thin steel rod, the smaller the better. This needs to be supported firmly in a horizontal position, and the bar or disc balanced on it through its fixing hole, as shown in the illustrations on page 56. For best results the rod must be of much smaller diameter than the hole, and of course it must be straight.

Having been thoroughly cleaned, the bar or disc is supported on the rod. First, test the dimensions. Fix a thin strip of metal or other suitable pointer alongside the tip of one of the blades so that it just touches. Turn the bar or disc through a half-circle until the other cutter is against the pointer. The difference shouldn't be more than 1.5mm (0.06in).

Before correcting any difference, check the balance. Set the blades at the same height, with the bar parallel to the floor, and release gently. Unless the cutter bar or disc has been damaged, it's most likely that the longer side will dip towards the floor, showing it's out of balance. If so, make a few strokes of a file across the end of the longer part and recheck the balance. Keep doing this until it no longer dips when released. As a check, turn it through a half-circle and check the balance again.

If the dimensions were correct – which is usually the case – but there's an indication of it being out of balance, file off the back of the bar or cutter, not the end. The secret with the filing is a little at a time. The better the all-round balance you can get, the more smoothly the mower will run and the less wear and strain there'll be on the engine.

With a disc with four fittings, say two cutters and two grass deflectors, balance with the cutters only and then with the deflectors only. A disc with three blades is more difficult, but do a particularly careful check on their dimensions first. Then spin the disc several times to check whether it always tends to settle with one blade nearer the bottom. If so, it's likely that the disc assembly is slightly heavier at that point.

IMPORTANT: *Bent blades, bent bars and uneven-length fittings or bars are best discarded and replaced.*

CYLINDER CUTTERS

No instructions are given for regrinding the blades of cutting cylinders, because this is one operation that can only be carried out satisfactorily on a machine made specially for the purpose, such as those used in lawnmower repair establishments. It's nevertheless worth considering the requirements for correct grinding.

The cutting cylinder may have anything from three blades, as on the smallest lightweight machines, up to twelve on larger models in the higher price brackets. The blades may be straight or slightly curved: either way, they're set at an angle to the axle of the cylinder. All these blades do the cutting by a scissor action against the bottom blade. As each cylinder blade comes round and strokes the bottom blade, it's in contact with it at only one point at any given moment. Contact must therefore be maintained between the angled blade on the cylinder and the straight bottom blade all along its length. Otherwise there'll be gaps in the cutting.

Another way of looking at it is from either end, along the axle. Every part of every blade must describe a perfect circle of exactly the same diameter as it spins, so that all the blades together are rather like a cylinder (hence the name), whose outside edge is always in contact with the bottom blade. And this is only the start.

The surface of the cutting edge of the bottom blade is at an angle. Each blade on the cylinder must therefore be ground at the same angle. Multiply these requirements by from three to twelve times and you'd need to be a masochist to want to do the job at home!

The special grinding machines referred to can be adjusted to an accuracy of at least 0.4mm (0.016in). The cutting cylinder is supported in its own bearings, so that it spins as precisely as it does when it's in the mower. A grinding wheel, set at the required angle and driven by an electric motor, is mounted alongside on an accurate slide and passes from end to end of the cylinder, which is steadily spinning. The cylinder has been sprayed with paint all over, so that as the grinding progresses it's easy to be sure when all the nicks and jags on the blades have been ground off, as only a straight, smooth and paint-free edge can then be seen. When all the blades have a complete cutting edge, smooth and clean and sharp, the machine is set to make several passes, grinding in both directions: this evens out any differences between the cutting edges and removes any slight roughness; it also dresses the grinding wheel itself in readiness for the next cylinder.

Bottom blade

It's possible to regrind a bottom blade that's in good condition, although this is seldom worthwhile. To obtain the best performance from the refurbished cylinder it's best to renew the blade. During use of a mower it may happen that a bottom blade, if rather lightweight and struck by some object, becomes bowed or dished. Obviously, in this condition the scissor action can't be achieved at all points, and poor cutting will result. It's sometimes possible to insert shims at the blade's mounting points so that when screwed down it tends to straighten out.

Set the bottom blade so that it only just makes contact with the cylinder blades as the latter rotate. Too firm a contact wears both blade and cylinder cutting edges, causes noisy operation and puts an extra load on the engine.

To check cutting efficiency, hold a single thickness of thin paper across the bottom blade's cutting edge, so that it points more or less at the cylinder axle, then carefully turn the cylinder by hand. *Be VERY careful*, as the blades are sharp enough to cause serious injury. The scissor action between fixed and moving blades should cut the paper. Repeat at various points along the bottom blade, using all the cylinder blades. Ideally the paper should be cut at any point along the bottom blade by any cylinder blade.

Some users may prefer to have a very slight clearance between the bottom blade and the cylinder blades; this gives very quiet operation while still giving a good cut, provided the blades are sharp.

Lapping

Grinding leaves slight roughness on one edge, which will be taken off against the bottom blade during mowing, the blade being further adjusted after 'running in'. If preferred, the cutting cylinder can be lapped.

Lapping compound can be obtained; it's usually oil mixed with grit of between 100 and 300 microns. This is applied to the blades and the cylinder is turned backwards, *ie* in the opposite direction to mowing. Usually this can be done by fitting a brace on a nut on its shaft, and turning by hand. The blades on the cylinder, the bottom blade and all the fittings must be cleaned thoroughly afterwards, as the grit will quickly damage moving parts such as bearings and chains. The bottom blade is set close for the operation, and after cleaning is readjusted and a paper-cutting test carried out, as described under the previous heading.

Lapping can also be used to sharpen up a slightly dulled set of blades. This can improve matters a little, and give better mowing for a time, but it can't compensate for any nicks or chips in the blades; only grinding will remove these. Patent devices for 'grinding' at home, the 'work of a few minutes' and 'saving yourself mower repair depot charges!', are really a variation of lapping and subject to the same limitations of being only a temporary solution that has to be repeated after a comparatively short time. Only a grinding machine will give durable resharpening that'll result in a high-quality finish to a lawn.

PROFESSIONAL SERVICING

When booking your machine in for repair or service, give as much information as possible about any particular faults that the machine may have, so that this can be conveyed to the service engineer when the machine arrives on the bench.

A typical common example might be: Machine owner: 'Can you fix the recoil on my petrol mower? The rope's snapped.'

Service dealer: 'Certainly, Sir, no problem.'

Sounds straightforward enough, and a simple, quick repair – except that the most important information hasn't been provided, and the transaction will likely end up with both parties frustrated and the same fault reoccurring within a very short period, because one of the most common reasons for a recoil rope breaking is because the engine's hard to start. If the rope is continually pulled, over and over, it will snap, wear out or break the recoil. So the fault is neither the rope nor the recoil, but lies with the engine's poor starting. If your engine doesn't start within three or four pulls, either there's a fault with it or you're doing something wrong. Modern mower engines in good order should start within a few pulls – some engine manufacturers now actually state that their engines will start on 'the first pull'. So, the owner should have mentioned the engine was hard to start, and the service dealer should have asked the owner if there were any starting problems. That way a lot of aggro, time and money would have been saved.

Another example might be: Machine owner: 'Can you fit a new start switch on my electric mower? It won't switch on.'

Service dealer: 'Certainly, Sir, no problem.'

But this isn't the best approach. The service engineer can carry out the customer's instructions, but the fault may not lie in a defective switch: there are several other possibilities, and you could end up paying for something you don't need. So don't try to self-diagnose problems. It's far better to book it in simply as 'Machine won't start.'

Other things to keep in mind when getting a full service are that in most cases the engineer won't know if any parts will be required until the job's been completed, so parts are normally quoted as extra. If you're unsure what the total cost might be ask for an estimate or a quotation before the work is carried out, keeping in mind that an estimate is a guess and may change, whereas a quotation should be the actual firm price for the job. In many cases on modern inexpensive mowers, if a machine requires major parts it may well be uneconomical to repair it, and the money would be better put towards buying a replacement machine. Finally, always ask if the price includes VAT.

Chapter 10

Tools

In an ideal world it would be possible to list the tools required for each stage of an overhaul. Unfortunately, however, mower design appears to be in a constant state of change, with frequent re-tooling of smaller parts. Even regarding such a simple matter as spanners it isn't possible to be specific: an engine of American design that's made in Europe may have both unified and metric bolts, and the next engine of the same make will be slightly different again.

Readers who regularly service their cars will probably have a reasonably good kit of tools, but remember that mower engines are small. The owners of motorbikes might be better off in some respects.

It isn't difficult to go all round the engine and mower, checking the fit of your tools, to see if you need to purchase something extra before starting on an overhaul. Use socket or ring spanners whenever possible – they're less likely to slip and damage the nuts. There aren't many nuts and bolts inside the engine, the principal ones being on the big-end bearing, and these tend to be robust because of their function.

The need for a solid bench or table and plenty of clean rags goes without saying!

◄ **A well-stocked tool box.**

ROUTINE MAINTENANCE AND MINOR REPAIR TOOLS

The tools on this list should be considered the minimum required for doing routine maintenance, servicing and minor repair work. Incidentally, if you have a choice it's a good idea to buy combination wrenches (ring and open-end combined in one wrench); while more expensive than open-end ones, they offer the advantages of both types. Also included is a complete set of sockets, which, though expensive, are invaluable because of their versatility (many types are interchangeable – accessories are available). We recommend ⅜in drive over ½in drive for general small engine maintenance and repair, although a ¼in drive set would also be useful (especially for ignition and carburettor work). Buy 6-point sockets, if possible, and be careful not to purchase sockets with extra-thick walls – they can be difficult to use when access to fasteners is restricted.

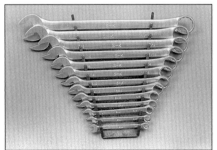

- Safety goggles/face shield: one of the most important items you'll need, but fortunately also one of the least expensive.
- Combination wrench set: buy a set with sizes from ¼in to ⅞in or 6mm to 19mm.
- Adjustable wrench, 10in: adjustable wrenches are very handy – just be

sure to use them correctly or you might damage fasteners by rounding off the hex head.

- Socket set (6-point): a ⅜in drive socket set with interchangeable accessories will probably be used more often than any other tool(s) – don't buy a cheap one.

- Reversible ratchet.
- Extension – 6in.
- Universal joint.
- Spark plug socket (with rubber insert).

- Spark plug gap adjusting tool: this will have several wire gauges for measuring the electrode gap and a device used for bending the side electrode to change the gap – make sure the one you buy has the correct size wire to check the spark plug gap on your engine.

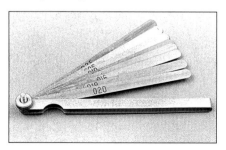

- Feeler gauge set: these have several blades of different thicknesses – if you need it to adjust air gaps, valves,

or contact breaker points, ensure the blades are as narrow as possible, and before buying check that the required thickness is included.

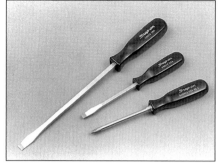

- Screwdrivers: a routine maintenance tool kit should have ⁵⁄₁₆in x 6in and ⅜in x 10in standard screwdrivers as well as a no 2 x 6in Phillips.

- Combination (slip-joint) pliers – 6in: common slip-joint pliers will be adequate for almost any job you end up doing.
- Oil can.
- Fine emery cloth.
- Wire brush.
- Funnel (medium size).

- Drain pan: a shallow pan for draining oil and for cleaning parts with solvent.

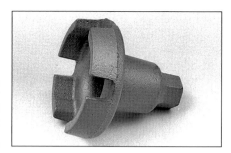

- Starter clutch wrench.*
- Flywheel holder.*

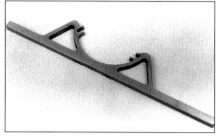

- Flywheel puller or knock-off tools.*

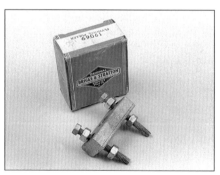

* Although these last three tools are normally available exclusively through distributors/dealers (so technically they're 'special factory tools'), they're included in this list because certain tune-up and minor repair procedures can't be done without them. For instance, a special tool (turned with a wrench) will be needed to remove the starter clutch used on Briggs & Stratton engines. Briggs & Stratton also sells a special flywheel holder for use when loosening the nut or starter clutch; the flywheel on a Briggs & Stratton engine can be removed with a puller or, although it's not recommended by the factory, a knock-off tool, which fits on the end of the crankshaft. Tecumseh flywheels can also be removed with one of these tools. Many Tecumseh and Honda engines require a three-jaw puller for flywheel removal.

Such factory tools may also be available at hardware and lawn and garden centres, and occasionally you'll come across imported copies of the factory tools – but examine them carefully before buying them.

REPAIR AND OVERHAUL TOOLS

These tools are essential if you intend to perform major repairs or overhauls and are intended to supplement those in the routine maintenance and minor repair tool kit listed above.

The tools in this list include many that aren't used regularly, are expensive to buy and need to be used in accordance with their manufacturers' instructions. Unless these tools are going to be used frequently it's not very economical to purchase many of them. One solution might be to split the cost and use between yourself and a friend or neighbour.

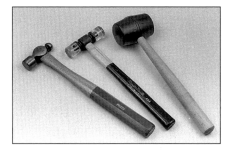

- Ring spanners: a set of ring spanners will complement the combination wrenches in the routine maintenance tool kit.
- Torque wrench (same size drive as sockets): a torque wrench will be needed for tightening head bolts and flywheel nuts (two varieties are available: the click type and the beam type).

- Ball pein hammer – 12oz: any steel hammer can be used in place of this.
- Soft-face hammer and rubber mallet.

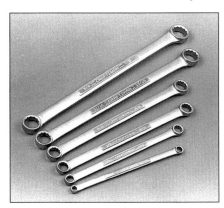

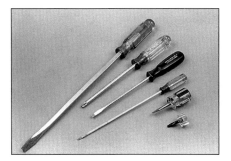

- Standard screwdriver: ¼in x 6in and stubby 5/16in.
- Phillips screwdrivers: no 3 x 8in and stubby no 2.
- Hand impact screwdriver and bits: a hand impact screwdriver (used with a hammer) and bits can be very helpful for removing stubborn, stuck screws and screws with deformed heads.

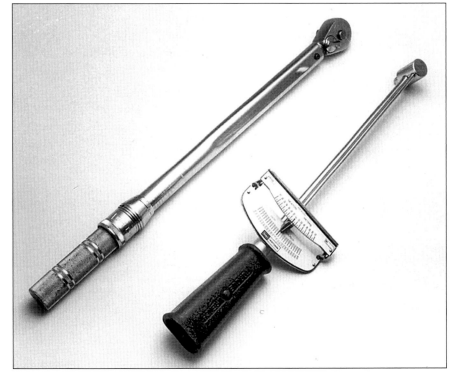

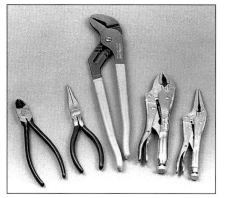

- Pliers – self-locking and needle-nose: 'water-pump', needle-nose, self-locking and wire-cutting pliers should be added to your tool collection as and when you can afford them.

disassembly – scouring pads can be used to rough up the gasket surfaces prior to reassembly.

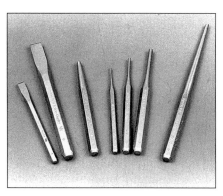

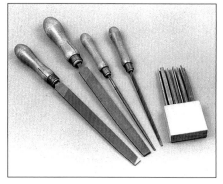

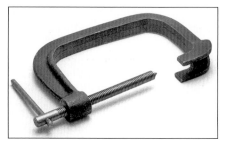

- Wire cutters.
- Cold chisels – ¼in and ½in.
- Centre punch.
- Pin punches – ¹⁄₁₆in, ⅛in and ³⁄₁₆in.
- Line-up tools (tapered punches).
- Scribe: used for making lines on

- Steel rule/straight edge – 12in.
- A selection of files: must be used with handles and should be stored so

- Piston ring removal and installation tool: some overhead valves (OHV) four-stroke engines require a tool like this to compress the springs so the valves can be removed.

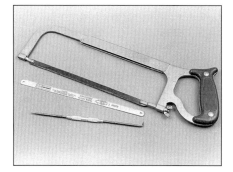

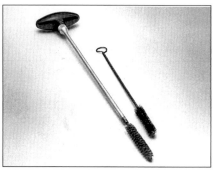

metal parts.
- Hacksaw and assortment of blades: needed for dealing with fasteners that won't unscrew.
- Gasket scraper: used for removing old gaskets from engine parts after

that they don't contact each other.
- A selection of nylon/metal brushes: for cleaning small passages in engine and carburettor parts.
- Small extractor set.
- Spark tester.
- Compression gauge.
- Ridge reamer.
- Valve spring compressor: required for side-valve Briggs & Stratton engines.
- Valve lapping tool: needed for any four-stroke engine overhaul.

- Piston ring compressor: these come in many sizes, so be sure to buy one that will work on your engine.
- Cylinder hone.
- Telescoping gauges.
- Micrometer(s) and/or dial/Vernier calipers.
- Dial indicator.
- Tap and die set.
- Torx socket(s).*
- Tachometer, or strobe timing light with rpm scale.

One of the most indispensable tools around is the common electric drill. One with a ⅜in capacity chuck should be sufficient for most repair work – it'll be large enough to power a cylinder-surfacing hone. Collect several different wire brushes to use in the drill and make sure you have a complete set of sharp bits (for drilling metal, not wood). Cordless drills, which are extremely versatile because they don't have to be plugged in, are now widely available and relatively inexpensive. You may want to consider one, since it'll obviously also be handy for other non-mechanical jobs around the house and workshop.

* Some Tecumseh two-stroke engines require a Torx socket (size E6) to remove the connecting rod cap bolts. If you're overhauling one of these engines, purchase a socket before beginning the disassembly procedure.

BUYING TOOLS

For the do-it-yourselfer just starting to get involved in small engine maintenance and repair, there are a number of options available when purchasing tools. If maintenance and minor repair is the extent of the work to be done, the purchase of individual tools is satisfactory. If, on the other hand, extensive work is planned, it would be a good idea to purchase a modest tool set. A set can usually be bought at a substantial saving over individual tool prices (and they often come with a tool box too). As additional tools are needed, add-on sets, individual tools and a larger box can be purchased to expand your collection. Building a tool set gradually in this way allows the cost to be spread over a longer period of time and gives the mechanic the freedom to acquire only such tools as will actually be used.

Tool stores and small engine distributors or dealers will be the only source of some of the overhaul and special factory tools needed, but regardless of where tools are bought, try to avoid cheap ones (especially when buying screwdrivers, wrenches and sockets) because they won't last very long. The expense involved in replacing cheap tools will eventually be greater than the initial cost of quality tools.

STORAGE AND CARE OF TOOLS

Good tools are expensive, so it makes sense to treat them with respect. Keep them clean and in usable condition and store them properly. Always wipe off dirt, grease and metal chips before putting them away. Never leave tools lying around in the work area.

Some tools, such as screwdrivers, pliers, wrenches and sockets, can be hung on a panel mounted on the garage or workshop wall, while others should be kept in a tool box or tray. Measuring instruments, gauges, cutting tools etc must be carefully stored where they can't be damaged by weather or impact from other tools.

When tools are used with care and stored properly they'll last a very long time. However, even with the best of care tools will wear out if used frequently. When a tool is damaged or worn out, replace it; subsequent jobs will be safer and more enjoyable if you do.

SPECIAL FACTORY TOOLS

Each small engine manufacturer provides certain special tools to distributors and dealers for use when overhauling or doing major repairs on their products. The distributors and dealers often stock some of these tools for the do-it-yourselfer and independent repair shops. A good example would be tools like the starter clutch wrench, flywheel holder and flywheel puller(s) supplied by Briggs & Stratton, which are needed for relatively simple procedures such as contact breaker points (they're required to get the flywheel off for access to the ignition parts). If the special tools aren't used, the repair either can't be done properly or the engine could be damaged by using substitute tools. Fortunately the tools mentioned aren't very expensive or hard to find.

Other special tools, like bushing drivers, bushing reamers, valve seat and guide service tools, cylinder sizing hones, main bearing repair sets etc, are prohibitively expensive and not usually stocked for sale by dealers. If repairs requiring such tools are encountered, take the engine or components to a dealer with the necessary tools and pay to have the work done, then reassemble the engine yourself.

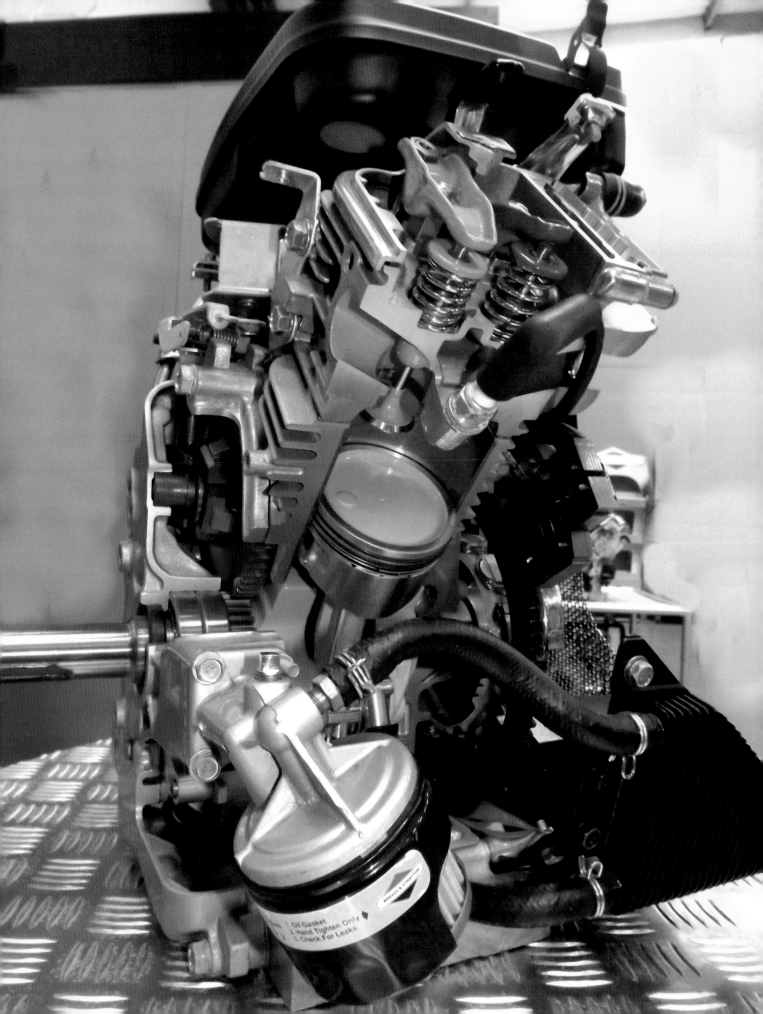

Chapter 11

Engine overhaul – general

Always work and service safely:

- Before draining oil, make sure it's cooled sufficiently so as not to scald you.
- Don't siphon toxic liquids such as fuel by mouth, and don't allow them to remain on your skin. Store petrol in approved metal or high-impact plastic petrol containers.
- Don't inhale clutch or brake lining dust.
- Don't turn the engine over unless the spark plug lead is detached and retained out of the way.
- Don't use petrol for cleaning parts, unless specified.
- Don't allow spilled oil, grease or fuel to remain on the floor – wipe it up before someone slips on it.
- Don't use ill-fitting spanners or tools that may slip and cause injury or damage parts.
- Don't attempt to lift a heavy component beyond your capability – always get help.
- Don't rush to finish a job, or take unverified short cuts.
- Take care when attempting to slacken a stubborn nut or bolt. It's generally

◀ **Briggs & Stratton V-twin**

better to pull on a spanner, rather than push – then if slippage occurs you'll fall away from rather than towards the mower.
- Wear eye protection when using power tools such as grinders, sanders and drills.
- Use a barrier cream or protective gloves prior to undertaking dirty jobs – it'll protect your skin from infection and make cleaning your hands easier. (Ensure plastic gloves are impervious to petrol when cleaning carburettors and fuel tanks and pipes.)
- Keep loose-fitting clothing and long hair well out of the way of moving parts.
- Keep your workplace tidy – it could be dangerous to fall over tools and components left lying around.
- Exercise caution when compressing springs for removal or installation. Apply and release tension progressively, and use tools that preclude violent escape of the spring and other components.
- Carry out work in a systematic sequence, checking as you go.
- Check that everything is assembled correctly and tightened afterwards.
- If, despite following all these precautions, you're unfortunate enough to hurt yourself, seek *immediate* medical assistance.

ADVANCE PREPARATIONS

Before starting any work, check round your machine and identify the major parts. Read this chapter for general procedures for dismantling, cleaning, inspection for wear, and reassembly advice. Read the sections covering your particular machine: many of the photographs show tools being used and the techniques for fitting parts.

These preparations will give a good idea of the tools and special materials, such as gasket jointing compounds, that you'll need, as well as information regarding when to lubricate and when not, and what to use. It's assumed that you'll have engine oil, if you have a four-stroke engine, and this can be used on all metal-to-metal surfaces when parts are assembled together. With a two-stroke, light machine oil should be used – not engine oil, which tends to be too heavy and has other disadvantages.

TIGHT SPOTS

We were surprised by how tight some of the crossheaded bolts were on some machines, and found an impact screwdriver helpful on numerous occasions.

Some flywheels were also tight, and usually required a puller. It should be noted that legged pullers aren't recommended by many manufacturers – all can supply their own flywheel puller, often a very simple device consisting of a flat bar with bolts that are tightened slowly in turn until the seal between the flywheel and the crankshaft gives.

The techniques given in this manual will work again and again without trouble, but some experience with such tools is needed: if in doubt, get the manufacturer's special tool.

'Release' fluids can be invaluable with really obstinate nuts, bolts and screws or those in awkward places, liable to get corroded.

A plastic or hide mallet is essential, to minimise the risk of damage during certain dismantling tasks.

MISTAKES TO AVOID

Every mower service station has a chamber of horrors where damaged, worn out or downright dangerous parts are thrown, discarded from mowers brought in for overhaul or repair. Service engineers are no longer surprised by what they find, and the owners haven't looked to see what's happened and so never know. The mower is returned (if worth repairing, of course) together with an unavoidably large bill, which would have been much smaller had the mower received regular maintenance. This section shows a small collection of such horrors.

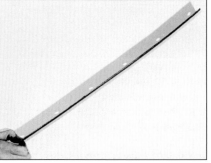

▲ Grassed areas are best raked or swept before mowing. This does two things: it prepares the grass for cutting and it clears stones and other hard objects that can damage the cutting edges or be thrown out at a dangerously high speed and cause injury. This bottom blade from a cylinder mower has been badly bent by striking a rock or concrete path at speed, through careless handling. It will no longer be in contact with the cutting cylinder blades all along its length and will cut unevenly.

▲ This cutting disc from a rotary mower shows two defects. Firstly, the grass deflectors mounted on top of the blades have been battered out of shape: because they weren't working properly, the mower deck kept getting clogged up with grass, making cutting inefficient and putting extra load on the engine as well.

▲ Secondly, the hopelessly blunt and chipped cutting edges gave poor cutting action. The engine was being run at full throttle all the time to try to compensate, and even then the grass was being torn off rather than cut. If some time had been spent straightening and sharpening, results would have been transformed, and the engine could have been run at about three-quarter throttle – less trouble and less wear and tear all round.

▲ Here the cutting edge is reasonably good but the blade has been chipped. There was other damage elsewhere and a noticeable lack of balance in the cutting disc, causing vibration and damage to the engine.

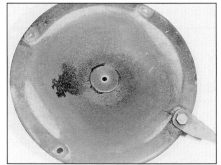

▲ An almost unbelievable example of neglect. This disc has four fixing points for two cutters and two grass deflectors. Running with only one cutting blade caused very serious vibration. Perhaps the owner was a pneumatic drill operator and felt more at home with it working like this! The crankshaft damage shown on the opposite page was the result of far less out-of-balance effects than this.

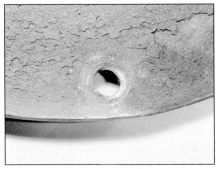

▲ Whilst on the subject of cutting discs, never use one with elongated fixing holes – it's very dangerous. The blades can work loose and fly off, and remember, they're travelling at an average speed of 200mph when rotating and will travel quite a distance if they get past the guards. So fit a new disc, and always use new bolts and fittings, even if the old blades are reusable.

▲ When a cutting disc or a cutter bar on a rotary mower is out of balance it's trying to shake the end of the engine crankshaft to and fro all the time. If this goes on, both crankshaft and bearings will be worn on two sides, one more than the other usually. This main journal has become deeply grooved round one half-circle...

▲ ... in just the same way as the bearing in the crankcase into which it fits. Here the wear is obvious, but long before it gets so bad the state of wear can be detected by running a fingernail along the bearing surface.

▲ The tremendous twisting action of the out-of-balance cutters is shown on this crankshaft, worn round one half-circle at one end and the opposite half-circle at the other.

▲ Wear on this crank pin had a simple cause: lack of lubrication. The oil in the sump was very dirty and there wasn't much of it. It's good practice to top up the sump every time the mower is used, and to change the oil at the recommended intervals. Oil is cheap; repairs aren't.

▲ Keep a lookout for wear and act before trouble develops. This belt on a cylinder mower is showing cracks on the edge running in the grooves of the pulleys, and will soon start to disintegrate.

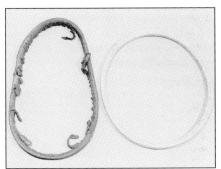

▲ Here's a really bad case alongside a new belt for comparison. If you spot trouble before it goes too far a belt can't snap and leave you with an unusable mower on the first fine Sunday for weeks.

▶ Investigate any unusual noise or action. Here, the owner should have noticed how the cylinder mower was snatching as the drive took up, so that the mower gave a jerk forwards. The holes in the large sprocket are getting enlarged because the bolts are slack; also, the chain is slack and snatches as the clutch is engaged. The small sprocket is showing signs of wear, which won't do the second chain much good.

WARRANTY CONSIDERATIONS

Following the lead of the automobile market, lawnmower manufacturers compete with each other to offer extended warranties on their products. Be wary of the small print, however, because some warranties involve taking the mower back to the supplying dealer for service if the extended warranty is to remain valid. Other manufacturers warrant the main body of the mower for an extended period but only warrant the engine for a shorter period; such arrangements can vary between one to ten years for the body and one to three years for the engine.

The purpose of a warranty is to cover breakdowns due to a manufacturing fault. Warranties very rarely cover breakdowns that result from normal wear and tear or misuse. It isn't unknown for manufacturers to accept liability for inbuilt shortcomings in design even when a recall hasn't been requested, so check first with the supplying dealer before undertaking any serious overhaul work.

Current legislation requires warranties to be transferable to second or successive owners during the warranty period. If there's no reason for there to be a problem, there'll be no reluctance to transfer the warranty, so make sure that you have this undertaking from the original supplying dealer in writing before purchasing any second-hand machine – whether buying privately or through a dealer.

> **NOTE**
> Unlike the automobile industry, many garden machine manufacturers don't make their own engines; therefore if there's an engine issue the warranty would mainly be covered by the engine manufacturer and not the mower manufacturer, and vice versa. Before undertaking any repair work beyond routine maintenance, make a point of checking with the supplying dealer about the warranty situation.

ENGINE IDENTIFICATION

To order spare parts or to gain help from a manufacturer or service dealer, the engine's identity will be needed. Every engine, regardless of manufacturer, leaves the factory with a model number (MN) stamped, cast or bonded on it somewhere, often on the cowl or crankcase. If the engine is dirty it may be obscured.

BRIGGS & STRATTON

The first one or two digits give the displacement of the engine in cubic inches (cu in, or in³). If the displacement in cubic centimetres (cc) is important for you to know, the conversion factor is 16.387 (eg 8in³ x 16.387 is approximately 131cc).

The digit following the displacement code indicates the 'basic design series' and may be interpreted as an engine family designation that defines configuration, cylinder type and ignition system.

The second digit after the displacement code defines the orientation of the crankshaft, the carburettor type and also the governor operation.

The third digit after the displacement gives the bearing type or gear reduction or the orientation of the auxiliary drive.

The fourth digit after the displacement defines the engine's starter type.

◄ **Deciphering Briggs & Stratton engine model identification numbers.**

▼ **Typical Briggs & Stratton model identification number. The MN may be interpreted by reference to the accompanying chart.**

BRIGGS & STRATTON MODEL NUMBER KEY

Displacement (cubic inches)*	First Digit After Disp. — Basic Design Series	Second Digit After Disp. — Crankshaft/ Carburettor/ Governor	Third Digit After Disp. — Bearings/ Reduction gears/ Auxiliary drive	Fourth Digit After Disp. — Starter type
6	0	0	0 = Plain bearing	0 = No starter
8	1	1 = Horizontal (Vacu-Jet)	1 = Flange mount plain bearing	1 = Rope starter
9	2	2 = Horizontal (Pulsa-Jet)	2 = Ball bearing	2 = Rewind starter
10	3	3 = Horizontal (Flo-Jet; pneumatic governor)	3 = Flange mount ball bearing	3 = Electric (110-volt; gear drive)
13	4	4 = Horizontal (Flo-Jet; mechanical governor)	4	4 = Electric starter/ generator (12-volt; belt drive)
	5	5 = Vertical (Vacu-Jet)	5 = Gear reduction (6 to 1)	5 = Electric starter only (12-volt; gear drive)
	6	6	6 = Gear reduction (6 to 1; reverse rotation)	6 = Wind-up starter
	7	7 = Vertical (Flo-Jet)	7	7 = Electric starter (12-volt; gear drive with alternator)
	8	8	8 = Auxiliary drive perpendicular to crankshaft	8 = Vertical-pull starter
	9	9 = Vertical (Pulsa-Jet)	9 = Auxiliary drive parallel to crankshaft	

* Cubic inches x 16·387 = Cubic centimetres (cc)

HONDA

Honda engines covered in the overhaul section are all from the 'G' series of engines rated up to 5.5hp. The model number is stamped into the side of the crankcase for engines with a vertical crankshaft orientation, and the serial number is stamped into the end of the crankcase. For horizontal crankshaft engines, the model and serial numbers are both stamped on the crankcase furthest away from the cylinder head.

TECUMSEH

Tecumseh stamp the engine number either on the engine cooling shroud or on a tag attached to the crankcase. The number is made up of a model/spec number (M/S No) followed by the serial number, which is prefixed 'SER'. The 'MODEL' group of letters and numbers gives information about the engine's general specification and its cubic capacity. The spec number provides detailed information about variations on the standard engine, and this number will need to be quoted when ordering parts. Finally, the serial number gives year, day and manufacturing plant information about the engine.

ORDERING SPARE PARTS

To ensure that the correct parts are ordered, both the model designation of the lawnmower and the model and serial number of the engine will generally be required. It's helpful to keep a note of these numbers handy when ordering. Where a spare part is required to replace a worn or damaged part, it'll help the service dealer or agent if the complete assembly is taken to his service depot. It's possible that the new part will form part of a new assembly that replaces the original. Dealers' parts stock records are retained today on computer records, and having sight of the original part and assembly will help the service dealer to ensure that the correct part is ordered.

DISMANTLING

The instructions given in the sections dealing with individual engines include guidance on dismantling and show tools in use, but problems can still arise with

▲ Typical Honda model identification number – vertical shaft engine.

▲ Typical Honda serial number – vertical shaft engine.

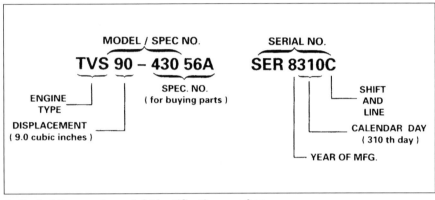

▲ Typical Tecumseh model identification number.

▼ Overhead-valve engine skeleton.

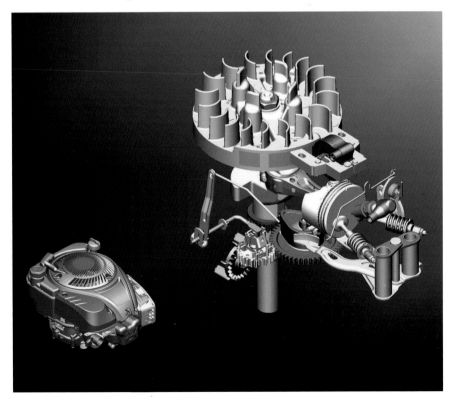

▲ **Briggs & Stratton V-twin.**

▲ **Briggs & Stratton V-twin.**

▲ **OHV linkage.**

parts that are so tight or badly stuck or contaminated that they can't be shifted.

Remember that if the force applied is concentrated in one spot and applied in one short sharp action, success can often be achieved, whereas the application of great strength or violent hitting usually results in something getting broken; skill sensibly applied is the answer. For example, one can lean heavily on a blade-type screwdriver and try to turn it with both hands and not succeed, but a flat-nosed punch placed against one end of the slot in the screwhead and a positive tap with a hammer will often suffice; if not, try alternate ends, several times. The use of six-point sockets will usually undo rounded bolts and nuts.

Cylinder heads should be eased off carefully, using a tool on both sides. Tap lightly all round with a soft mallet

first, to break the seal. The same applies to flywheels, especially those on a tapered shaft. The shock from a series of quite light taps will usually break the grip and other methods will then have a chance, for example pullers (see 'Flywheels' opposite).

Heat can work wonders. A gas torch can be used for a few moments to expand the area gripping a shaft, followed by tapping with a soft mallet; but apply the heat *very* briefly, especially if vulnerable parts such as electrical fittings and connections are underneath.

Accurately applied heat can be useful. Small screws and bolts can be heated up with a solder gun without affecting the surrounding area too much. This is a good way of releasing screws held with Loctite: the reed valves in two-stroke engines are often mounted with this, and the screws secured with it as well.

▼ **Silencer cutaway.**

▼ **Governor cutaway.**

▲ **Con rod cutaway.**

▲ **See-through carb.**

▲ **Carb cutaway.**

The stems of exhaust valves may have got so gummed up that the valves can't be drawn up out of their guides. Clean the stems with a fine abrasive tape or a file. Then, when removed, finish off cleaning them so that they won't get gummed up as quickly when replaced.

Always make notes during dismantling. So many changes take place in mower design that this is essential in order to avoid mishaps when reassembling: your mower may have an older type (or the latest type) of fitting. A piece of card can be useful – the parts can be taped on to it in their correct sequence, to be cleaned at leisure later. In the case of parts such as valves and bolts, a simple sketch of the top of the engine can be made, holes made in the card, and each placed in its correct position.

FLYWHEELS
Removing the flywheel from the crankshaft is a common task in small engine repair. The flywheel is usually located on the crankshaft by a key and tightened on to a taper that's usually very tight and requires considerable force to remove. Ideally this can be achieved by use of the manufacturer's recommended pullers, many of which are simple devices consisting of a metal plate with bolts that screw into the flywheel; then the nuts are tightened evenly to push the plate on to the crankshaft, which forces the flywheel from the taper. Most manufacturers advise against the use of legged pullers.

An alternative method is as follows. Remove the flywheel nut and washer, then replace the nut until it's flush with the end of the crankshaft and lever the flywheel gently away from the engine. Now tap the end of the crankshaft sharply with a soft-faced hammer. Be careful to hit it squarely, or damage will be done to the crankshaft. This should free the flywheel from its taper. This method isn't recommended by manufacturers, but it works well if applied correctly. If in doubt, obtain the correct puller for your engine.

RECOIL STARTERS
These are dealt with in specific engine sections, on pages 127, 135, 143 and 157, as there are wide variations in their details.

However, when renewing starter cords or fitting new handles to most starters that require a knot to secure them, the figure-of-eight knot is the most effective method, and less likely to pull through. Heat-seal the end of the cord to prevent fraying, by holding it momentarily in a naked flame.

▼ **Triple V-twins, or a 'V12'!**

CLEANING AND INSPECTING PARTS

CARBURETTORS

Clean all parts in clean petrol. If metal parts won't clean, use a solvent. Don't use a solvent on plastic parts, and don't use wire to clean jets.

1 Examine all needles of float valves and of the mixture and slow-running jets as applicable, according to the carburettor design. Look very closely then run a fingernail along the slope of the needle point. If ridged, replace the needle and its seat, the latter of which is usually a screw-in fitting.

2 This needle is quite badly ridged and should be replaced, and a new seating to match it screwed into the top plate. Check that the needle isn't bent.

3 This type of carburettor has a different needle and float arrangement, but the same principles apply to needle and seating replacement.

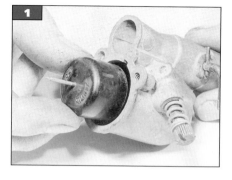

4 Some carburettors are fitted with a removable bowl. This is held in position over the float by a central bolt, and incorporates a tickler in the base. Check the condition of the rubber washer of the tickler, and that the tickler works freely. Check the condition of fibre washers in the bowl.

5 In diaphragm-type carburettors, visually check the state of the diaphragm. It must be in good condition and not hardened or cracked. If it's defective, replace it.

6 Always renew all gaskets and O-rings where fitted on a carburettor. The manufacturers usually supply a complete carburettor kit containing all the parts that they recommend renewing as a matter of routine when overhauling.

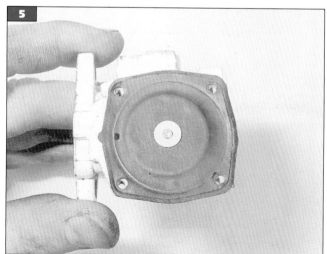

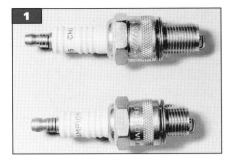

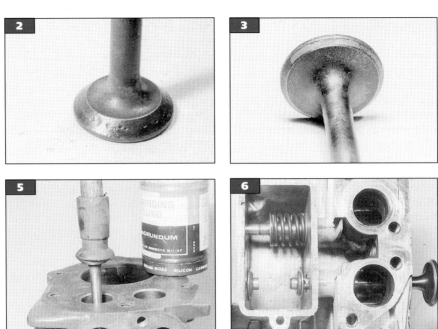

SPARK PLUGS AND VALVES

Clean with a wire brush, never in a sandblasting machine; some engine manufacturers warn that the use of a sandblaster will invalidate their guarantee. It's almost impossible to get all the abrasive particles out of the plug. If plug points are worn, or the porcelain insulation around the centre terminal is cracked or damaged, fit a new plug. It's probably better to fit a new plug even if it was renewed not long ago.

1 Be sure to get the correct plug type. Plugs have different reaches, as shown here, and the use of one with an incorrect reach may foul the engine parts. They also have different performance features, so the manufacturer's recommendations should always be followed.

2 If your engine's been performing badly, giving little power, and its exhaust valve looks like this, an overhaul is overdue.

3 This is slightly better, but the sloping face that provides the seal with its seat in the cylinder head is uneven and marked.

4 If the margin – the vertical piece above the slope – isn't worn down to 0.4mm (0.016in), and the valve is otherwise in good condition, with the stem not worn or bent, it'll be worth regrinding the valve and its seat.

5 The tool is rotated to and fro between the palms of the hands, and the valve lifted and turned round slightly every 15–20 rotations, to even out the grinding all round. Coarse grinding paste is used first, then, when an even face starts to appear, it's cleaned off and fine paste is used.

6 This valve being refitted has an even, very fine, smooth face all round and will seal well. Because metal has been removed, the valve will be sitting slightly lower and the valve clearance between the end of its stem and the tappet must be checked...

7 ...with a feeler gauge (doing this before the spring is fitted is easier). Make sure the valve is pressed home (by hand, or with the valve spring). If the gap is smaller than that specified for the engine, the stem of the valve must be ground down to give the correct figure.

8 Drill a hole in a block of wood, taking care to keep it at right angles, and use it like this. Rub slowly on the grinding block, and pause frequently: too fast and too long at one time may overheat the stem and destroy its temper, and it might then wear more rapidly. Note that one thumb is keeping the stem hard against the grinding block while the other hand slides the wood block to and fro. The hole in the wood keeps the stem vertical all the time.

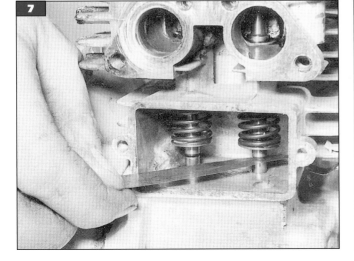

PISTONS AND RINGS

1 Pistons should be cleaned off, the rings removed by easing them gently out of their grooves, and the grooves cleaned with an old piece of piston ring ground down to a chisel edge. Also clean the backs of the piston rings. Great care is necessary, as the cast iron rings are very brittle.

2 These grooves are clean, the bottom oil ring has been fitted and the parts assembled to check for wear. Always note which way round the piston fits in the cylinder, which end of the gudgeon pin is at which side of the piston, and which way round the connecting rod fits inside the piston. This rod has identification marks on one side; mark that side of the piston (inside) if there's no way of identifying it. The two halves of the split big-end bearing must go together the same way they came off.

3 Note that the two piston rings don't have their gaps in line with one another: one faces the camera, the other is at the top at about 90°. With three sets of rings, stagger them at about 120°, evenly round the piston. The pistons of most two-strokes (but not all) have pegs in their ring grooves so that the rings will only fit in one position and can't move when fitted: this is to prevent them from fouling the ports inside the cylinder.

NOTE: *On some engines the gudgeon pin is a tight fit, and the piston will need warming up in hot water before the pin will go in. Don't strike it or use force – pistons can be fairly fragile, and it's all too easy to bend the connecting rod.*

4 Note the three ports of this two-stroke engine cylinder. Note also they've been cleaned in preparation for the rebuild. A piston ring is being measured with a feeler gauge: as it wears, the gap between its ends increases. The Technical Data table in each chapter gives the limits at which new rings should be fitted.

5 A safe way to insert a ring for measurement in the cylinder bore is vertically, then turn it carefully while it's inside the cylinder. A good method for getting it level in the bore is to insert the piston upside down and push the ring into position for measurement. Usually the place to measure is with the ring about 19mm (0.75in) below the top, but on Victa two-strokes it should be near the bottom of the cylinder. For Victas it's recommended that you don't just fit a new piston ring – always fit new rings too.

NOTE: *If in any doubt about the state of the cylinder, piston and rings, or any similar group of parts, take the complete set and the cylinder block to your service station. They have special tools for accurate measurement and can, if necessary, supply complete sets of matched parts to the manufacturer's specification, to suit the condition of your engine. This applies also to the crankshaft and camshaft.*

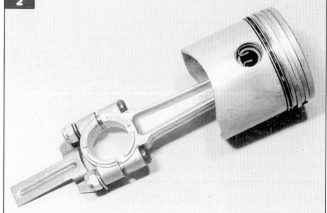

CYLINDER HEAD

Various tools have been suggested for cleaning off cylinder block surfaces, heads and the tops of valves and pistons, among them a coin, which is relatively soft and, used with care, shouldn't damage even aluminium engines; and an old blunt screwdriver, used with a little pressure. Possibly the best of all is a wire brush in a drill head, with plenty of oil. The series of surfaces, fitted with a gasket ready to receive the cylinder head, is in perfect condition and was prepared by this last method. Never use caustic soda solution – it'll dissolve aluminium and produce an explosive gas.

ENGINE CASTINGS

Check engine castings for cracking and stripped threads – threads can be restored by fitting the correct size of thread insert, but cracked castings should be replaced.

CRANKSHAFT AND CAMSHAFT

1 Examine the bearing surfaces on the crankshaft and camshaft. If there's grooving through wear or lack of lubrication, causing an accumulation of dirt in the bearings, run a fingernail along. If grooving is only just detectable it may be left as it is, but if it's grooved badly, as on the crankpin in the photograph, take the advice of your service agent. Crankshafts can be reground and a connecting rod supplied to

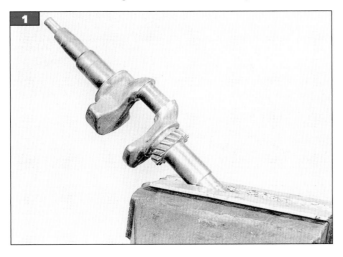

fit in most cases, but it may be cheaper to replace the engine – your service dealer will advise.

NOTE: *Never fit a new crankshaft or a reground crankshaft in the original bearings.*

2 Note the soft aluminium plates in the vice to protect the surfaces of the crankshaft. Never clamp a part in a vice without protection.
3 Examine the bushes (or ball bearings) in which the shafts run. They should be a close fit and not show any wear. Clean ball bearings in solvent to remove all lubrication, then spin them close to the ear: they should run reasonably freely and without noise when unloaded by a shaft like this. Renew a bearing if it shows undue movement along the axis (along the length of the shaft when fitted), or is noisy. If plain bushes are used in the crankcase for the shafts, and these are worn, it's uneconomic to repair them.
4 Examine the lobes of the cams, which should be of uniform shape and not worn. Examine the gears of the camshaft and crankshaft for wear: is there undue play/backlash between them? If there is, then depending on the engine the common remedy nowadays would be an engine replacement, especially on budget mowers. Such wear is commonly caused by lack of lubrication, a poor oil grade or overheating in heavy wear-and-tear conditions.

REED VALVES

Many two-strokes have reed valves that consist of thin flexible springs looking rather like the blades of a feeler gauge. If cleaning is needed it should be carried out very carefully. The blades should have a gap under them – they spring slightly outwards from their mounting, the gap usually being around 0.125 to 0.25mm (0.005 to 0.010in). If they're bent or kinked, or the gap is greater than this, replacements should be fitted. Reed valves close off the crankcase from the carburettor inlet manifold while the new petrol and air mixture is being moved to the combustion chamber and the exhaust gases are being discharged, so their operation is important to the efficiency of the engine. Some two-stroke engines have a three-port arrangement in the cylinder and don't need reed valves.

POINTS

Check the gap between the contact breaker points if the engine is fitted with a conventional breaker ignition. The gap should be 0.51mm (0.02in) or as recommended by the engine manufacturer. Before checking the gap, make sure the points are clean, *ie* there isn't a pip on one point and a crater on the other. Small pips and craters can be cleaned off using a fine carborundum stone, but if large ones are present fit new points. If new points quickly develop another pip and crater, the condenser is weak and should be renewed. If the spark at the plug appears weak and yellowish rather than strong and blue, this could also mean a weak condenser. This is often confirmed by the engine starting when cold, but misfiring and refusing to spark as it gets hotter. The fibre heel of the moving point should be lubricated with a small blob of grease where it bears on the cam sleeve. On most engines the contact breakers are located underneath the flywheel. Refer to the relevant engine section for instructions on removing flywheels.

Briggs & Stratton points

1 Fit the capacitor under the clamp, but leave the clamp untightened. Push the fibre cam follower rods alongside and push it home.

2 Fit the coil spring over the centre contact of the capacitor. Fit the post; the lug in the boss fits into the slot of the post.

3 Fit the end of the moving contact arm into the slot of the post and hook the coil spring into the arm and over the second post.

4 Feed the wire from the magneto, with the earthing wire, through the centre post of the capacitor, which is held by a small coil spring. The cable slots into the casting.

5 Check the points gap. This should be 0.51mm (0.02in). The easiest way to position the engine on compression (both valves closed) with the points fully open is to turn it by means of the flywheel, which will have to be removed to adjust the fixed contact to the required setting.

6 Setting completed. Note the key in the keyway of the shaft, needed to turn the shaft by the flywheel. Always use an aluminium key, never a steel one.

7 Fit the contact breaker cover.

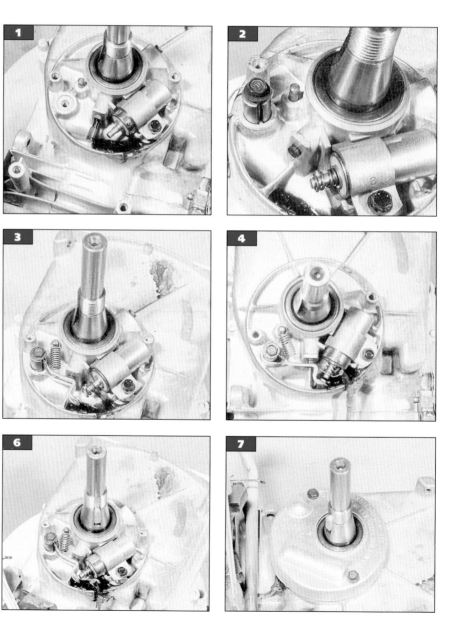

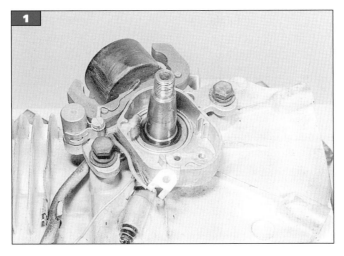

Tecumseh points

1 Fit the contact breaker assembly. Line up with the marks made when dismantling, and tighten it down.

2 Slide the contact breaker cam over the shaft. Fit the fixed contact but don't tighten.

3 Fit the moving contact assembly. The plastic mounting fits into a recess, the cam follower over the pivot on the fixed contact assembly.

4 Turn the crankshaft until the follower is exactly on top of the cam lobe. Move the fixed contact until the gap is 0.51mm (0.02in). Tighten the fixed contact locking screw.

5 Recheck the contact breaker gap. Connect the brown wire, the black wire and the black shorting-out wire to the terminal post.

6 Fit the cover and secure it with the clip.

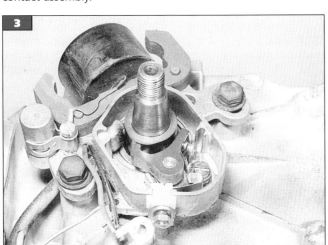

LUBRICATION SYSTEM

1 Always renew oil seals: sometimes there's a dust cover on the outside. Note very carefully which way round it fits. If inserted the wrong way the engine sump will empty itself quite rapidly, in all probability making a horrible mess of the mower (and of the engine, if the leak isn't noticed soon enough).

2 Examine very closely all bearing bushes, big-end bearings and connecting rods, to look for oilways drilled in them. Make sure these are clear after cleaning the part; quite often the dirt is washed into the oilway and sits there, blocking the oil and causing rapid wear of the parts not receiving lubrication. There are always oilways in engines with oil pumps, and shafts are sometimes drilled through, end to end, as a passage for the oil.

3 Check self-aligning bearings are free to rock in all directions, and grease them well. They're often used to give freedom of movement to a drive shaft and its connection with a driven shaft – as when an engine crankshaft is driving the chain sprocket shaft of a cylinder mower, for example.

4 Cylinder mowers have numerous oiling points to lubricate the bearings of the cutting cylinder, roller and other parts. As shown here, it's sometimes possible to tap a thread in the oiling hole and fit a nipple. Using a grease gun has advantages in that it forces the grease or oil on to the moving surfaces and at the same time helps to force the dirt and other contaminants away from

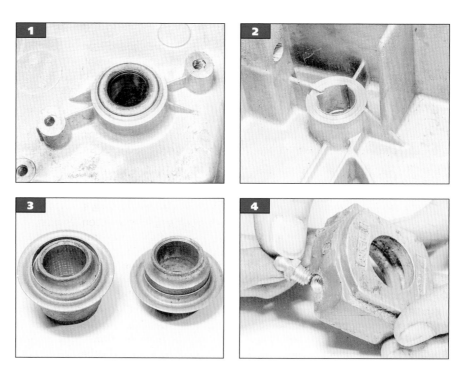

the outside of the bearing. Furthermore, the admission point of the lubricant will be sealed off automatically.

5 Always treat the springs of starters with respect. If they come out they'll unwind very rapidly and can cause injury. This spring is in a container: keep it in the container if it's necessary to remove it from the housing. Put a strip of wood across and tie it round to prevent any possibility of its unwinding.

6 In numerous places in this manual

it's advised to mark the position of the contact breaker mounting plate before any dismantling takes place, immediately after the flywheel has been removed. This position determines the time that the spark will jump the terminals of the spark plug and fire the petrol–air mixture. Precise timing is essential for correct engine operation. A worn flywheel-to-crankshaft key can affect timing and cause poor ignition. Fit a new key if wear is present.

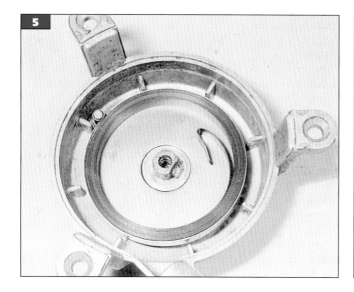

REASSEMBLY

LUBRICATION

1 All rotating and rubbing surfaces of the engine and mower must be lubricated during their assembly, unless instructions are to the contrary. Ball bearings and roller bearings must be greased. Plain bearings, shafts, gudgeon pins, big-end bearings and piston rings must be oiled: use engine oil for four-strokes, light machine oil for two-strokes. If this isn't done considerable wear will be caused during the first run-up of the engine, or even worse may happen, such as a partial seizure.

2 Oil seals must be oiled before insertion, and before passing the shaft through. If this isn't done it's possible to split the lip of the seal, so that it will no longer embrace the shaft closely all round, and the oil will get through. In passing, it should be mentioned that seals have a right way and a wrong way of being fitted: this will have been noted with the old seal. Sometimes the seals have instructions printed on one surface.

3 Drive chains on cylinder mowers should be thoroughly cleaned, then re-greased. Belts shouldn't be lubricated; if noisy, use French chalk dusted on the rubbing surfaces. Remember that chains and belts that are adjusted too tightly will absorb engine power, besides wearing the chain and sprockets or belt and pulleys unnecessarily rapidly. If no specific figure is given, about 13mm (0.5in) of slack in the middle of the longest run is a general guide. With spring-loaded idlers taking up the slack, of course, adjustment is automatic, and some models have these on chains and belts.

4 The assembly of cylinder mowers gives an excellent opportunity to grease all the working parts very thoroughly. This not only lubricates the rubbing surfaces but helps to keep out grass juices, grit and other contaminants.

FITTING

As when dismantling, reassembly needs careful attention and slow, gentle handling. Force is seldom needed and never sensible, whereas a sharp tap at the right places – once everything is lined up in the correct position – is strength used intelligently. If anything won't go together and you encounter a positive obstruction, stop and investigate.

TIGHTENING

1 It's possible to find the correct degree of torquing, or exact amount of tightening required, for most nuts and bolts, but few owners will have tools of the sizes required if they have any at all. Figures are usually given for the more important fasteners.

2 The technique of tightening correctly without a torque wrench is to be aware of the feel you're getting from the spanner. Tighten first as far as is easy, until a definite stop is felt. Then give a firm, steady pull as far as it feels it wants to go. A violent jerk isn't the action required, because momentum can carry you too far; simply maintain a firm grip and firm pressure until the fixing also feels firm.

3 On rotary mowers the bolts fixing the cutter bar or the disc, and the blades on discs, require somewhat greater force – but again, not a violent pull, just a more positive tightening action.

4 When there are a number of bolts or nuts to the fixing tighten them in turn, quite lightly, then more firmly, then tightly. On cylinder heads, tighten in turn diagonally and work round the head, crossing from side to side.

5 Be sure to fit shakeproof washers if they were found when dismantling. At some points on some engines slotted locking plates with ears (tabs) are used under nuts or bolt heads: this is the case with some oil spoilers on big ends. Turn the ears up against one face after tightening.

6 After tightening, always check the freedom of moving parts, to be sure there's no binding. After tightening big-end bearings, for example, check that the connecting rod can be slid slightly from side to side along the crankpin: and when released, it should fall down below the crankpin by its own weight, quite freely.

7 Check the freedom of the camshaft and crankshaft in their bearings before connecting them up, engaging the gears, and so forth. Common sense, in short, is a good guide to good rebuilding.

TESTING AND CARBURETTOR ADJUSTMENTS

1 Mower engines are relatively simple mechanisms and don't have many adjustments. One reassembles them the way they were, with the throttle, governor and other controls in the same positions.

2 These are permanent settings, for the most part. Certainly the governor connections shouldn't be disturbed, but having overhauled the engine it's likely to perform in a different manner from that when it was last used. One item that may need attention is the carburettor.

3 Some carburettors have no adjustment, while others have only one adjustment, the idler screw. This spring-loaded screw presses on the carburettor control, to which the cable throttle control is fitted, and determines the speed of the engine when the hand throttle is closed. Run the engine until thoroughly warm, and adjust to give a reliable tickover.

4 Other carburettors may have one or two more adjusters, also spring-loaded. One is likely to have most effect when the engine is running at about half speed, fairly fast, the other on tickover. The latter, slow-running control of the petrol supply is normally left alone. Run the engine until really warm, from three to five minutes depending on the weather.

5 Remember not to screw in the adjusting screw too tightly – you can damage the seating. Be gentle. With the engine running fairly fast, screw in until it will go no further or until the engine starts to falter or stalls, whichever happens first. Then turn it in the opposite direction until the engine starts to 'hunt' with an uneven beat, counting the number of turns. Finally, set the screw halfway between the two positions.

6 The above procedure takes care of variations in the condition of engines, the effect of fitting new parts and other variables, and will normally result in a satisfactory adjustment. If, however, the engine seems to lack power under load, unscrew a further quarter turn to give a slightly richer mixture.

7 Some operating instructions issued with a mower give quite explicit guidance on adjusting the carburettor: if so, then obviously that advice must be followed. A crude guide is that if the engine lacks power, the mixture is too weak (too little petrol in the petrol–air mixture); if it seems to run roughly and/or produce smoke, especially on speeding up, and the exhaust system gets clogged quickly with soft carbon, the mixture is too rich.

NOTE: *The above procedure follows an overhaul, when it's known that valve clearances (on a four-stroke) and contact breaker and spark plug gaps have just been set. At any other time, remember that satisfactory running may be impossible unless these are correct.*

Chapter 12

Engine overhaul

1 BRIGGS & STRATTON MAX 4HP VERTICAL CRANK FOUR-STROKE ENGINE OVERHAUL

Model/spec number on engines: 110700, 111700, 112700, 114700

Mower application

Every effort has been made to ensure the list of models that use this engine is as comprehensive as possible. Due to model and engine supply changes, however, you may have a mower that isn't listed. Refer to 'Engine identification' on pages 96 and 170 to identify the engine that you have, or contact an engine supply dealer to assist with identification.

Atco
Flymo
Hayter Harrier
Hayter Harrier 2
Hayter Hawk
Hayter Hunter 48
Husqvarna
Mountfield Emperor
Mountfield Empress

Technical data

Spark plug gap	0.75mm (0.030in)
Armature air gap	0.25–0.36mm (0.010–0.014in)
Valve clearance	
Inlet	0.13–0.18mm (0.005–0.007in)
Exhaust	0.23–0.28mm (0.009–0.011in)
Breather disc valve clearance	1.10mm (0.043in)
Wire gauge must not enter space between valve and body	
Ring gap not to exceed	
Compression rings	0.80mm (0.031in)
Oil ring	1.14mm (0.045in)
Cylinder wear	
Rebore if oversize greater than	0.08mm (0.003in)
Or ovality greater than	0.06mm (0.0024in)
Oil	SAE 30 or SAE 10W-30

Dismantling

Read Chapter 11 for hints and tips on dismantling and reassembly before starting to dismantle. The information given there will assist an orderly and methodical approach to engine overhaul.

1 Remove battery.
2 Unclip starter cord from handle.
3 Disconnect the electrical connection from starter.
4 Remove air filter.
5 Remove power drive belt cover.
6 Remove the two bolts securing the power drive shaft bearing under the cover.
7 Tip mower backwards to stand on grass deflector.
8 Remove cutter bar and friction disc. A puller may be needed – take care not to bend the disc.
9 Remove Woodruff key from crankshaft.
10 Remove engine drain plug, drain oil into suitable container, refit the drain plug.
11 Remove throttle cable, after noting its position.
12 Undo three engine mounting bolts and remove engine. Support the engine while undoing the last bolt to avoid it falling out. Release belt from power drive pulley as you're removing the engine.

13 Remove starter cover.
14 Remove fuel tank assembly held by three small bolts and one larger one. Disconnect fuel pipe from tap.
15 Remove engine cowl and dipstick tube.
16 Remove battery charging coils. Note the small spacer under the coil on the back bolt.
17 Take off air filter housing, disconnect engine breather pipe from rear.
18 Unhook stop wire from throttle control plate.
19 Unbolt and remove electric starter unit.
20 Remove carburettor and throttle control plate, carefully noting positions and order of governor links and spring.
21 Remove ignition coil.
22 Remove mesh screen from starter clutch.
23 Unscrew and remove starter clutch. Flywheel may be jammed with screwdriver in starter teeth against rear post. Turn starter with large stilsons or special removing tool. Remove washer.
24 Remove flywheel (see advice in Chapter 11).
25 Remove exhaust screen then bend back locking tabs and remove two exhaust mounting bolts.

26 Remove engine breather from valve chest. Note steel plate attached to top bolt.
27 Slacken and remove remaining cylinder head bolts. Remove cylinder head and gasket.
28 Turn the engine over and remove power drive cover and gasket.
29 Remove shaft retainer from slot, then shaft may be slid inwards to give access to sump bolt inside sump.
30 Clean any rust or debris from the crankshaft with emery cloth to avoid damaging the seal when you take the sump off.
31 Remove six sump bolts and remove sump.
32 Remove camshaft with governor and oil slinger. Make notes of any shims that may be on the end of the camshaft.
33 Remove cam followers.
34 Remove big-end cap.
35 Remove any carbon from top of cylinder bore and push piston out through the top, taking care not to damage the bore. Remove crankshaft. Remove valve springs using special valve tool or spanner head, push plate up valve stem and pull towards notch to release. Note that the exhaust valve spring is longer than inlet spring.
36 Finally, remove the valves.

Reassembly

1 Clean all parts in paraffin or engine degreaser. Remove all traces of old gaskets from mating faces of sump, engine block and cylinder head. Do this very carefully so as not to damage the aluminium castings. Clean carbon from valves, exhaust port and piston crown, and lap in valves as explained in Chapter 11, but don't refit the springs yet, as the valve clearances will have to be checked later.

2a Check the condition of all bearings in the engine (pictures show bearing locations) and check the crankshaft for wear on big end and main bearing journals as described in Chapter 11.

2b Check condition of cylinder bore for deep scratches. Check castings for cracks, and also check condition of crankshaft seals and PTO shaft seal.

3 Refit gear on power take-off shaft. Roll pin goes through the gear and hole in the shaft, locking the two together.

4 Carefully remove piston rings, noting which way up they were and their position in the grooves. Slide them one by one about 25mm (1in) down cylinder bore and check that the gap between the ends of the rings doesn't exceed the limits in the specifications – replace the rings if the ring gap is excessive.

5 Check small-end bearing for wear by holding the piston in one hand and twisting the connecting rod in the other. The piston should slide freely on the pin but not rock. If worn, the connecting rod and gudgeon pin must be replaced.

6 Lubricate the main bearing in the crankcase and the tapered end of the crankshaft with engine oil. Fit crankshaft into the crankcase.

7 Lubricate piston and cylinder bore and refit piston. A piston ring clamp will have to be fitted to compress the piston rings before sliding the piston into bore. The open end of the big-end cap should face the valves, as shown in this picture. Lower piston carefully into the bore, taking care not to scratch it. Push piston out of clamp with hammer handle. This should happen reasonably easily – if any obstruction is felt, stop to investigate the cause.

8a Oil the big-end bearing and refit big-end cap.

8b Be sure to tighten securely, as there are no locking tabs. Rotate the crankshaft to check for free movement.

9 Lubricate and refit cam followers, making sure they're replaced in their original holes.

10 Rotate crankshaft so timing dimple in the gear is facing towards the camshaft bearing hole.

11 Fit camshaft so that the timing marks in crankshaft and camshaft align, remembering any shims that were on the camshaft when dismantled.

12 Note the position of oil slinger/ governor. Fit new sump gasket and lubricate the main bearing with engine oil.

13 Slide the sump gently down the crankshaft. Make sure the oil slinger and camshaft are in their correct positions and that the locating dowels line up with their holes.

14 Fit the sump bolts, the short one goes into the hole beside the power take-off gear. Tighten the bolts evenly to avoid cracking or distorting the sump.

15a Slide the power take-off shaft carefully and twist it to engage gear.

15b The shaft locating plate may now be placed in its slot to lock the shaft in position.

16 Fit a new gasket and secure the power take-off cover with the four small bolts.

17a Check valve clearances. The valve must be held down firmly in its seat, with the piston at top dead centre on the firing stroke (with both valves closed). Feeler gauge should slide between valve stem and cam followers without moving the valve. Clearances are given in specifications at the end of this section. If the clearance is too small, the end of the valve stem must be filed off slightly to give the correct gap (as described in Chapter 11).

17b Refit valve springs.

18 Remove all the carbon from the cylinder head, using a soft scraper or wire brush to avoid scratching the aluminium. Place a new gasket on the cylinder. Fit the cylinder head but leave out the bolts as shown – these will be used to secure the carburettor later.

19 Remove the carburettor from the throttle control plate – two bolts. Check condition of O-ring between plate and carburettor. Check condition of the needle valve, mixture screw and float. Clean all parts in petrol and blow through jets. Don't use wire to clear jets, as this will change the size of the holes.

20 Refit needle valve and float, slide in pivot pin to secure. Screw in mixture-adjusting needle gently to avoid damage to seat. Turn out 1½ turns for initial setting of mixture.

21 Refit float bowl with large rubber ring seal on the carburettor body and fibre washer and bolt. Fit carburettor throttle control plate, remembering to put the O-ring back between carburettor and plate.

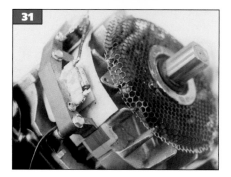

22 The correct position of governor links and spring are shown.

23 Refit carburettor to engine. Wipe inlet pipe end with oil to help it to enter the carburettor. Hook governor link back to plastic lever and slide carburettor on to manifold. Fit remaining cylinder head bolts and tighten in diagonal sequence.

24 Inspect the flywheel key for signs of shear or other damage. If necessary replace the key with the correct replacement. Don't use a steel key. Place the key in the slot in the crankshaft.

25 Fit the flywheel on to the crankshaft taper, making sure that the keyway lines up with the key in the crankshaft.

26 Fit the washer to the crankshaft. If it's a domed washer, fit the dome upwards.

27 Screw on the recoil starter clutch. It'll be necessary to jam the flywheel with a large screwdriver placed in the teeth of the flywheel and rested against one of the lugs on the back of the engine. Tighten the starter securely.

28 Fit electric starter to the engine and tighten the two bolts that secure it.

29 Fit the mesh screen to the starter clutch and secure with the two bolts.

30 Fit ignition coil and charging coils, remembering the small spacer on the charging coil. Don't tighten the bolts yet.

31 Set the air gap on the ignition coil and charging coil. Place a piece of plastic or card of the correct thickness (as given in the Technical Data table) between the coil and the flywheel magnets. The magnets will attract the coil and hold it against the card. Tighten the bolts and then rotate the flywheel to slide out the card. This process is repeated for the charging coils.

32a Fit the stop wire to throttle control plate. The spring contact should be pushed up towards the plate; the wire is then put through the hole. When the contact is released the wire is held in position.

32b Fit the engine breather with a new gasket. Remember to place the plate under the top bolt.

33 Fit the exhaust silencer. Place the locking strip on the silencer then tighten the bolts and bend over the locking tabs to secure.

34 Fit the exhaust cover with three small screws.

35 Fit the starter cover after checking operation of recoil start (see the end of this section for full information on renewing the spring or rope). Be careful not to trap spark plug lead or charging lead under the cover. Reconnect charging lead.

36 Check the O-ring seal at the base of the dipstick tube for cracks or other damage, and replace where necessary. Fit the dipstick tube to the engine cowl with two bolts.

37 Fit the air filter housing, reconnecting the breather pipe at the back when it's in position with the carburettor. Secure with the two bolts.

38 Reconnect the fuel pipe to the fuel tap and fit the fuel tank, securing with three small screws and one larger one.

39 Fit the plastic cover over the recoil starter.

40 Check the condition of the air filter, and if it's dirty or contaminated with oil replace it. Place the air filter in its cover and fit to the engine.

41 Refit engine to mower, engaging the power drive belt as you're putting the engine on. Make sure the power drive shaft bearing is the right way

up. Insert metal spacers in the plastic bearing carrier. Fit belt retainer and bolt the assembly to the mower deck.

42 Fit the Woodruff key in the crankshaft keyway, tapping it gently home with a soft-faced hammer if necessary.

43 Grease the end of the crankshaft. Slide on the cutter friction disc and twist it gently to align the keyway with the crankshaft key. Slide it fully home.

44 Check the cutting blade for nicks or cracks. Sharpen and balance the blade as described in Chapter 9, but if it's

damaged it's always worthwhile to fit a new blade.

45 Fit blade with special washer. Tighten the blade bolt.

46 Hook the end of the throttle cable into its hole in the control lever and secure the outer sheath under the cable clamp. Operate the throttle control to ensure that the choke is fully closed when the control is set to choke.

47 Fit the plastic drivebelt cover over the exposed end of the power take-off shaft and secure it with the bolt.

48 Fill the sump with new engine oil to the correct level. Replace the spark plug and reconnect the spark plug cap. Put fresh petrol in the fuel tank.

Recoil starter repair

If the recoil starter cord fails to wind back into the rewind housing after being pulled, the most likely cause is a broken recoil spring. The spring is situated on top of the rope pulley. To renew the spring, proceed as follows:

1 Pull the rope fully out and clamp the pulley to hold the spring tension. Keep the knot aligned with the rope outlet hole. Cut off the knot and remove rope.

2 Slacken spring, releasing slowly with a square piece of wood as described. Take a

15cm (6in) length of batten, 15mm (¾in) square. Drive a 10cm (4in) nail through one end (to enable controlled turning) and insert the other end into the centre of the pulley. Bend tangs up and remove pulley.

3 To fit new spring pass the end of the replacement spring through the hole in the side of the starter and engage in the pulley.

4 Bend down the tangs to secure the pulley. Wind the pulley anticlockwise to pull the spring in.

5 When fully wound in, the end of the spring will engage in the narrower section in the hole in the cover.

6 Wind up the spring until tight, then back one turn or until the hole lines up with the rope outlet. Lock with self-locking pliers or a clamp and thread rope through.

7 Fit handle to the other end of the rope. Hold the cord and release the self-locking pliers or clamp. Allow the rope to draw back the starter.

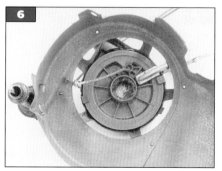

Electric starter dismantling

1 Mark position of end plate to motor body and motor body to gear housing as an aid to reassembly.
2 Remove circlip securing main gear.
3 Pull off gear and engaging spiral, check gear for wear or broken teeth.
4 Undo three bolts to remove gearbox cover.
5 Slide off the large and small gears, noting which way up they are.
6 Undo two screws securing motor back plate and slide motor away from housing. Note there are two washers on each end of the armature, one plastic on the outside then one steel. On the drive end, the steel one is a dished washer.
7 Remove the brush plate carefully and slide out the cable insulator.
8 Remove the armature and check the copper commutator for burning and wear.
9 Check the brushes for free movement and wear. If they're badly worn or burnt they should be replaced.

Electric starter reassembly

1 Put a drop of oil on bronze bush in brush plate.

2 Spread brushes and insert armature into bearing. Fit motor body to armature – carefully, as the magnets will pull the armature in. Align brush plate with locating notch and slide in the insulated wire outlet.

3 Assembled armature and motor body.

4 Fit washers to end of motor shaft, lubricate shaft with oil and refit to gear housing. Make sure the locating notches are aligned.

5 Reassembled motor and greased gears ready for refitting.

6 Refit gears in housing, making sure the small one is located correctly on the motor shaft.

7 Fit cover and gasket and tighten the three screws. Refit starter gear and spiral – this engages in the large gear under the cover. It is fully home when the circlip groove on the shaft is visible.

8 Fit circlip to secure the starter gear to the shaft.

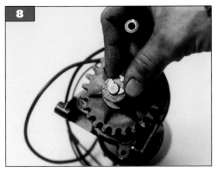

Model/spec number on engine: 121602

Mower application

Every effort has been made to ensure the list of models that use this engine is as comprehensive as possible. Due to model and engine supply changes, however, you may have a mower that isn't listed. Refer to 'Engine identification' on pages 96 and 170 to identify the engine that you have, or contact an engine supply dealer to assist with identification.

Hayter Harrier 48
IBEA 5361
Mountfield MPR series
TORO Re-cycler
26637/20791/20789/20826/20827

Technical data

Spark plug gap	0.75mm (0.030in)
Spark plug type	NGK B2LM
Cylinder bore ovality limit	0.038mm (0.0015in)
Piston ring gap limit	0.8mm (0.031in)
Valve clearances	
Inlet (cold)	0.13–0.18mm (0.005–0.007in)
Exhaust (cold)	0.18–0.23mm (0.007–0.009in)
Armature air gap	0.25mm (0.010in)
Oil grade	SAE 30
Oil capacity	0.6 litres

Dismantling

Before starting to dismantle, read Chapter 11. The procedures outlined apply to all engines, and if adopted will ensure an orderly and methodical approach that will make both dismantling and reassembly much easier. Remove the engine from the mower, and proceed as follows:

1 Unscrew the two bolts and remove the air filter cover.

2 Remove the fuel filler cap and the two bolts securing the plastic engine cover. Lift off the cover. Replace the fuel filler cap.

3 Release the clip and pull the supply pipe from the fuel tank. Be prepared for fuel spillage. Unscrew the four bolts securing the fuel tank. Note the position of the spacer fitted to the lower mounting bolt.

4 Using a ⅜in square drive tool, undo the sump plug and drain the engine oil into a suitable container.

5 Unscrew the three bolts and remove the exhaust shield.

6 In order to remove the engine cowling the oil filler neck must first be removed. Unscrew the one retaining bolt and lift the filler neck away. Note the O-ring at the base of the neck. Unscrew the four bolts and remove the cowling.

7 Unscrew the four retaining bolts, and remove the exhaust system.

8 Disconnect the engine breather pipe from the air filter housing. Unscrew the two retaining bolts and remove the housing.

9 Remove the two carburettor mounting bolts, and unhook the governor linkage as the carburettor is withdrawn.

10 Unscrew the float bowl nut and remove the float bowl. Be prepared for fuel spillage.

11 Push out the float pivot pin, and carefully lift out the float with the needle valve.

12 Check the condition of the needle valve and seat for any damage or wear (refer to Chapter 11). Examine the float bowl O-ring for any cracks, etc. The float bowl nut incorporates the main jet. Check that the holes are clear. If necessary, clear the holes by blowing or by the use of a thin nylon bristle – never use a needle or wire to clean a jet. Check the float for damage or leaks.

13 Disconnect the engine stop wire from the ignition magneto, and unscrew the carburettor mounting/linkage plate-retaining bolt. Lift the plate away.

14 Remove the engine cowling panel by unscrewing the one retaining bolt and unhooking the governor linkage.

15 Carefully pull the HT cap from the spark plug. Unscrew the two bolts and remove the ignition magneto.

16 In order to remove the flywheel retaining nut, it's necessary to prevent the flywheel from turning. In the absence of the manufacturer's special tool, this can be done by using a strap wrench around the circumference of the flywheel. Don't be tempted to lever a screwdriver against the flywheel fins – being made of aluminium they're easily damaged.

17 Remove the plastic cooling fin disc from the flywheel. Note the two locating dowels.

18 With reference to Chapter 11, pull the flywheel from the crankshaft. If you're using the manufacturer's puller, it may be necessary to cut the threads in the flywheel. The puller holes are clearly labelled in the flywheel, and the puller bolts are specially formed to cut the threads. Recover the key from the crankshaft.

19 Unscrew the four bolts and remove the breather chamber cover.

20 Unscrew the two bolts and remove the breather cover/valve.

21 Undo the four bolts and remove the rocker cover.

22 Remove the rocker arm mounting nuts and hemispherical washers. Carefully remove the rocker arms, pushrods and valve cap pads. Note or label which components are for the inlet and exhaust valves; it's important that if they're reused they're refitted to their original locations.

23 Unscrew the four bolts and remove the cylinder head. It may be necessary to gently tap the cylinder head away from the engine block, but avoid levering

between the block and cylinder head cooling fins. Note the cylinder head locating dowels.

24 In order to remove a valve, depress the valve collar and push it towards the notch in the rim of the collar. Although a special valve spring compressor is available, due to the size of the spring it's quite possible to compress them sufficiently by hand. The valve collars have two adjoining holes, one of which is larger than the other. This allows the valve stem to slide through the collar. Remove the spring and slide the valve from the cylinder head. It's important to label or arrange the components so that if reused they're refitted to their original locations. Note the seal/spring seat fitted to the inlet valve.

25 Undo the two bolts and remove the rocker mounting plate. Inspect the valve guides for scoring and excessive wear. Examine the valve seats and renovate as necessary (refer to Chapter 11).

26 Undo the retaining bolt and remove the remaining engine block cowling.

27 Slide the belt drive pulley from the crankshaft, and recover the Woodruff (half-moon) key.

28 Remove any dirt or rust from the crankshaft, unscrew the seven retaining bolts and remove the sump. It may be necessary to gently tap the sump with a soft hammer or piece of wood. Note the two locating dowels.

29 Slide the governor/oil slinger assembly from the end of the camshaft and lift the camshaft from the crankcase.

30 Remove the cam followers. Note or label each follower as exhaust or inlet as appropriate.

31 Slide the camshaft drive gear from the crankshaft. If the Woodruff (half-moon) key is loose, remove it.

32 Unscrew the retaining bolts and remove the big-end cap.

33 Remove any carbon build-up at the lip of the cylinder bore using a soft tool, and gently push the connecting rod and piston assembly up and out of the cylinder. Take care not to mark the bore with the connecting rod.

34 If required, remove the piston rings from the piston by carefully expanding the rings at their ends and sliding them from the piston. Note the orientation of the rings for reassembly.

35 Remove the circlip and push the gudgeon pin from the piston.

36 Carefully withdraw the crankshaft from the crankcase.

37 The crankshaft oil seals can now be prised out from the crankcase and sump. Note which way round they fit.

38 Prior to removing the governor arm and lever, mark the position of the lever on the shaft. It's essential that the lever be refitted in its original position. Remove the lever pinch-bolt and pull the lever from the shaft. Prise off the steel 'push-on' clip and remove the governor arm/shaft from the crankcase.

39 Check the condition of the crankshaft bearing, camshaft bearing and cylinder bore for wear, scores or cracks. If the bore is damaged, worn oval or oversized, then professional skills and special equipment will be necessary to restore it. The same applies to worn or damaged bearings. These can be reamed out to accept bushes obtainable from spares stockists, but special reaming equipment and knowledge are essential. Check all threaded holes for damaged threads, and repair if necessary by fitting a thread insert of the correct size (refer to Chapter 11).

Reassembly

1 Fit new oil seals into the crankcase and sump by carefully pushing them into place using an appropriate-sized socket. The seals should be fitted with the sharp rubber edge of the seal towards the inside of the engine.

2 Fit the governor arm into the crankcase. Note the washer fitted between the arm and the crankcase on the inside.

3 Fit a new 'push-on' clip on the arm on the outside of the case.

4 Smear the crankcase bearing journal and lip of the oil seal with new engine oil, and fit the crankshaft into the crankcase, tapered end first.

5 If previously removed, fit the gudgeon pin into the piston/connecting rod assembly. The piston is fitted with the arrow on its crown towards the tapered end of the crankshaft, and the 'open' side of the connecting rod towards the camshaft bearing. Always fit a new piston circlip. If the gudgeon pin is reluctant to move, immerse the piston in hot water for a few minutes. This causes the aluminium to expand, enabling the gudgeon pin to slide easily.

6 Fit the piston rings on to the piston. The oil control (lowest) ring should be fitted first, by carefully expanding the coiled element just enough to slide down over the piston and into its groove.

7 Next fit the second element of the oil control ring in the same manner, positioning it so that the coiled element is inside the second element. Next fit the compression ring into the middle groove. This ring must be fitted with the internal chamfer facing down. Finally, fit the top compression ring with the internal chamfer facing up. Arrange the three ring-end gaps so that they're spaced out around the circumference of the piston at 120° intervals.

NOTE: *Beware! Piston rings are very brittle, and if they're expanded too much they'll break.*

8 Smear the piston rings and cylinder bore with oil.

9 Using a piston ring clamp, fit the piston into the cylinder from the top by feeding the connecting rod through first. Make sure that the arrow on the top of the piston points towards the tapered end of the crankshaft, and that the connecting rod doesn't scratch the cylinder walls. Press the piston firmly into the cylinder, sliding it out of the clamp as the rings enter the bore. If necessary, use a piece of wood or hammer handle to gently tap the piston out of the clamp and into the cylinder, but stop and investigate any undue resistance you encounter.

10 Smear some oil on the crankshaft journal and engage the big end on to the journal.

11 Fit the big-end cap, arrow mark pointing towards the piston (arrowed), and secure it with the two bolts. Tighten the bolts securely, as there are no locking devices, but don't over-tighten. Rotate the crankshaft to ensure freedom of movement.

12 If previously removed, fit the Woodruff (half-moon) key to the crankshaft, and fit the camshaft drive gear to the crankshaft with the timing mark facing outwards (arrowed).

13 Put a drop of oil on to the cam followers, and insert each follower into the same hole from which it was removed.

14 Turn the crankshaft until the timing mark on the gear is pointing at the middle of the camshaft bearing hole in the crankcase (arrowed). Smear some oil on the camshaft bearing journal, and install the camshaft. The timing dimple drilled in the camshaft gear must be aligned exactly with the mark on the crankshaft gear when the gears are meshed. Rotate the crankshaft two revolutions to ensure correct movement.

15 Fit the governor/oil slinger assembly on to the camshaft. Align the head of the bob-weight assembly with the governor arm.

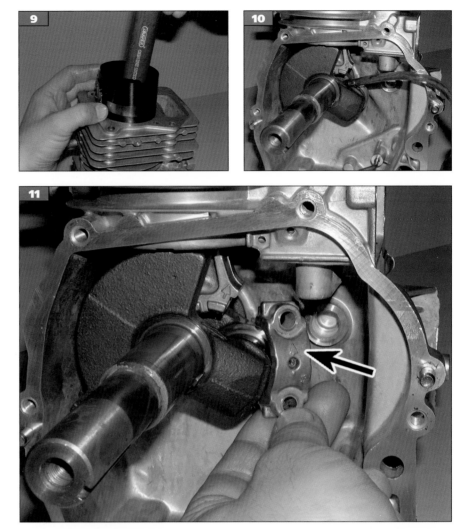

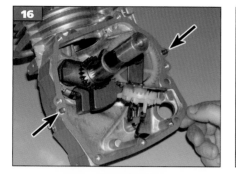

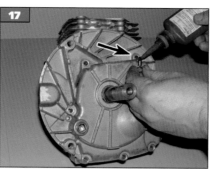

16 Fit a new sump gasket to the crankcase, noting the locating dowels.

17 Smear some oil on to the crankshaft and camshaft journal. Carefully fit the sump, ensuring that the locating holes engage with the crankcase dowels, and the oil seal lip isn't damaged during the process. Tighten the seven bolts securely, using threadlocking compound on the bolt that screws into the engine breather chamber (arrowed).

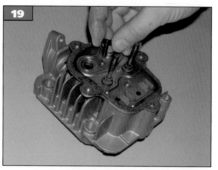

18 With a new gasket in place, fit the rocker mounting plate to the cylinder head.

19 Secure the rocker mounting plate with the two bolts.

20 Refit the valves into the cylinder head, and a new valve seat/seal to the inlet valve.

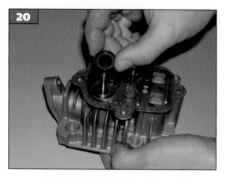

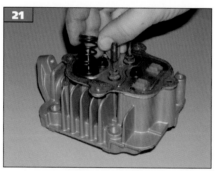

21 Fit the springs to their respective valves and compress them.

22 Locate the valve collars over the valve stems. Move the collars away from the notch on the rims and slowly release the springs. Ensure that the valve stems have located correctly in their collars.

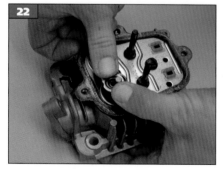

23 With a new gasket, fit the cylinder head on to the cylinder block. The gasket isn't symmetrical, and therefore will only fit one way correctly. Don't use any jointing compound. Ensure that the locating dowels on the underside of the cylinder head engage the gasket and block correctly.

24 Refit the four cylinder head bolts and tighten securely in a diagonal pattern.

25 Insert the pushrods through the holes in the rocker mounting plate, making sure they locate in the ends of the cam followers. Providing that they're inserted close to vertically, the ends of the pushrods should 'self-locate' in the cam followers. Once the pushrods have been correctly fitted, great care should be taken not to dislodge the protruding ends, as there's a danger of them falling through an oil drain hole and into the crankcase.

26 Fit the contact pads to the valve collars. It's essential that the valve pads and pushrods be refitted to their original locations.

27 Refit the rocker arms, hemispherical washers and mounting nuts to their original locations.

28 Adjust the valve clearances. The clearances are adjusted by turning the rocker arm mounting nut. The exhaust valve clearance should be adjusted when the inlet valve is fully open, and the inlet valve clearance adjusted when the exhaust valve is fully open. Turn the crankshaft to open and close the valves. The clearance dimensions are given in the Technical Data table.

29 With a new gasket, refit the rocker cover. Tighten the four bolts securely.

30 Refit the cylinder block cowling. Tighten the bolt securely.

31 Check the fibre disc valve in the engine breather for distortion or cracks. The gap between the disc valve and the body shouldn't exceed 1.1mm (0.043in). The valve is held in place by an internal bracket, which will distort if too much pressure is applied to the disc. If the valve is defective, renew the complete breather assembly.

32 Renew the gasket and refit the valve/cover using the two bolts. Tighten securely.

33 With a new gasket, refit the breather chamber cover. Tighten the four bolts securely.

34 Refit the Woodruff (half-moon) key to the crankshaft, and slide on the belt drive pulley.

35 Fit and tighten the oil drain plug to the sump, using a ⅜in square drive tool.

36 Refit the governor lever to the arm, aligning the previously made marks. Tighten the pinch-bolt securely. If the aligning marks have been lost, turn the governor shaft until the arm inside the crankshaft comes into contact with the bob-weight assembly. Then push the

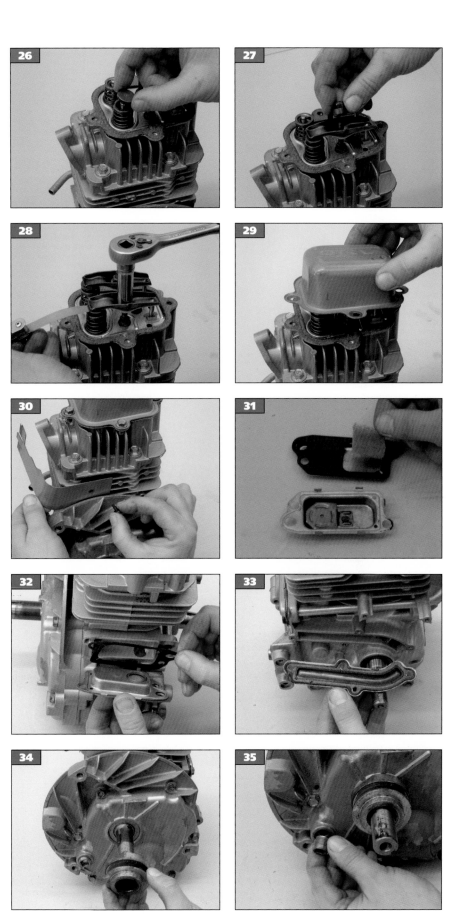

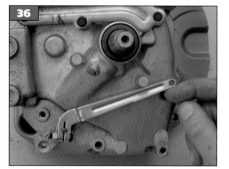

lever against its stop and tighten the pinch-bolt.

37 Slide the flywheel over the tapered end of the crankshaft and insert the key.

38 Fit the plastic cooling fin disc to the flywheel, ensuring that the locating pins have engaged correctly.

39 Fit the starter flange over the end of the crankshaft and fit the retaining nut. Tighten the nut very securely, preventing the flywheel from turning by means of a strap wrench around its circumference.

40 Refit the ignition magneto. The magneto body is marked 'Cylinder side' on one side, and 'This side out' on the other. Before tightening the two mounting bolts, turn the flywheel so that the magnets are on the opposite side to the magneto, and use a feeler gauge to measure the air gap between the two legs of the magneto's armature and the flywheel. The correct air gap is 0.254mm (0.01in). The mounting holes in the armature legs are slotted. Move the armature until the correct gap is achieved. Tighten the bolts securely.

41 Connect the governor linkage to the governor lever and refit the crankcase cowling, secured with a single bolt.

42 Place a new gasket around the inlet port, and refit the carburettor mounting/linkage plate securing the single bolt. Reconnect the magneto earthing wire from the linkage plate to the ignition magneto.

43 Reassemble the carburettor by refitting the needle valve into its holder in the float and carefully lowering the assembly into place.

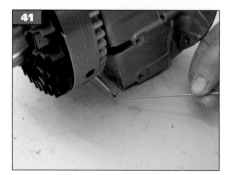

44 Insert the float pivot pin. There's no provision for adjusting the float height.

45 Refit the float bowl and secure with the nut. Do not over-tighten. Note the fibre washer between the nut and float chamber (arrowed).

46 Engage the end of the governor linkage with the relevant hole in the carburettor throttle arm.

47 Holding the heat shield in place, fit the carburettor using a new gasket. Tighten the two bolts securely.

48 Reconnect the end of the governor linkage spring to the relevant hole in the linkage plate.

49 Fit the air filter housing to the carburettor using a new gasket. Note the locating pins on the housing gasket face. Tighten the two bolts.

50 Connect the crankcase breather pipe to the air filter housing.

51 Using a new gasket, refit the exhaust system. The two self-tapping bolts fit into the crankcase and the side of the cylinder head, whilst the remaining two bolts secure the system to the exhaust port.

52 Fit the spark plug to the cylinder head and reconnect the HT lead.

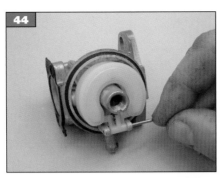

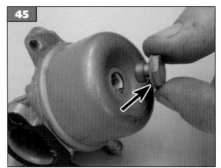

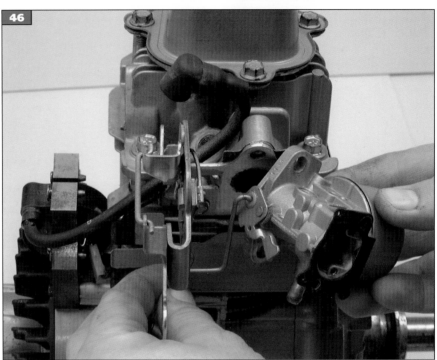

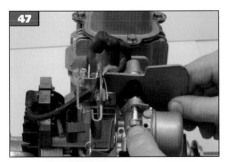

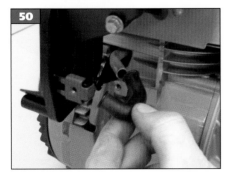

53 Refit the engine cowling and secure with the four bolts. Ensure that the edge of the cowling interlocks with the crankcase cowling already fitted.

54 Fit a new O-ring to the base of the oil filler spout, and secure the spout in place with the bolt.

55 Refit the exhaust heat shield. Tighten the three bolts securely.

56 Fit the air filter element. One side is marked 'Top'.

57 The fuel tank is secured by four bolts – three on the top and one longer bolt on the underside. Note the spacer that locates between the bottom mounting bracket and the crankcase.

58 Fit the fuel pipe between the fuel tank and the carburettor. Secure the ends of the pipe with the two clips.

59 Remove the fuel tank cap and fit the plastic engine cover. Tighten the two bolts and refit the fuel tank cap.

60 Refit the air filter cover and tighten the two bolts.

61 Remember to fill the engine sump with the correct grade and quantity of oil.

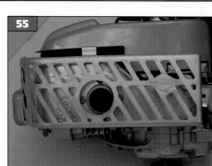

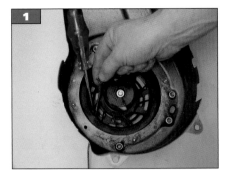

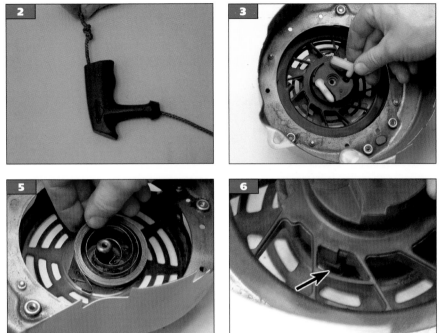

Starter repair

1 With the starter/engine cowling removed, pull the starter rope to its full extension. Lock the rope pulley in this position by inserting a screwdriver (or similar) through the spokes of the pulley and the slots of the engine cowling.

2 To replace the rope: Where the rope goes through the pulley, cut off the knot and pull the rope from the starter. Feed the new rope through the outer hole in the cowling and the hole in the pulley. Tie the knot. Feed the other end of the rope through the hole in the starter handle, and tie the knot again. Tension the rope and remove the screwdriver from the pulley spokes. Be prepared for the spring to violently rewind the starter rope. Refit the starter/engine cowling.

3 To replace the recoil spring: Where the rope goes through the pulley, untie the knot and pull the rope from the starter. Pull the screwdriver from the pulley. Unscrew the central bolt from the pawl mechanism and lift off the guide plate. Note the position of the pawls and remove them.

4 Carefully lift out the pulley, noting the locating slot for the end of the spring. Lift out the spring.

5 Insert the new spring, locating the inner end around the lug on the cowling.

6 Fit the pulley, locating the outer end of the spring in the slot on the pulley (arrowed).

7 Check the starter pawls for damage or excessive wear and refit them to the pulley. Refit the guide plate on to the pawls, ensuring that the pawl locating pins engage with the slots on the underside of the guide plate. Tighten the central bolt.

8 Using a screwdriver (or similar), very carefully wind the pulley approximately seven full turns and align the rope hole in the pulley with the hole in the cowling. The exact number of turns is dependent on the length of rope. Lock the pulley in place by inserting a screwdriver (or similar) through the spokes of the pulley and the slots of the engine cowling. Exercise extreme caution during this procedure. It will take some effort to wind up the spring, and should the screwdriver slip the pulley will unwind violently.

9 Feed the rope through the outer hole in the cowling and the hole in the pulley. Tie a knot in the end of the rope. Tension the rope and remove the screwdriver from the pulley spokes. Be prepared for the spring to violently rewind the starter rope. Refit the starter/engine cowling.

3 BRIGGS & STRATTON I/C 'L' HEAD 5HP HORIZONTAL CRANK FOUR-STROKE ENGINE OVERHAUL

Model/spec number on engine: 135232

Mower application

Every effort has been made to ensure the list of models that use this engine is as comprehensive as possible. Due to model and engine supply changes, however, you may have a mower that isn't listed. Refer to 'Engine identification' on pages 96 and 170 to identify the engine that you have, or contact an engine supply dealer to assist with identification.

Atco Club
Atco Royale
Kompact 90S

Technical data

Valve clearances (cold)	
Inlet	0.13–0.18mm (0.005–0.007in)
Exhaust	0.23–0.28mm (0.009–0.011in)
Spark plug type	NGK B2LM
Spark plug gap	0.75mm (0.030in)
Crankshaft end float	0.05–0.20mm (0.002–0.008in)
Magneto armature air gap	0.254–0.355mm (0.010–0.014in)
Piston ring gap	
Compression rings	0.80mm (0.031in) max
Oil control ring	1.14mm (0.045in) max
Oil grade	SAE 30, SAE 10W–30
Oil capacity	0.62 litres
Torque wrench settings	
Big-end bolts	11Nm
Cylinder head bolts	16Nm
Flywheel nut	88Nm
Crankcase end plate bolts	10Nm

Dismantling

Before starting to dismantle, read Chapter 11. The procedures outlined apply to all engines, and if adopted will ensure an orderly and methodical approach that'll make both dismantling and reassembly much easier.

1 Unscrew the two bolts and remove the air filter cover. Lift out the filter element.
2 Remove the air filter housing.
3 The engine cowling/starter is secured by four bolts, two on the top and one on each side at the crankcase base. Remove the cowling.
4 Bend back the tab washers and undo the exhaust system mounting bolts. Remove the system.
5 Loosen the Torx screw securing the carburettor to the fuel tank sufficiently to allow the engine breather pipe to be disconnected and removed.
6 Unscrew the two Torx screws and remove the remote control panel. Disconnect the linkage and the magneto earthing wire as the panel is removed.
7 Disconnect the magneto earthing wire under the fuel tank by unscrewing the retaining nut.

8 Remove the carburettor and fuel tank together. Two bolts secure the carburettor to the cylinder head, and one, under the fuel tank, secures the tank to the crankcase. As the assembly is withdrawn recover the heat shield, and disconnect the governor arm-to-throttle butterfly linkage and the spring between the governor arm and pivot plate.
9 To separate the carburettor from the fuel tank, undo the Torx screws and disengage the throttle linkage. Lift the carburettor from the tank. Be prepared for fuel spillage.
10 Remove the wire gauze over the main jet, and clean if required. To gain access to the pilot jet for cleaning, undo the brass cover screw.
11 Inspect the screen in the base of the fuel pickup pipe for damage and cleanliness. Don't brush or rub the screen, as it's very delicate.
12 The fuel pump is integral with the carburettor. Remove the four Torx screws and withdraw the cover, diaphragm, cup and spring. Check for cleanliness and diaphragm damage.
13 Unscrew the two magneto retaining

bolts, disconnect the HT cap from the spark plug and remove the magneto. Note how the deflector plate slots under the armature post.
14 The nut retaining the flywheel to the crankshaft can be extremely tight. To prevent the flywheel from turning, in the absence of the manufacturer's special tool use a strap wrench around the circumference of the flywheel, and undo the nut. The help of an assistant to steady the engine may be necessary.
15 Remove the starter flange and mesh.
16 To remove the flywheel, tap the back of it with a soft hammer whilst pulling it away from the crankcase. Do not tap the aluminium element or the magnets of the flywheel. Recover the key from the crankshaft.
17 Unscrew the two retaining bolts and remove the crankcase cowling.
18 In order to remove the cylinder block cowling, unscrew the three cylinder head bolts and the bolt on the side of the cylinder block.
19 Remove the remaining five bolts and lift away the cylinder head. Note that

the three bolts around the exhaust valve are slightly longer than the others.

20 Unscrew the two retaining bolts and prise away the tappet cover/breather valve.

21 Turn the exhaust valve spring collar until the notch in its rim faces out. The valve collars have two adjoining holes, one of which is larger than the other. This allows the valve stem to slide through the collar. Using a pair of thin-nosed pliers or similar, compress the spring, move the collar away from the cylinder, slide the collar off the end of the valve stem and remove the valve. Repeat for the inlet valve. It's important to label or arrange the components so that if reused they're refitted to their original locations.

22 Inspect the valve guides for scoring and excessive wear. Examine the valve seats and renovate as necessary (refer to Chapter 11).

23 Using a ⅜in square drive tool, undo the sump plug and drain the engine oil into a suitable container.

24 Remove all rust and dirt from the crankshaft. Unscrew the six retaining bolts and remove the crankcase end plate.

25 If required, the governor cup assembly can be removed from the end plate by pulling.

26 Unscrew the big-end bolts. Recover the oil dipper and the bearing cap.

27 Remove any carbon build-up at the lip of the cylinder bore using a soft tool, and gently push the connecting rod and piston assembly up and out of the cylinder. Take care not to mark the bore with the connecting rod. If required, remove the piston rings from the piston by carefully expanding the rings at their

ends and sliding them from the piston. Note the orientation of the rings for reassembly. Remove the circlip and push the gudgeon pin from the piston.

28 Align the timing mark on the crankshaft counterweight with the drilling on the camshaft gear, and withdraw the crankshaft and camshaft together.

29 Slide out the cam followers. It's important to label or arrange the followers so that if reused they're refitted to their original locations.

30 If it's necessary to remove the governor lever from the shaft, mark the position of the lever on the shaft before undoing the pinch-bolt. Pull out the 'R-clip' and withdraw the governor shaft from the crankcase.

31 If required, prise out the crankcase and end plate oil seals. Note which way round they're fitted.

32 Check the condition of the crankshaft bearing, camshaft bearing and cylinder bore for wear, scores or cracks. If the bore is damaged, worn

oval or oversized, then professional skills and special equipment will be necessary to restore it. The same applies to worn or damaged bearings. It may be possible to have these reamed out to accept bushes obtainable from spares stockists, but special reaming equipment and knowledge are essential. Check all threaded holes for damaged threads, and repair if necessary by fitting a thread insert of the correct size (refer to Chapter 11).

33 If the output side crankshaft main ball bearing requires replacement, a bearing press will be needed, as the bearing is a press-fit on the shaft. To install a new bearing, suspend the bearing in hot oil at 120°C. Take all necessary safety measures to protect your skin from hot oil splashes. With the crankshaft clamp in a soft-jawed vice, slide the bearing on to the shaft with the shield side inwards. As the bearing cools it'll tighten on the journal. Do not quench the bearing.

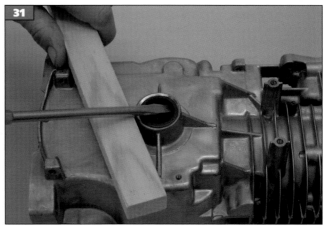

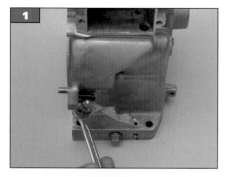

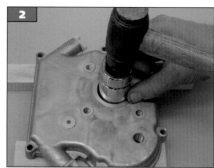

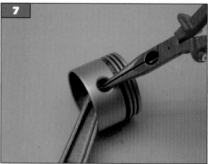

Reassembly

1 If removed, refit the governor arm into the crankcase and secure with the 'R-clip'. Refit the governor lever to the arm, aligning the previously made marks. Tighten the pinch-bolt.

2 Fit new oil seals into the crankcase and sump by carefully pushing them into place using an appropriate-sized socket. The seals should be fitted with the sharp rubber edge of the seal towards the inside of the engine.

3 Refit the cam followers to their respective holes. A smear of grease can be useful to hold the followers in place.

4 Oil the crankshaft and camshaft bearing journals. The crankshaft and camshaft must be inserted together. Prior to fitting the shafts into the crankcase, mesh the drive gear on the crankshaft with the camshaft gear, and align the timing marks. Fit the shafts into the crankcase.

5 If previously removed, fit the gudgeon pin into the piston/connecting rod assembly. If the gudgeon pin is reluctant to move, immerse the piston in hot water for a few minutes. This causes the aluminium to expand, enabling the gudgeon pin to slide easily.

6 The piston is fitted with the circlip groove towards the tapered end of the crankshaft, and the connecting rod with the cast lug (arrowed) at the big-end journal towards the camshaft bearing.

7 Always fit a new piston circlip.

8 Fit the piston rings on to the piston. The oil control (lowest) ring should be fitted first, by carefully expanding the ring just enough to slide down over the piston and into its groove. The oil control ring is symmetrical in profile.

9 Next fit the compression ring into the middle groove. This ring must be fitted with the step in its circumference facing down. The top compression ring is symmetrical in profile. However, if the rings are marked with a dot, fit the ring with the dot facing up. Remember that piston rings are very brittle, and if they're expanded too much they'll break. Arrange the three ring-end gaps so that they're spaced out around the circumference of the piston at 120° intervals.

10 Smear the piston rings and cylinder bore with oil. Using a piston ring clamp, fit the piston into the cylinder from the top by feeding the connecting rod through first. Make sure that the connecting rod doesn't scratch the cylinder walls. Press the piston firmly into the cylinder, sliding it out of the clamp as the rings enter the bore. If necessary, use a piece of wood or hammer handle to gently tap the piston out of the clamp and into the cylinder, but stop and investigate any undue resistance you encounter.

11 Smear some oil on the crankshaft journal and engage the big end on to the journal. Fit the big-end cap with the cast lug (arrowed) towards the camshaft.

12 Fit the oil dipper, and, if you have a suitable torque wrench, tighten the bolts to the torque given in the Technical Data table. If not, tighten the bolts securely, but don't over-tighten. Rotate the crankshaft to ensure freedom of movement.

13 If removed, push the washer and governor cup assembly on to its mounting shaft on the inside of the crankcase end plate.

14 Liberally grease the main bearing ball race. Place a new gasket over the locating dowels and refit the crankcase end plate. As the cover engages on the locating dowels, it may be necessary to rotate the governor cup gear in order for it to mesh with the camshaft gear.

15 Tighten the crankcase end plate bolts evenly, in a diagonal sequence, to the torque given in the Technical Data table. Check that the crankshaft end float is within the limits given in the specifications. If it's less than the lower limit, an additional paper gasket must be fitted under the crankcase end plate. If it's more than the upper limit, a thrust washer is available, and must be fitted on the crankshaft between the camshaft drive gear and the main bearing.

16 Prior to fitting the valve springs, turn the crankshaft until the piston is

at TDC on the compression stroke. Slowly continue to turn the crankshaft until the piston has moved down the bore approximately 6mm. Insert the valves into their respective guides and, with reference to Chapter 11, check both valve clearances. The dimensions are given in the Technical Data table. Once the correct clearances have been achieved, remove the valves.

17 Fit the inlet valve spring and collar into place in the tappet chest. Ensure that the notch in the rim of the collar is facing out.

18 Using a pair of thin-nosed pliers or similar, compress the valve spring, slide the collar over the end of the valve stem and move the collar in towards the cylinder. Slowly allow the spring to uncompress, and check that the collar has located correctly on the end of the valve stem. Repeat this procedure for the exhaust valve, noting that a spring seat should be fitted on top of the exhaust spring.

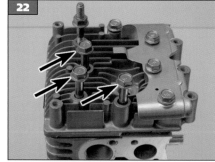

19 Check the fibre disc valve in the engine breather for distortion or cracks. The gap between the disc valve and the body should not exceed 1.1mm (0.043in). The valve is held in place by an internal bracket, which will distort if too much pressure is applied to the disc. If the valve is defective, renew the complete breather assembly. Renew the gasket and refit the valve/cover using the two bolts. Tighten securely.

20 Place the new head gasket in the correct position. The gasket will only align with the bolt holes one way round. Don't use any jointing compound.

21 Fit the cylinder head and cowling.

22 The three long bolts (arrowed) fit into the holes around the exhaust valve. The bolt with the stud extension is located as shown. Tighten the cylinder head bolts evenly, in a diagonal sequence, to the torque given in the Technical Data table.

23 Tighten the bolt retaining the cylinder block cowling.

24 Refit the crankcase cowling using the two retaining bolts.

25 Fit the flywheel over the tapered end of the crankshaft and insert the square-section key into the keyway.

26 After fitting the flywheel mesh and starter flange, tighten the flywheel nut to the torque given in the Technical Data table. Use a strap wrench around the circumference of the flywheel to prevent it from turning. The help of an assistant will be necessary.

27 Refit the ignition magneto. The magneto body is marked 'Cylinder side' on one side, and 'This side out' on the other.

28 Fit the deflector plate over its locating post on the armature.

29 Before tightening the two mounting bolts, turn the flywheel so that the magnets are on the opposite side to the magneto, and use a feeler gauge to measure the air gap between the two legs of the magneto's armature and the flywheel. The correct air gap is given in the Technical Data table. The mounting holes in the armature legs are slotted. Move the armature until the correct gap is achieved. Tighten the bolts securely. Refit the HT cap to the spark plug.

30 Refit the fuel pump spring, cup and diaphragm to the carburettor. Secure the cover with the four Torx screws.

31 Using a new gasket, refit the carburettor to the fuel tank. The carburettor is secured to the tank by two Torx screws – a long one down through the body of the carburettor, and a short one through the mounting flange.

32 Reconnect the throttle linkage.

33 Refit the carburettor and fuel tank assembly. As the assembly is fitted, reconnect the governor linkage and spring.

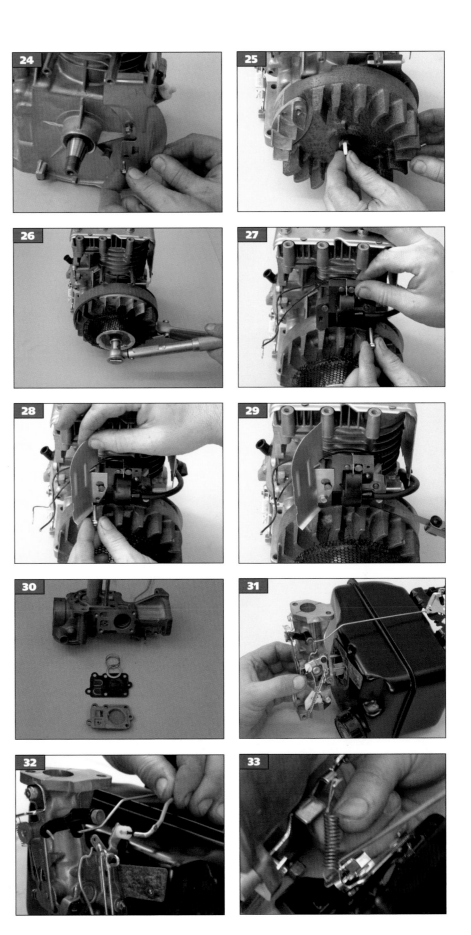

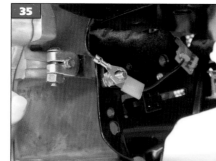

34 Fit the heat shield between the carburettor and cylinder head. Secure with the two retaining bolts. The fuel tank is secured with one bolt to the crankcase base.

35 Reconnect the magneto earthing wire under the fuel tank.

36 Refit the remote control panel to the carburettor/fuel tank assembly. Reconnect the choke linkage as the panel is fitted, and ensure that the throttle lever pin engages with the sliding linkage. Secure the panel with the two Torx screws.

37 Reconnect the magneto earthing wire. Check for correct operation.

38 Install the engine breather pipe between the breather valve cover and air intake. The pipe is retained by a clamp under a carburettor-to-fuel tank mounting Torx screw.

39 Fit the exhaust system. Tighten the retaining bolts and secure them by bending the tabs of the locking washer.

40 The engine cowling/starter is secured to the crankcase by four bolts, two on the top and one on each side. Before tightening the bolts, ensure that it interlocks correctly with the cylinder block cowling already fitted, and that the HT lead hasn't been trapped.

41 Refit the air filter housing using the four bolts with integral shakeproof washers.

42 Refit the air filter element. One side is marked 'UP'.

43 Secure the air filter cover with two bolts.

44 Remember to fill the sump with the correct grade and quantity of oil.

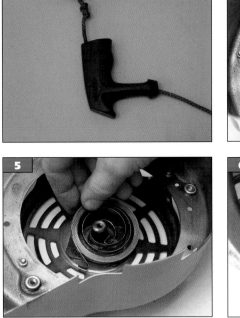

Starter repair

1 With the starter/engine cowling removed, pull the starter rope to its full extension. Lock the rope pulley in this position by inserting a screwdriver (or similar) through the spokes of the pulley and the slots of the engine cowling.

2 To replace the rope: Where the rope goes through the pulley, cut off the knot and pull the rope from the starter. Feed the new rope through the outer hole in the cowling and the inner hole in the pulley. Tie the knot. Then feed the other end of the rope through the hole in the starter handle, and retie the knot. Tension the rope and remove the screwdriver from the pulley spokes. Be prepared for the spring to violently rewind the starter rope. Refit the starter/engine cowling.

3 To replace the recoil spring: Where the rope goes through the pulley, untie the knot and pull the rope from the starter. Pull the screwdriver from the pulley. Unscrew the central bolt from the pawl mechanism and lift off the guide plate. Note the position of the pawls and remove them.

4 Carefully lift out the pulley, noting the locating slot for the end of the spring. Lift out the spring.

5 Insert the new spring, locating the inner end around the lug on the cowling.

6 Fit the pulley, locating the outer end of the spring in the slot on the pulley (arrowed).

7 Check the starter pawls for damage or excessive wear, and refit them to the pulley. Refit the guide plate on to the pawls, ensuring that the pawl locating pins engage with the slots on the underside of the guide plate. Tighten the central bolt.

8 Using a screwdriver (or similar), very carefully wind the pulley approximately

seven full turns, and align the rope hole in the pulley with the hole in the cowling. The exact number of turns is dependent on the length of rope. Lock the pulley in place by inserting a screwdriver (or similar) through the spokes of the pulley and the slots of the engine cowling. Exercise extreme caution during this procedure. It will take some effort to wind up the spring, and should the screwdriver slip the pulley will unwind violently.

9 Feed the rope through the outer hole in the cowling and the hole in the pulley. Tie a knot in the end of the rope. Tension the rope and remove the screwdriver from the pulley spokes. Be prepared for the spring to violently rewind the starter rope. Refit the starter/engine cowling.

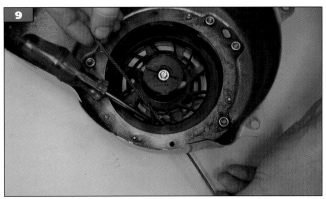

4 BRIGGS & STRATTON 35 SPRINT/CLASSIC 2.6KW FOUR-STROKE ENGINE OVERHAUL

Model/spec number on engines: 9D902, 10D902, 98902

Mower application

Every effort has been made to ensure the list of models that use this engine is as comprehensive as possible. Due to model and engine supply changes, however, you may have a mower that isn't listed. Refer to 'Engine identification' on pages 96 and 170 to identify the engine that you have, or contact an engine supply dealer to assist with identification.

Efco LR series
Flymo
Harry 313
Hayter
Lawnflite by MTD 383
Lawnflite by MTD GE40
Lawn-King NG series
Macalastair
McCulloch
Mountfield Emblem 15
Mountfield Laser Delta 42/46
Oleomac G43

Partner 431
Rover 100
Stiga Multiclip Pro 48
Suffolk Punch P16
and many more...

Technical data

Spark plug gap	0.76mm (0.030in)
Spark plug type	NGK B2LM
Valve clearances (cold)	
Inlet	0.13–0.18mm (0.005–0.007in)
Exhaust	0.18–0.23mm (0.007–0.009in)
Armature air gap	0.15–0.25mm (0.006–0.010in)
Oil grade	SAE 30
Oil capacity	0.6 litres
Torque wrench settings	
Flywheel nut	74Nm
Big-end bolts	11Nm
Cylinder head bolts	16Nm

Dismantling

Before starting to dismantle, read Chapter 11. The procedures outlined apply to all engines, and if adopted will ensure an orderly and methodical approach that'll make both dismantling and reassembly much easier.

1 Undo the retaining bolt and remove the cutting blade.
2 Slide the blade mounting flange from the shaft and remove the Woodruff (half-moon) key.
3 Disconnect the engine stop cable from the flywheel brake assembly by squeezing the retaining tabs of the cable ferrule and pulling it from the bracket. Disengage the cable end fitting from the arm.
4 Unscrew and remove the three engine mounting nuts and bolts.
5 Lift the engine away from the mower body. Recover the three washers between the engine and body.
6 Using a ⅜in square drive tool, remove the sump plug and drain the oil into a suitable container.
7 Undo the retaining bolt and remove the air filter/cover assembly. Recover the sealing washer.

8 Remove the flywheel brake cover.
9 Unscrew the two retaining bolts and remove the exhaust shield.
10 The engine cowling/starter is secured by two bolts, one into the cylinder head and the other into the crankcase at the side. Unscrew the bolts and remove the cowling/starter.
11 After noting their location, disconnect the two throttle springs from the throttle linkage.
12 Undo the two mounting bolts and remove the carburettor and fuel tank together. As the assembly is withdrawn, disengage the throttle linkage from the engine governor.
13 To separate the carburettor from the fuel tank, undo the six mounting screws and very carefully prise the carburettor from the fuel tank. As the carburettor is removed, take care not to lose the spring that fits between the carburettor body and the mounting gasket/diaphragm. Be prepared for fuel spillage.
14 Remove the wire gauze over the main jet, and clean if required. Carefully clean the wire gauze in the end of the fuel pickup pipe. Clean any obscured jets or air/fuel passages by blowing only.

15 The carburettor has fixed main and pilot jets, and no further dismantling is possible.
16 Remove the crankcase cowling between the fuel tank and crankcase.
17 Carefully pull the HT cap from the spark plug.
18 Undo the two retaining bolts and remove the ignition magneto together with the governor arm. As the magneto is removed, disconnect the earthing wire.
19 In order to remove the flywheel brake assembly, use a screwdriver to wedge the brake in the 'Off' position. Unscrew the two retaining bolts and remove the brake. Disconnect and remove the magneto earthing wire.
20 Bend back the two tab washers, undo the bolts and remove the exhaust system.
21 The nut retaining the flywheel to the crankshaft can be extremely tight. To prevent the flywheel from turning, in the absence of the manufacturer's special tool use a strap wrench around the circumference of the flywheel, and undo the nut. The help of an assistant to steady the engine may be necessary.

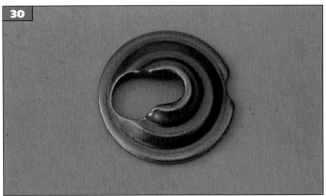

22 Remove the starter flange. With reference to Chapter 11, pull the flywheel from the crankshaft. If you're using the manufacturer's puller it may be necessary to cut the threads in the flywheel. The puller holes are clearly labelled in the flywheel, and the puller bolts are specially formed to cut the threads. Recover the key from the crankshaft.

23 Remove the inlet manifold.

24 Undo the two retaining bolts and prise away the engine breather valve/ tappet cover.

25 Remove the spark plug.

26 Unscrew the eight cylinder head bolts and lift away the head with the cowling.

27 Turn the exhaust valve spring collar until the notch in its rim faces out. The valve collars have two adjoining holes, one of which is larger than the other. This allows the valve stem to slide through the collar. Using a pair of thin-nosed pliers or similar, compress the spring, move the collar away from the cylinder, slide the collar off the end of the valve stem and remove the valve. Repeat for the inlet valve. It's important to label or arrange the components so that if reused they're refitted to their original locations.

28 Inspect the valve guides for scoring and excessive wear. Examine the valve seats and renovate as necessary (refer to Chapter 11).

29 Unscrew the engine breather pipe from the crankcase.

30 Ensure that the crankshaft is free of dirt and rust. Unscrew the six retaining bolts and remove the sump. A light tap from a soft hammer may be necessary, as the sump locates over two dowels in the crankcase gasket face.

31 Remove the oil slinger from the end of the camshaft.

32 Align the timing mark on the camshaft gear with the mark on the camshaft drive gear fitted to the crankshaft. Carefully remove the camshaft.

33 Slide out the cam followers. It's important to label or arrange the followers so that if reused they're refitted to their original locations.

34 The camshaft drive gear should slide easily from the crankshaft.

35 Unscrew the big-end bolts and withdraw the bearing cap.

36 Remove any carbon build-up at the lip of the cylinder bore using a soft tool and gently push the connecting rod and piston assembly up and out of the cylinder. Take care not to mark the bore with the connecting rod.

37 If required, remove the piston rings from the piston by carefully expanding the rings at their ends and sliding them from the piston. Note the orientation of the rings for reassembly. Remove the circlip and push the gudgeon pin from the piston.

38 Prise the oil seals from the crankcase and sump.

39 Check the condition of the crankshaft bearing, camshaft bearing and cylinder bore for wear, scores or cracks. If the bore is damaged, worn oval or oversized, then professional skills and special equipment will be necessary to restore it. The same applies to worn or damaged bearings. It may be possible to have these reamed out to accept bushes obtainable from spares stockists, but special reaming equipment and knowledge are essential. Check all threaded holes for damaged threads, and repair if necessary by fitting a thread insert of the correct size (refer to Chapter 11).

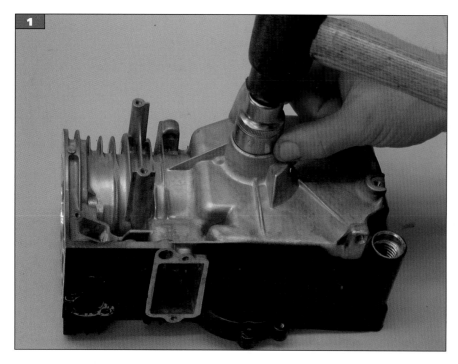

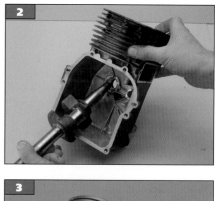

Reassembly

1 Fit new oil seals in the crankcase and sump by carefully pushing them into place using an appropriate-sized socket. The seals should be fitted with the sharp rubber edge of the seal towards the inside of the engine.

2 Oil the main bearing journal in the crankcase and insert the crankshaft, tapered end first.

3 If previously removed, fit the gudgeon pin into the piston/connecting rod assembly. The piston is fitted with the circlip groove towards the non-tapered end of the crankshaft, and the 'open' side of the connecting rod towards the camshaft bearing. If the gudgeon pin is reluctant to move, immerse the piston in hot water for a few minutes. This causes the

aluminium to expand, enabling the gudgeon pin to slide easily.

4 Always fit a new piston circlip.

5 Fit the piston rings on to the piston. The oil control (lowest) ring should be fitted first, by carefully expanding the coiled element just enough to slide down over the piston and into its groove. Next fit the second element of the oil control ring in the same manner, positioning it so that the coiled element is inside the second element. Next fit the compression ring into the middle groove. This ring must be fitted with the step in its circumference facing down. The top compression ring is symmetrical in profile. However, if the rings are marked with a dot, fit the rings with the dot facing up.

Remember that piston rings are very brittle, and if they're expanded too much they'll break. Arrange the three ring-end gaps so that they're spaced out around the circumference of the piston at 120° intervals.

6 Smear the piston rings and cylinder bore with oil. Using a piston ring clamp, fit the piston into the cylinder from the top by feeding the connecting rod through first. Make sure that the connecting rod doesn't scratch the cylinder walls. Press the piston firmly into the cylinder, sliding it out of the clamp as the rings enter the bore. If necessary, using a piece of wood or hammer handle, gently tap the piston out of the clamp and into the cylinder, but stop and investigate any undue resistance you encounter.

7 Oil the crankshaft journal and engage the big end on to the journal. Fit the big-end cap. Due to the stepped shape of the cap, it will only fit one way round (arrowed). If you have a suitable torque wrench, tighten the bolts to the torque given in the Technical Data table. If not, tighten the bolts securely but don't over-tighten. Rotate the crankshaft to ensure freedom of movement.

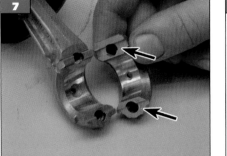

8 Slide the camshaft drive gear over the end of the crankshaft with the timing mark facing outwards (arrowed). The gear locates over a pin in the crankshaft.

9 Oil the cam followers and refit them to their original locations.

10 Turn the crankshaft until the timing mark on the gear is pointing at the middle of the camshaft bearing hole in the crankcase. Smear some oil on the camshaft bearing journal and install the camshaft. The timing dimple cast in the camshaft gear must align exactly with the mark on the crankshaft gear when the gears are meshed (arrowed). Rotate the crankshaft two revolutions to ensure correct movement.

11 Refit the oil slinger assembly to the end of the camshaft.

12 Fit a new gasket over the locating dowels in the crankcase gasket face, and carefully refit the sump. Take care not to damage the lip of the oil seal. Secure the sump with the six bolts, using thread sealer on the bolt that enters the engine breather chamber (arrowed). Refit the sump plug and filler/dipstick.

13 Prior to fitting the valve springs, turn the crankshaft until the piston is at TDC on the compression stroke. Slowly continue to turn the crankshaft until the piston has moved down the bore approximately 6mm. Insert the valves into their respective guides and, with reference to Chapter 11, check both valve clearances. The dimensions are given in the Technical Data table. Once the correct clearances have been achieved, remove the valves.

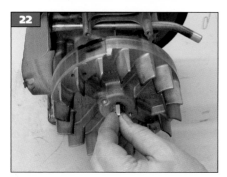

14 Fit the exhaust valve spring and collar into place in the tappet chest, with the close-coiled end of the spring towards the valve head. Ensure that the notch in the rim of the collar is facing out. Insert the exhaust valve. Using a pair of thin-nosed pliers or similar, compress the valve spring, slide the collar over the end of the valve stem and move the collar in towards the cylinder. Slowly allow the spring to uncompress, and check that the collar has located correctly on the end of the valve stem. Repeat this procedure for the inlet valve.

15 Check the fibre disc valve in the engine breather for distortion or cracks. The gap between the disc valve and the body shouldn't exceed 1.1mm. The valve is held in place by an internal bracket, which will distort if too much pressure is applied to the disc. If the valve is defective, renew the complete breather assembly. Renew the gasket.

16 Refit the valve/cover and crankcase cowling using the two bolts. Tighten securely.

17 Grease the threads of the engine breather pipe and screw it into the breather chamber.

18 Place the new head gasket in the correct position. The gasket will only align with the bolt holes one way round. Don't use any jointing compound.

19 Refit the cylinder head and cowling.

20 Tighten the eight retaining bolts evenly, in a diagonal sequence, to the torque given in the Technical Data table. Refit the spark plug.

21 Using a new gasket, refit the inlet manifold.

22 Fit the flywheel over the tapered end of the crankshaft, align the keyway and slide the square-sectioned key into place.

23 Refit the screen mesh, starter flange and retaining nut to the crankshaft. Using a strap wrench to prevent the flywheel from turning, tighten the retaining nut to the torque given in the Technical Data table. The help of an assistant will be required to steady the engine during this procedure.

24 Check the condition of the gasket and refit the exhaust system. The two retaining bolts are locked in place by bending the tabs of the locking washer.

25 Using a screwdriver, wedge the flywheel brake assembly in the 'Off' position and refit it to the crankcase using the two retaining bolts. Remove the screwdriver.

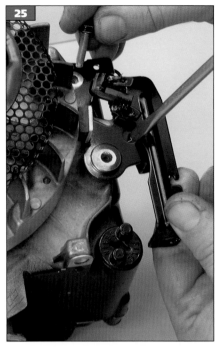

26 Route the magneto earthing wire under the engine breather pipe and through the retaining clip, and reconnect it to the engine stop element of the flywheel brake assembly.

27 Refit the magneto and engine governor using the two retaining bolts. The magneto body is marked 'Cylinder side' on one side, and 'This side out' on the other. Before tightening the two mounting bolts, turn the flywheel so that the magnets are on the opposite side to the magneto, and use a feeler gauge to measure the air gap between the two legs of the magneto's armature and the flywheel. The correct air gap is given in the Technical Data table. The mounting holes in the armature legs are slotted. Move the armature until the correct gap is achieved. Tighten the bolts securely. Reconnect the magneto earthing wire. Refit the HT cap to the spark plug.

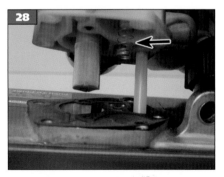

28 Refit the carburettor to the fuel tank using a new gasket. As the carburettor is fitted, ensure that the spring is correctly located in the carburettor body (arrowed). Tighten the six retaining bolts securely.

29 The carburettor-to-inlet manifold joint is sealed by an O-ring, retained by a collar in the carburettor outlet. Carefully prise out the collar and check the O-ring for signs of damage or wear. Fit a new O-ring if in any doubt. Refit the collar by pushing it into place.

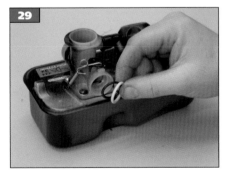

30 As the carburettor and fuel tank assembly is fitted, reconnect the throttle arm-to-governor linkage and reconnect the engine breather pipe. Retain the assembly with the end mounting bolt, but don't tighten.

31 Fit the crankcase cowling and spacer, insert the fuel tank-retaining bolt, and tighten both mounting bolts.

32 Reconnect the governor return spring...

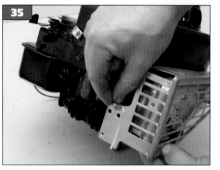

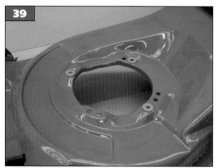

33 ...and the throttle spring.

34 Refit the engine cowling/starter using two retaining bolts, one into the top of the cylinder head and the other into the crankcase, which also retains the crankcase cowling.

35 Fit the exhaust shield using the two retaining bolts, one into the cylinder head and the other into the crankcase, which also secures the engine cowling.

36 Note the locating peg (arrowed), and fit the flywheel brake cover.

37 Refit the air filter assembly, not forgetting the sealing washer between the housing and carburettor.

38 If the air filter element is dirty, clean it with fresh petrol and soak it in clean engine oil. Squeeze the excess oil from the foam and refit it into the housing.

39 Position the three washers around the relevant body mounting holes, and refit the engine to the body. Tighten the nuts and bolts securely.

40 Refit the Woodruff (half-moon) key to the keyway nearest the end of the shaft, and fit the blade mounting flange.

41 Mount the blade on the flange using the locating lugs, and tighten the retaining bolt securely.

42 Reconnect the flywheel brake/ engine stop cable by engaging the inner cable in the hole in the lever, and pushing the outer cable ferrule into the locating hole in the bracket.

43 Remember to add the correct quantity and grade of engine oil.

Starter repair

1 With the starter/engine cowling removed, pull the starter rope to its full extension. Lock the rope pulley in this position by inserting a square-sectioned piece of wood through the cowling next to the lug on the pulley rim. The lug jams against the wood, and the pulley is held.

2 To replace the rope: Where the rope goes through the pulley, cut off the knot and pull the rope from the starter. Feed the new rope through the outer hole in the cowling and the inner hole in the pulley. Tie the knot. Then feed the other end of the rope through the hole in the starter handle and again tie the knot. Tension the rope and remove the piece of wood. Be prepared for the spring to violently rewind the starter rope. Refit the starter/engine cowling.

3 To replace the recoil spring: Where the rope goes through the pulley, untie the knot and pull the rope from the starter. Unscrew the central bolt from the pawl mechanism and lift off the guide plate. Note the position of the pawls and remove them.

4 Carefully lift out the pulley, noting the locating slot for the end of the spring. Lift out the spring.

5 Insert the new spring, locating the inner end around the lug on the cowling.

6 Fit the pulley, locating the outer end of the spring in the slot on the pulley (arrowed).

7 Check the starter pawls for damage or excessive wear and refit them to the pulley. Refit the guide plate on to the pawls, ensuring that the pawl locating pins engage with the slots on the underside of the guide plate. Tighten the central bolt.

8 Using a screwdriver (or similar), very carefully wind the pulley approximately seven full turns and align the rope hole in the pulley with the hole in the cowling. The exact number of turns is

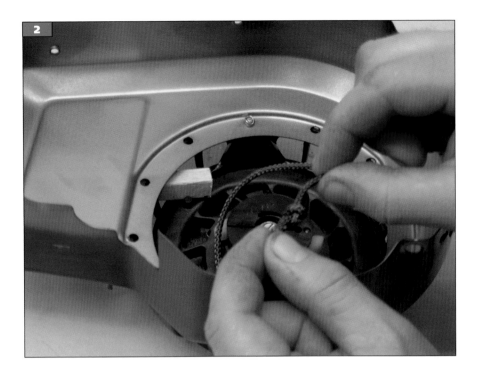

dependent on the length of rope. Lock the pulley in place by inserting a piece of square-sectioned wood through the cowling, jamming the lug on the pulley rim. Exercise extreme caution during this procedure. It will take some effort to wind up the spring, and should the piece of wood slip the pulley will spin violently.

9 Feed the rope through the outer hole in the cowling and the hole in the pulley. Tie a knot in the end of the rope. Tension the rope and remove the piece of wood from the cowling. Be prepared for the spring to violently rewind the starter rope. Check for correct operation. Refit the starter/engine cowling.

5 HONDA GXV120 OHV FOUR-STROKE ENGINE

Model/spec number on engine: GXV120

Mower application

Every effort has been made to ensure the list of models that use this engine is as comprehensive as possible. Due to model and engine supply changes, however, you may have a mower that isn't listed. Refer to 'Engine identification' on page 97 to identify the engine that you have, or contact an engine supply dealer to assist with identification.

Honda HR194
Honda HRA214
Honda HR214
IPU 400 series
Rover (various)
Tracmaster Camon and many more...

Technical data

Spark plug gap	0.7–0.8mm (0.028–0.031in)
Valve clearances	
Inlet	0.08–0.13mm (0.003–0.005in)
Exhaust	0.13–0.18mm (0.005–0.007in)
Armature air gap	0.25mm (0.010in)
Piston ring gap (standard)	0.23–0.525mm (0.009–0.021in)
Roto-stop brake cable adjustment (free play at tip of lever)	5–10mm (0.20–0.39in)
Drive clutch cable (free play at handle bar)	5–10mm (0.20–0.39in)
Speed change cable (free play at tip of lever)	1–3mm (0.04–0.12in)
Oil	SAE 10W-40

Dismantling

Before starting to dismantle, read Chapter 11. The procedures outlined apply to all engines, and if adopted will ensure an orderly and methodical approach that'll make both dismantling and reassembly much easier.

1 Disconnect the plug lead. Drain the oil from the engine.
2 Remove the handle bars. Be careful not to damage or kink the control cables.
3 Loosen the handle bar locknuts of the Roto-stop cable, and unscrew the adjuster to release tension in the cable.
4 Free the throttle cable from the carburettor.
5 Remove the cutter blade.
6 Remove the cover panel from the transmission. Remove the plastic cover from the drive shaft.
7 Remove the engine mounting bolts.
8 Slide the engine forward so that the transmission drive shaft slides off the serrations on the final drive unit shaft.
9 Undo the two nuts securing the air cleaner duct to the carburettor. Remove the bolt securing the air cleaner to the engine. Remove the air cleaner complete with the engine breather pipe.
10 Remove the fuel filler cap.
11 Remove the engine cover.
12 Remove the petrol tank from the engine. Disconnect the fuel pipe from the tank, withdrawing the filter from the tank connector as the pipe is removed. Handle the filter with great care, as it's very fragile.
13 Remove the clutch central bolt. Withdraw the cover plate, spring, clutch plate and pressure plate.
14 Make a careful note of the positions of all springs and links to assist reassembly in the same holes.
15 Remove the linkage mounting plate from the engine.
16 Remove the carburettor and the plastic insulator plate.

Remove the float chamber, float and needle valve for inspection. Dismantle the fuel tap.
17 Remove the ignition unit.
18 Remove the exhaust muffler assembly (consisting of a shield, muffler box and gasket).
19 Remove the central bolt holding the brake assembly together and lift off the Roto-stop brake components.
20 Remove the Woodruff key from the crankshaft.
21 Unscrew the three flange bolts and springs from the brake housing and lift off the housing.
22 Lift the ball retainer from the ball control plate.
23 Remove the Roto-stop return springs and lift off the ball control plate.
24 Remove the circular spacer from the crankshaft.
25 As a precaution, make a permanent mark on the governor lever and the shaft. If the lever ever becomes loose it's then easy to set it to the original datum.
26 Remove the flywheel nut from the crankshaft and lift off the rotating screen/starter hub and the flywheel and impeller. Remove the key from the crankshaft taper.
27 Remove the overhead valve cover and gasket.
28 Remove the cylinder head complete with valves.
29 Remove the crankcase cover. Make a careful note of where the bolts of differing lengths fit, to assist reassembly.
30 Mark the big end of the connecting rod and the cap before removing the latter, as the cap will fit both ways. It must be reassembled the same way round as originally fitted.
31 Withdraw the piston and connecting rod through the top of the cylinder, taking care not to scratch the bore.
32 Withdraw the camshaft and then the crankshaft. Pull the R-shaped clip off the drive shaft. Withdraw the drive shaft from the crankcase cover. To remove and dismantle the final drive unit, remove the right-hand rear wheel.

33 Remove the height-adjusting plate pivot bolts from both back wheels.
34 Remove the torque reacting bracket.
35 Lift the back axle clear.
36 Disconnect the speed change cable and the drive engage cable.
37 Remove the protector plate from the axle.

38 Remove the final drive case bolts, split the two halves of the casing and remove the internal components.
NOTE: *If any difficulty is experienced in carrying out these instructions, refer to the photographs in the reassembly instructions that follow. Used in the reverse sequence, these photographs indicate the steps in dismantling and will help to identify the components mentioned above.*

Reassembly

1 The governor components are shown in the photo. Fit the C-clip into the groove in the shaft; it's easier to do this at this stage.

2 Slide the carrier wheel on to the governor shaft from the end with the slot in it. The weights on the wheel must be facing away from the slot. Fit the smaller washer on to the shaft after the wheel. With the wheel and washer as far on to the shaft as they'll go, fit the shaft into the crankcase cover. The slot in the shaft mates on to a key machined in the cover casting. Fit the shaft clamp with the fork in the end engaged on the peg on the cover. (The gear seen in the photo won't have been fitted at this stage.) Place the larger washer in the shaft, then fit the slider on to the shaft with its flange engaged between the weights.

3 Insert the drive shaft into the crankcase cover.

4 The gear and its fixing components are shown in the photo.

5 Fit the washer with the smaller hole on to the shaft so that it'll be between the first bearing and the gear. Slide the shaft into the gear.

6 Fit the washer with the larger hole on to the end of the shaft then push the shaft into the second bearing.

7 Insert the clip between the gear and the washer. Fit the straight leg of the clip into the hole in the shaft and press until it clicks fully home.

8 Fit a new oil seal to the crankcase cover bearing if necessary, in the same way as described previously for other engines.

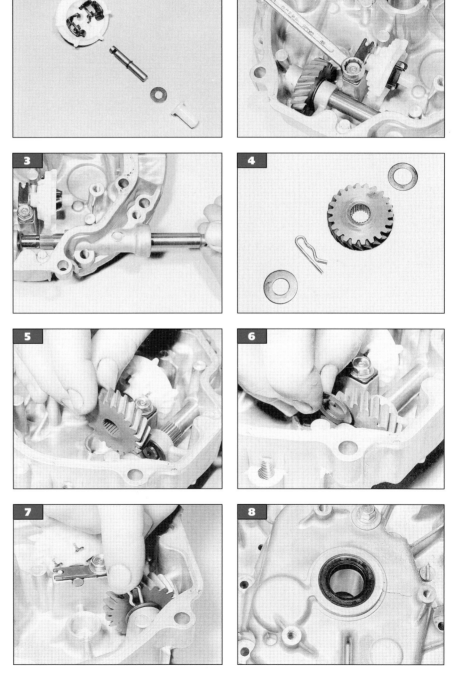

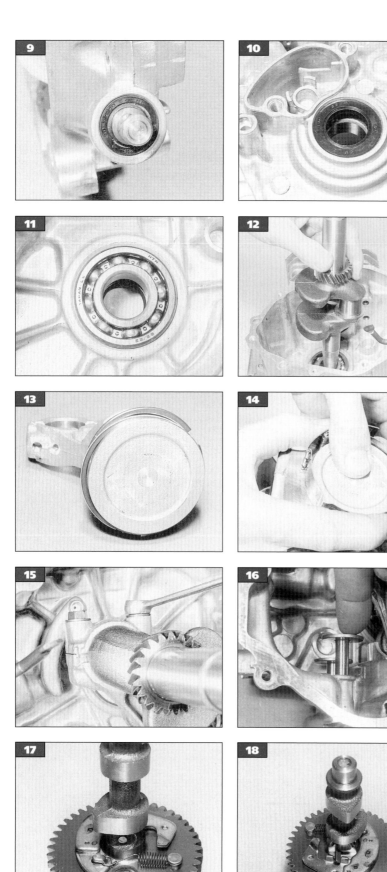

9 The drive shaft is also fitted with an oil seal. If necessary, renew the seal before fitting the drive shaft.

10 Fit a new oil seal to the crankcase flywheel bearing if necessary.

11 The flywheel bearing in the crankcase is a ball bearing. To renew it, remove the oil seal and drive the old bearing in towards the crankcase interior. Fit the new bearing from the interior. Drive it into the housing with a piece of tube that bears on the outer race only. If the ball cage or the inner race are struck, the bearing will be damaged. Keep the bearing square as it's driven into the casting.

12 Smear a little oil on the crankshaft parallel portion at the tapered end. Insert the crankshaft into the crankcase bearing.

13 Assemble the connecting rod to the piston the same way round as when removed, *ie* with the oil hole on the same side as the arrow on the piston crown. If the gudgeon pin has been removed, fit it in the conventional manner, the same way round as when it was removed, and replace the circlips securely.

14 Fit a piston ring clamp to the piston. Oil the bore of the cylinder and insert the piston into it, taking care not to scratch the bore with the connecting rod. Press the piston out of the clamp and into the bore. Tap it gently with a piece of wood if necessary, but stop and investigate any obstruction or the piston rings may break. The arrow on the piston crown must be pointing towards the OHV pushrod hole in the casting.

15 Invert the engine and oil the crank pin, engage the big end on it and fit the big-end cap the same way round as marked when dismantling. Note that the cap will fit the wrong way round. Tighten the bolts firmly.

16 Oil the cam followers and fit them into the holes in which they were originally fitted (marked during dismantling).

17 Check the action of the decompressor on the camshaft gear. Ensure that the spring is undamaged, not stretched and imparts a positive return action.

18 Check that the toe of the decompressor lever and the two prongs on the weight lever aren't worn, and that they remain engaged throughout full travel of the weight lever.

19 Lay the engine on its side, oil the camshaft bearing and insert the camshaft into the crankcase.

20 Mesh the cam gear with the crankshaft gear, with the timing marks aligned.

21 Place a new gasket on the crankcase. Oil the camshaft bearing and the crankshaft bearing. Fit the dowel into the crankcase.

22 Fit the OHV oil return pipe into the elongated hole in the crankcase.

23 Fit the crankcase cover, ensuring that the governor slider and washer don't fall off. Guide the internal governor lever into the space between the governor slider and the side of the crankcase. Engage the cover on the dowel and seat the cover on to the crankcase.

24 Secure the crankcase cover with the six bolts. Tighten diagonally opposite bolts a little at a time to avoid distorting or cracking the cover.

25 Insert the valves into the cylinder head. The exhaust valve has the smaller head of the two.

26 Place a small block of wood in the cylinder head to hold the valves on the seats while the springs are fitted. Turn the cylinder head on to its face with the wooden block in position.

27 Fit the pushrod guide plate on to the two studs in the cylinder head and

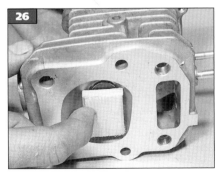

secure with the two nuts. Place the valve spring over the valve stem.

28 Press the collar down on to the spring, slightly off to one side so that the larger, offset hole in the collar can pass down on to the valve stem, then centralise the collar with a sideways movement so that the smaller hole fits under the shoulder near the tip of the valve stem.

29 Place the two dowels in the top of the cylinder.

30 Place a new gasket on the cylinder.

31 Fit the assembled cylinder head on to the cylinder.

32 Secure the cylinder head with the four bolts, tightening them diagonally to avoid distortion or cracking.

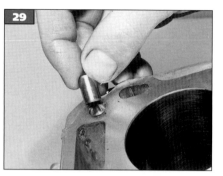

33 Insert the pushrods through the retainer plate and locate them in the concave holes in the followers.

34 Place the rocker arms on to the studs with the smaller dimple seated on the top of the pushrod.

35 Screw the shouldered nuts on to the studs.

36 Fit the locknuts and set the valve clearances as given in the Technical Data table. Lock the locknuts. This operation must be carried out at top dead centre of the firing stroke.

37 Fit a new valve cover gasket, then fit the valve cover but don't tighten down, as two of the four bolts are used later to install the cowl.

38 Inspect the breather disc valve for damage or distortion. Renew if necessary.

39 Rinse the gauze in solvent, dry thoroughly and insert it into the cavity in the breather housing.

40 Fit a new gasket to the breather cover and secure the cover in position.

41 Place the Woodruff key in the slot in the crankshaft taper. If there are any shear marks or serious burrs, use a new key.

42 Install the flywheel and the impeller on the crankshaft, aligned with the key. The impeller has four locating pegs that fit into four holes in the flywheel.

43 Fit the rotary screen and starter hub on to the impeller, with the screen located in the hole in the impeller. The three holes in the hub fit on to three pegs on the impeller. Fit the flywheel nut.

44 Install the ignition unit.

45 Using a non-ferrous feeler gauge, set an air gap as given in the Technical Data table, between the armature legs and the flywheel.

46 Remove the main jet and metering tube and examine them for dirt or gummy deposits. Clean by rinsing and blowing them. Don't poke the openings with a needle or wire, or they may be damaged and the accurate metering lost. Replace the metering tube and the main jet in the carburettor body.

47 To remove the float, pull out the hinge pin. Remove the needle valve by pushing against the coil spring and sliding it out of the slot in the float. Examine the needle head for ridging or wear and renew if necessary.

48 Fit the needle valve back into the slot in the float. Place the float hinge in position between the carburettor hinge posts, with the needle in the hole between the posts. Press the hinge pin through the holes and check it for free movement.

49 Examine the float chamber gasket for distortion or other damage. Renew it if necessary. Ensure that it's properly seated in the groove. Fit the float

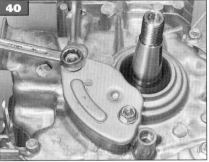

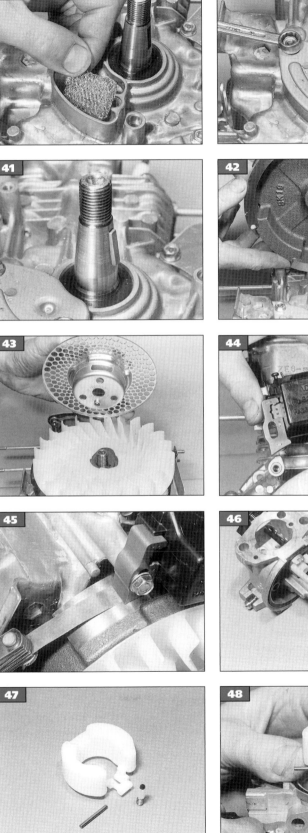

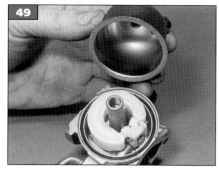

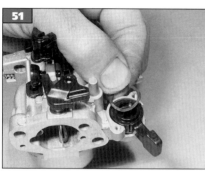

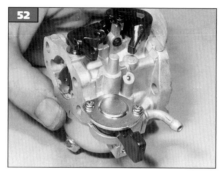

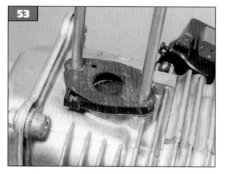

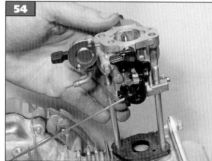

chamber with the drain plug towards the choke butterfly. Secure it with the bolt and fibre washer.

50 Inspect the four-hole seal in the fuel tap and renew it if torn, distorted or hardened. Place it on the two shallow studs.

51 Place the lever valve body in the housing. Fit the wave washer on top of the body.

52 Fit the cover plate on to the housing.

53 Fit a new gasket on the inlet port and place the plastic insulator block on top of it, then fit another new gasket on the insulator block – the small hole in the insulator block must be pointing towards the bottom of the engine.

54 Position the carburettor near the studs and connect the governor link to the larger hole in the throttle butterfly lever. Connect the governor spring to the smaller hole in the lever. Slide the carburettor on to the studs.

55 Fit the gasket, spacer and second gasket to the carburettor intake.

56 Fit the linkage plate to the engine. Connect the short link from the choke butterfly to the lever on the plate. Connect the coil spring from the hole marked 'STD' in the control lever to the small lever at the bottom of the governor lever.

57 Fit the guard over the linkage plate.

58 Place the heat shield gasket on the exhaust port studs, with the slanted edge positioned as shown.

59 Place the muffler on the studs.

60 Finally, fit the heat shield. Secure with the two nuts.

61 Gently rinse the fuel pipe filter mesh in clean petrol. Blow down the pipe from the other end to remove any particles left on the filter. Don't brush or rub it or the mesh will be damaged. Connect the pipe to the tank and secure with the clip.

62 The fuel tank attaching parts are shown in the photo.

63 Place the washer on the bolt, then the spacer tube. Fit a rubber grip on the tube. Insert the tube and bolt through the hole in the fuel tank, through the other rubber grip and screw the bolt into the mounting bracket on the crankcase.

64 Pass the fuel pipe behind the linkage plate and press the pipe support clip into the hole in the linkage plate. Connect the pipe to the carburettor and secure it with the spring clip. Fit the cowl to the engine with the five bolts.

65 Position the air cleaner duct on the carburettor mounting studs.

66 Secure the air cleaner to the studs with the two nuts. Bolt the air cleaner mounting lug to the linkage plate.

67 Place the spacer on the crankshaft.

68 Fit the Roto-stop ball control plate on to the crankshaft.

69 Connect the two Roto-stop return springs to the two levers and to the anchor bolts.

70 Place the ball retainer on the ball control plate, with the balls located in the three concave pressings.

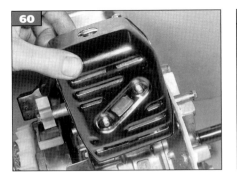

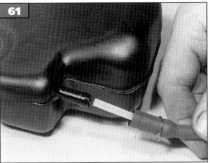

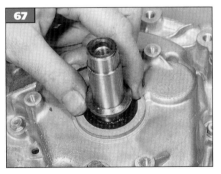

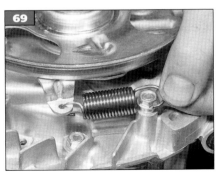

71 Place the brake housing in position with its blisters located on the balls.

72 Place the brake springs on the flange bolts.

73 Align the brake housing with its three bolt holes in line with the threaded holes in the crankcase cover. Fit the flange bolts.

74 Tighten them down. Fit the Woodruff key into the crankshaft slot.

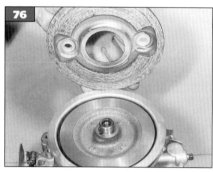

75 Fit the drive disc on to the crankshaft, aligned with the key.

76 Place the brake lining plate on the drive disc.

77 Place the clutch spring on the brake lining plate. Fit the driven disc on the brake lining plate, with the two pegs in the holes in the brake lining plate. The driven disc has a ball bearing and an oil seal in its centre. Renewal of these is straightforward and the same as for the crankcase bearings described previously.

78 Fit and tighten the central bolt.

79 Examine the seal in the final drive case for damage or distortion. Ensure that it's properly seated in the groove.

80 Renew the oil seal at the bevel drive shaft bearing if necessary. Insert the bevel drive shaft.

81 Place the thrust washer in the casing.

82 Install the bevel gear.

83 Insert the drive selector fork into the bearing in the case.

84 The drive gear shaft and clutch ratchet hub are shown in the photo. The internal coil spring can be renewed by withdrawing the cross key from the slots.

85 Slide the ratchet hub on to the gear shaft splines. Oil the end of the gear shaft and insert it through the bevel gear into the bearing in the case. Engage the hub in the selector fork as the shaft is inserted.

86 Engage the hub ratchet with the bevel gear ratchets.

87 Fit the larger gear flange upwards on to the gear shaft.

88 Fit the smaller gear on to the shaft.

89 Fit the thrust washer. The cross key in the shaft fits into the cross of the small gear.

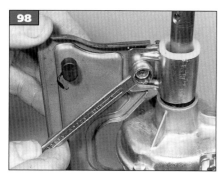

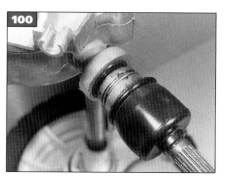

90 Insert the drive actuating plunger into the gear shaft.

91 Insert the hollow dowel in the case lip. Fill the case with a light transmission oil.

92 Slide the other half of the case on to the axle, engage it on the dowel and mate the two halves together. Secure with the five bolts. Two are longer and are fitted one over the extended torque reactor bolt, and the other at the opposite end of the case.

93 Clamp the speed selector lever to the selector fork shaft. The index mark on the end of the shaft must coincide with the centre pop mark on the lever.

94 Fit the washer into the hub of the ratchet-drive rear wheel.

95 Fit the ratchet freewheel unit into the wheel hub.

96 Place the cover over the hub with the lip pointing outwards.

97 Slide the clamp bracket for the protector plate on to the axle.

98 Bolt the protector plate to the bracket. The tabs on the clamp bracket must be entered in the matching holes in the protector plate.

99 Fit the universal joint on to the drive shaft and secure it by pushing the shear pin through the hole in the shaft.

100 Spring the clip into the groove to retain the pin.

101 Turn the mower frame upside down and lift the axle assembly into position on it. Connect the speed selector cable to the selector fork lever.

102 Connect the drive engage cable to the plunger actuating lever.

103 Remove the left-hand back wheel to improve access. Fit the shouldered bolt through the curved end plate of the height adjusting lever. Pass the bolt through the height pivoting plate. Fit a washer on to the bolt between the pivoting plate and the boss on the mower frame. Insert the bolt into the higher of the two bosses on the frame and secure it with the nut.

104 Locate the slot in the torque plate on the extended torque reactor bolt on the drive case.

105 Secure the torque plate with the two bolts.

106 Fit the wheel cup on to the axle with the flange lip inward. Insert the drive pin into the axle hole.

107 Fit the wheel on to the axle so that the drive pin engages the slots in the hub.

108 Secure the wheel with the central bolt and fit the hubcap.

109 To fit the Roto-stop operating cable to the bottom of the engine, connect the nipple in the slot first...

110 ...then pull the bracket into position and secure it with the two screws. Don't remove the cable sheath retaining spring disc unless a spare is available, as these discs can only be used once. Note that it isn't possible to assemble this bracket after the engine has been mounted on the chassis.

111 Mount the engine and secure it with the four bolts.

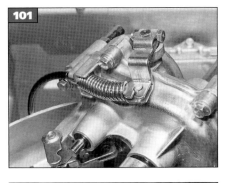

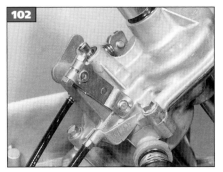

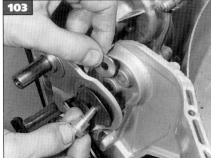

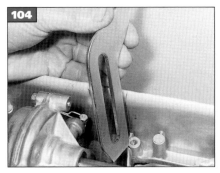

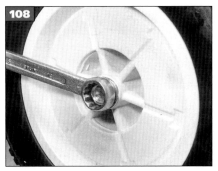

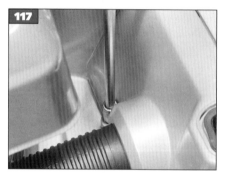

112 Mount the blade holder on the crankshaft with the blade attachment holes aligned with the holes in the driven disc.

113 Fit the cutter blade. Hold it with a piece of rag to avoid injury from the cutting edge.

114 Place the spring clip in position next to the groove on the drive shaft. Slide the drive shaft on to the serrations on the drive bevel shaft.

115 Connect the forward universal joint of the drive shaft on to the engine output shaft, align the drive pin hole and insert the pin.

116 Fit the drive shaft guard with the throttle cable located in the slot.

117 Secure it with the screw.

118 Connect the throttle cable to the lever on the link plate. Clamp the cable sheath in the clip in a position that gives full range of movement. Push the engine breather pipe on to the air cleaner duct and secure it with the spring clip. Push the other end of the breather pipe into the hole in the crankcase.

119 Adjust the cables as necessary to give correct operation (see Technical Data table). The cables on the underside of the control quadrant in the photo above are, from left to right, the Roto-stop, self-propel drive, throttle and speed change.

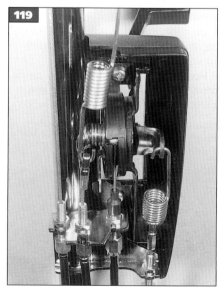

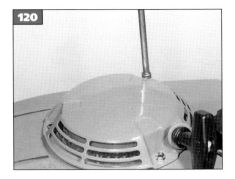

120 Fit the recoil starter on to the engine cowl.

121 Place the element in the air cleaner housing and fit the cover.

122 Fill the engine with oil to the level shown on the filler plug dipstick.

Starter repair

To fit a new recoil spring or starter cord, proceed as follows:

1 Remove the recoil starter from the engine cowl.

2 Bend up the tang near the cord exit hole to allow the rope to be unwound.

3 Release pulley tension by pulling the cord out about 60cm (2ft), holding the pulley and unwinding the cord. Gently release the pulley.

4 Remove the central bolt and lift off the cover. There's no need to lift out the pawls or their spring unless they need renewing, which is straightforward and can be seen in the following views.

5 Lift the pulley from the shaft. Remove the recoil spring.

6 Hook the outer end of the new spring into the slot in the housing. Wind the spring anticlockwise into the housing,

working in towards the middle. Put a blob of grease in the coils. Attach a new cord to the pulley if necessary and wind it anticlockwise round the pulley. Place the pulley on the stub shaft and turn it gently anticlockwise until it engages with the hook on the inner end of the recoil spring.

7 If a new cord was fitted, thread the end through the exit hole and knot the handle in place. Inspect the pawls and their spring – renew if damaged. To tension the pulley, wind it about three turns anticlockwise, hold it and wind the

slack in the cord anticlockwise on to the pulley, then release the pulley.

8 Fit the cover with the two legs of the clip on either side of the peg on the pawl...

9 ...then fit and tighten the bolt.

10 Bend the tang down over the cord. Pull the starter handle and check for freedom of movement and a positive return action. Install the starter on the engine cowl with the handle facing the left side of the mower.

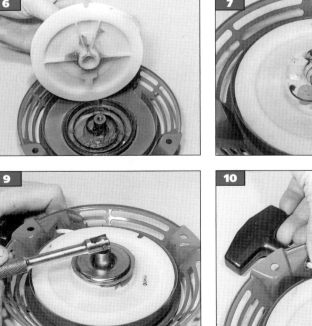

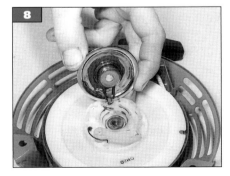

6 TECUMSEH 3.5HP/VANTAGE 35 FOUR-STROKE ENGINE

Model/spec number on engines: E-31, E-41, E-36, E-46, E-56

Mower application

Every effort has been made to ensure the list of models that use this engine is as comprehensive as possible. Due to model and engine supply changes, however, you may have a mower that isn't listed. Refer to 'Engine identification' on page 97 to identify the engine that you have, or contact an engine supply dealer to assist with identification.

AL-KO (various)
Castel (various)
Efco LR series
Flymo 42cm/46cm
Harry (various)
Hayter Hobby
Kompact 90
Mountfield Emblem
Mountfield Empress
Mountfield M3
Mountfield Laser
Oleomac G43
Qualcast Quadtrak 45
Qualcast Trojan
The Club 470 T35/40
Valex Daytona

Technical data

Spark plug gap	0.8mm (0.031in)
Armature air gap	0.37mm (0.015in)
Valve clearance: Inlet and exhaust	0.25mm (0.010in)
Piston ring gap	0.18–0.43mm (0.007–0.017in)
Oil	SAE 30 or SAE 10W-30
SAE 10W is an acceptable substitute. Do NOT use SAE 10W-40	

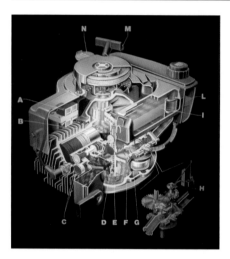

◄ **Tecumseh four-stroke BVS 143/153 engine.**

Dismantling

Before starting to dismantle, read Chapter 11. The procedures outlined apply to all engines, and if adopted will ensure an orderly and methodical approach that'll make both dismantling and reassembly much easier.

1 Disconnect the plug lead. Drain the oil from the engine.
2 Disconnect the power drive clutch cable from the drive casing.
3 Remove the cutter, the drive sleeve and the key. Remove the exhaust box.
4 Disconnect the throttle cable from the carburettor.
5 Remove the engine mounting bolts. Remove the engine from the deck by unscrewing the bolts in the power drive cover mounting bracket, and have some assistance to pull sideways on the drive cover while the engine is moved sideways to disconnect the power drive. Lift the engine clear when the power drive is disconnected.

Remove the plastic dust shield from the power drive shaft.
6 Disconnect the fuel pipe from the tank.
7 Disconnect the air cleaner housing from the carburettor inlet.
8 Remove the engine cowling complete with the air cleaner housing, leaving the fuel tank and recoil starter behind on the engine.
9 Remove the recoil starter from the engine. Remove the fuel tank with the starter handle in it.
10 Note the positions of the governor spring and the link from the governor lever to the throttle butterfly lever, so that they can be reassembled in the same holes. Disconnect the spring and the link and remove the carburettor.
11 Grip the engine drive shaft in a soft jaw vice and remove the flywheel nut. Don't over-tighten the vice. If the shaft turns while loosening the flywheel nut, replace the cutter sleeve and key on the drive shaft and grip the sleeve in the vice.

12 Remove the flywheel from the taper (see Chapter 11).
13 Remove the offset key from the drive shaft; remove the plastic sleeve from the shaft.
14 Remove the valve cover.
15 Remove the cylinder head.
16 Remove the crankcase cover, disengaging the power drive pinion as it's withdrawn. Remove the oil pump from the camshaft.
17 Remove the camshaft.
18 Mark the big-end cap for reassembly in the same position, then remove it.
19 Withdraw the piston upwards from the cylinder. Ensure that the connecting rod doesn't score the bore as it passes through.
20 Mark the cam followers for reassembly in the same holes, then remove them.
21 Remove the valves.
22 Remove the breather assembly from the lower part of the crankcase.

Reassembly

1 Fit new oil seals in the crankcase if necessary, as described for previous engines.

2 The valve components are shown in the picture in order of assembly.

3 The valve marked with an 'I' in the centre is the inlet valve. Be careful not to transpose the valves.

4 Insert the valve into the guide.

5 Fit the plain-hole collar on to the valve stem, dished side to the valve chest. Place the spring against the collar. Fit the slotted collar on to the valve stem, dish into the spring, and offset to allow the valve stem through the wide end of the slot. Lever up the collar and move it sideways so that the narrow end of the slot engages under the shoulder on the valve stem. This locks the spring on to the valve. Fit both valves in an identical manner (this picture shows an exhaust valve).

6 Smear the crankshaft with oil and insert into the crankcase bearing.

7 Assemble the piston rings and connecting rod on the piston. The rings must be fitted the same way round in the same grooves as when removed. The gudgeon pin and connecting rod must be the same way round as when removed. Ensure circlips are located securely. When assembled in the cylinder, the serial numbers on the connecting rod must face the open end of the crankcase.

8 Fit a piston ring clamp to the piston. Oil the cylinder walls. Insert the piston from the top, taking care not to scratch the bore with the connecting rod. Press the piston out of the clamp, tapping gently with a piece of wood if necessary. If an obstruction occurs, don't force the piston in – stop and investigate.

9 Oil the crankpin and engage the big end on it. Fit the cap the correct way round, as marked during dismantling. Tighten the two bolts firmly.

10 Oil the cam followers and insert them in the same holes in which they

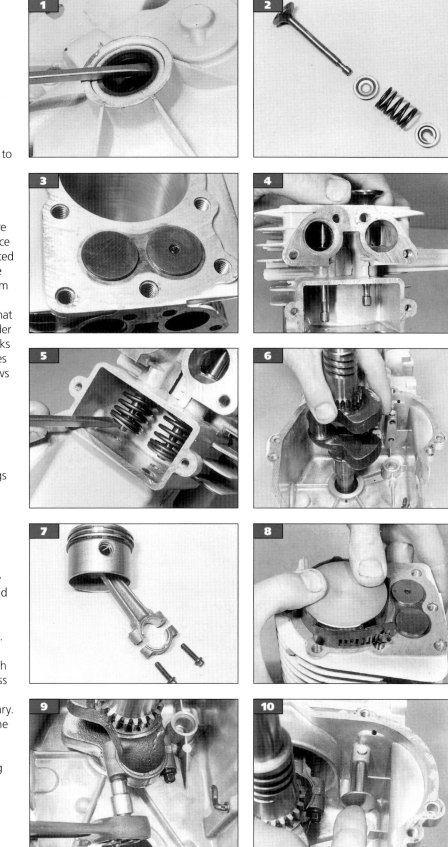

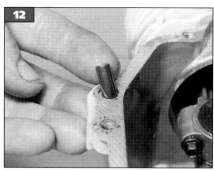

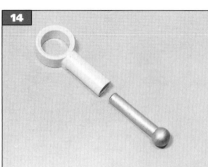

were originally fitted, as marked during dismantling.

11 Oil the camshaft bearing and insert the camshaft into the crankcase. Mesh the cam gear timing mark in line with the mark on the crankshaft gear.

12 Fit the two dowels into the holes in the crankcase.

13 Fit a new crankcase gasket.

14 Insert the oil pump plunger into the housing.

15 Fit the pump on to the camshaft, with the chamfered side of the hole in the white plastic housing facing down on to the cam gear.

16 The final drive shaft and pinion assembly is held in the crankcase by a circlip with a flat washer behind it.

17 The pinion is keyed to the shaft and has a thrust washer on either side of it, one with an anti-spin angled leg. Removal and installation to fit a new pinion or shaft is straightforward and can be carried out from the picture.

18 Check the governor slider and weights for freedom of operation and signs of wear. If faulty, the governor should be renewed as a complete unit. To remove the governor, prise the C-clip out of the groove in the shaft, withdraw the spool, remove the second circlip and lift off the gear assembly and the washer under it. Reassembly is the opposite sequence.

19 The crankcase cover ready for installation is shown in the picture.

20 Oil the crankshaft and the camshaft bearings, then slide the cover on to the

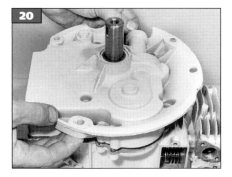

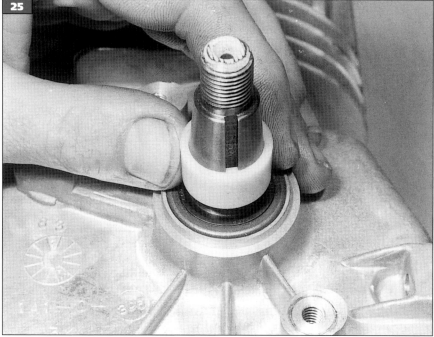

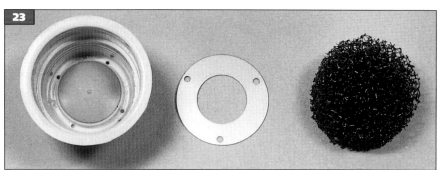

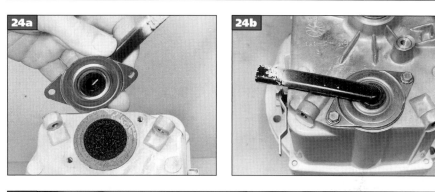

crankshaft. Turn the pinion shaft slightly to engage the pinion with the worm on the crankshaft if necessary. Locate the cover on the dowels. Check through the engine breather hole that the oil pump plunger ball-end is correctly in its housing, and that the governor lever is resting correctly against the governor spindle. Fit and tighten diagonally the six bolts and spring washers that secure the housing.

21 Check the valve clearances. Both valves should have a clearance of 0.25mm (0.010in). Adjustment of valve clearance is by grinding the tip of the valve stem to increase it or grinding in the valve seat to reduce it, but there are limits to the amount of seat grinding possible. In bad cases, new valves may need fitting. This requires professional attention and the use of special tools.

22 Replace the valve cover with the chamfered corner in the bottom left position.

23 Check the engine breather assembly. The valve in the bottom of the cup must be free, clean and undamaged. Wash the steel wool element in solvent and dry it. Place the circular baffle on the shoulder halfway down the cup. Insert the element on to the baffle.

24a Insert the baffle cup assembly into the hole in the crankcase. Fit a new gasket...

24b ...then fit the cover and tube, and secure with the two bolts and shakeproof washers. Ensure that 'Top' stamped on the cover is towards the top of the engine.

25 Fit the plastic sleeve on the crankshaft with its key in the crankshaft groove.

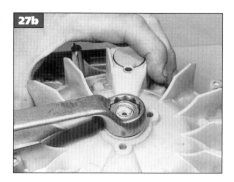

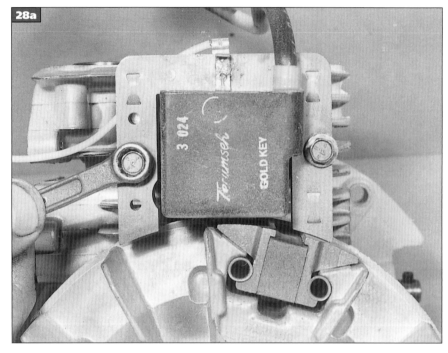

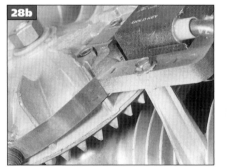

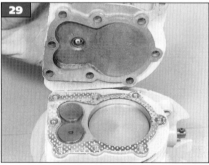

26 Fit the offset key in the slot as shown in the photo, with the longer offset to the left.

27a Fit the flywheel on to the crankshaft aligned with the key...

27b ...and secure with the nut and flat washer.

28a Fit the ignition unit and, using a non-ferrous feeler gauge...

28b ...set an air gap of 0.37mm (0.015in).

29 Fit a new cylinder head gasket and fit the cylinder head, tightening down a little at a time on each bolt in a diagonal sequence.

30 The float components are shown in the picture. Check the end of the needle valve for ridging or other damage and renew if necessary.

31 Assemble the needle valve on the float with the clip.

32 Position the float hinge between the carburettor hinge lugs, with the needle valve inserted in the fuel entry hole. Insert the hinge pin.

33 Inspect the float bowl seal for damage

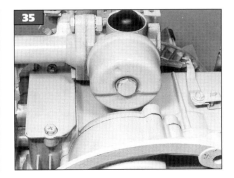

or distortion and renew if necessary. Fit the bowl on to the carburettor.

34 The bowl is secured with the threaded main jet. Check the main jet for cleanliness and damage. Rinse and blow to clean it. Do not use a pin or wire on the metered holes or they will be damaged and accurate metering lost.

35 The step on the float bowl must be located as shown in the photo to allow full movement of the float.

36 Fit the carburettor and linkage plate to the engine using a new gasket. Two screws and spring washers are used to secure the carburettor.

37 Connect the link from the throttle butterfly to the hole at the tip of the governor lever. Connect the spring to the next hole in the governor lever, and the link to the lever on the control plate.

38 Connect the earth lead to the spade connector on the linkage plate.

39 Connect the fuel pipe to the carburettor. If the recoil starter needs attention, this should be carried out now as it's difficult to deal with the starter cord after the fuel tank and engine cowl have been installed. The main components of the starter are shown in the picture.

40 Drive the central pin out by tapping on the chamfered end, then remove the pulley and recoil spring capsule.

41 Lift the capsule off the pulley.

42 To free the cord, prise out the staple in the pulley. Fit the new cord and tap the staple in again.

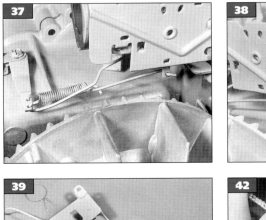

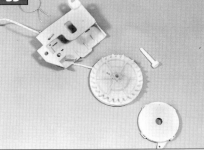

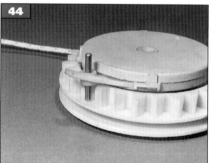

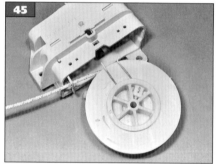

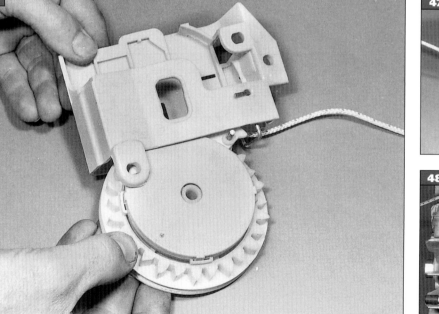

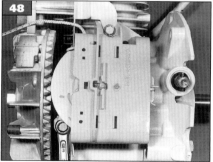

43 Fit the new spring capsule on to the pulley and turn it anticlockwise until the hook on the spring engages in the slot on the pulley hub. This can be verified by increasing tension when turning the capsule.

44 Turn the capsule about four turns to tension the pulley. Use a pin through the hole in the stop lever to hold the tension. Wind the cord clockwise on to the pulley when viewed from the capsule side. Leave enough cord free to pass through the hole in the fuel tank and fit the handle.

45 Fit the large clip on to the pulley. Enter the pulley assembly into the housing, ensuring that the legs of the clip are located either side of the divider plate (in the picture the tip of the divider plate can just be seen on the top edge of the housing).

46 Seen from the other side, the photo shows the pulley assembly being entered into the housing with the pin still in the stop lever. Thread the cord under the wire guide.

47 Fit the central pin. Don't withdraw the pin from the stop lever yet.

48 Install the recoil starter on the engine with the two bolts and shakeproof washers, fitting the engine fairing plate at the same time, as it's secured by the same screws. Take the pulley tension and withdraw the temporary pin from the stop lever. Pull out some more cord then anchor it temporarily.

49 Fit the engine cowl with the four bolts and shakeproof washers.

50 Fit the dipstick tube and secure it to the cowling with the bolt.

51a Thread the cord through the fuel tank hole...

51b ...slide the fuel tank into the slides on the cowl and secure it with the three bolts. Fit the handle to the cord with the removable staple. Free the cord from its temporary anchorage. Pull the starter handle to check correct operation and a positive return action.

52 Connect the fuel pipe to the tank and secure it with the spring clip.

53 Insert the air cleaner inlet duct through the hole in the cowling.

54 Check that the rubber ring is in position on the air cleaner housing elbow duct. Connect the engine breather pipe to the tube on the corner of the air cleaner housing. Position the housing elbow on the carburettor inlet flange and secure with the two screws.

55 Wash the air cleaner foam element in solvent and squeeze it dry. Place it in the housing.

56 Fit the press-on lid.

57 If the power drive unit needs removing, turn the front left-hand wheel backplate until the hole in it exposes the roll pin. Drive the roll pin out and remove the wheel. Withdraw the complete drive unit from the axle.

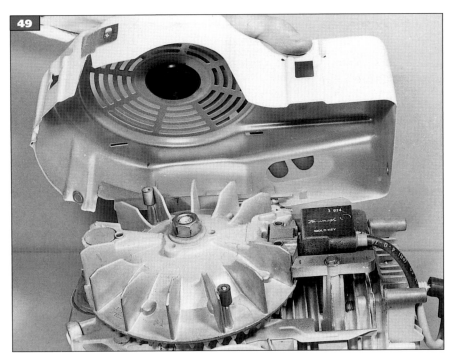

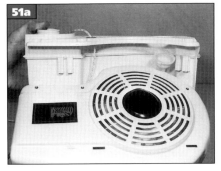

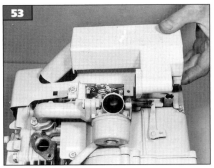

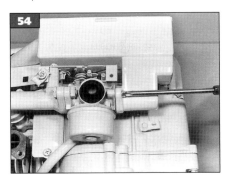

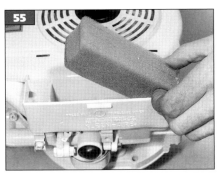

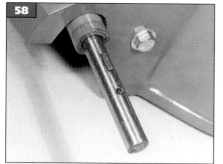

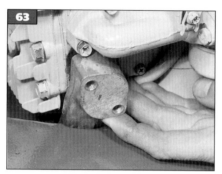

58 To reinstall the drive unit or fit a new one proceed as follows: fit the Woodruff key into the slot in the axle.

59 The groove in the power drive shaft engages the key on the axle.

60 Place the washer on the plastic bush. Place the bush on the power drive sprocket shaft; push the shaft along the slot until the flats on the plastic bush enter the slot in the drive unit casing. Repeat this operation for the other face of the casing.

61 Slide the housing on to the axle, engaging the groove with the key on the axle.

62 Enter the roll pin into the wheel hub, fit the wheel on to the axle and align the pin with the hole in the axle. Drive the pin into the axle with a hammer and punch, taking care not to damage the pin. Fit the wheel cover plate.

63 Fit the exhaust manifold to the engine, using a new gasket.

64 Secure the manifold with two bolts and a locking tab.

65 Lower the mower to the minimum cutting height position. Place the engine on the deck. Fit the plastic sleeve on the power drive unit shaft. Enter the engine shaft into the sleeve and engage the drive dogs in the drive unit shaft slots.

66 Bolt the power drive unit to the decking.

67 Fit three of the engine mounting nuts, bolts and flat washers. Connect the exhaust silencer into the manifold pipe and secure it with the fourth engine mounting nut, bolt and flat washers.

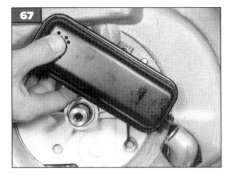

67

68a

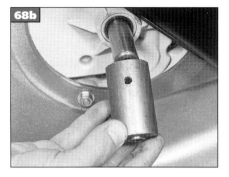

68b

68c

69

68a Fit the Woodruff key in the engine drive shaft, then...

68b ...fit the drive sleeve on to the shaft aligned with the key, and fit the cutter using the shouldered spacer, flat washer and bolt.

68c Use a rag to hold the cutter while tightening it to protect your hand from the cutting edge.

69 Connect the clutch cable to the lever and quadrant.

70 Connect the throttle cable to the lever on the linkage plate.

71 The height-adjusting knob attachment fittings are shown in the photo.

72a Screw the knob on to the threaded rod until the shoulder nears the edge of the casting. Place the half collet in the groove. Continue screwing the knob and collet down into the hole in the boss, until the hole in the collet aligns with the threaded hole in the boss. Then screw the grubscrew into the boss so that it intercepts the hole in the collet. Tighten the grubscrew, and...

72b ...operate the knob to check for free rotation and correct operation of the height adjustment.

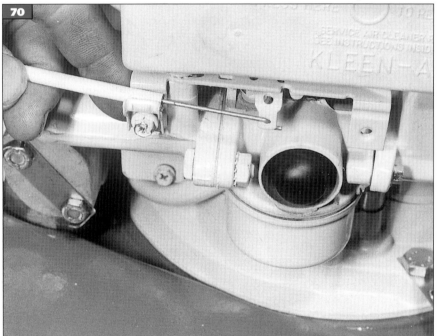

70

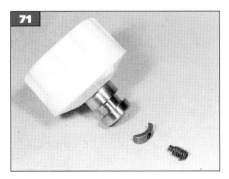

71

72a

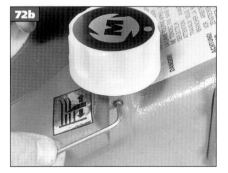

72b

Mower application

The Kawasaki FJ100D OHV engine was fitted from 2008 onwards when the Tecumseh engine company ceased production, and is currently fitted to all 14in, 17in and 20in Allett Kensington and Atco Balmoral models; 14in, 17in and 20in Webb models (2012 onwards); 14in and 17in Qualcast Classic and Suffolk Punch (2008–12) models; then the less expensive Lonsin engine was fitted from 2012 onwards to 14in and 17in Qualcast and Suffolk 5 blade models for the mass market.

1 The Kawasaki engine is currently the quietest, smoothest and most reliable engine that's been fitted on this popular range of lawnmowers. Having overhead valves and low compression, it has a very light initial rope-pull for easy starting, dispensing with the need for an electric start, and suffers very few engine faults. Nevertheless, like any other engine on the planet, even a Rolls-Royce, it still requires general maintenance.

▲ Kawasaki FJ180D internals.

▼ Kawasaki OHV cutaway.

▼ Kawasaki fuel tap.

▲ **Kawasaki fuel tap and filter.**

▲ **Kawasaki air filter.**

2 Check the air filter every 25 hours (more often if used in dusty conditions). Remove the filter cover and remove the filter element carefully. Large grass debris can be tapped off the element. If the filter has turned grey or is clogged, replace it.

3 The FJ100D engine series doesn't have a fuel filter in the tank or in the fuel pipe. It's situated at the base of the carburettor, integral within the tap. Ideally clean or check the filter every 50 hours. Clean in a well-ventilated area, and ensure that there's no flame and no sparks anywhere near the appliance.

4 If pump fuel is used, it's best to drain the fuel for winter storage. This will prevent gum deposits forming on essential carburettor parts and the fuel system: (a) carburettor bowl, (b) drain screw, (c) container.

5 Empty the fuel from the fuel tank with a siphon or pump. Place a suitable container under the carburettor. Loosen the drain screw (b) of the carburettor and drain completely. After draining the fuel, refit and retighten the drain screw firmly.

6 Remove the spark plug; pour approx 1–2ml of new engine oil through the plughole. Slowly pull the recoil starter a few times. This will coat the internal engine parts, protecting them from condensation and corrosion. Refit the spark plug, then slowly pull the starter

till you feel resistance on the rope, and leave it there. This leaves the engine on the compression stroke with the piston positioned at the top of the engine, leaving none of the bore surface exposed to moisture. Also, in this position all the valves are closed. Placing the choke lever in the 'On' position will also help prevent moisture ingress to the carburettor.

▶ **Kawasaki fuel tap service. Close the fuel tap lever to the off position. Loosen nut (a) and remove the cup (b), gasket (c) and filter (d). Remove any sediment, wipe clean, and reinstall the fuel tap. Caution: parts can be tight – don't over-force any that are.**

▼ **Carburettor drain.**

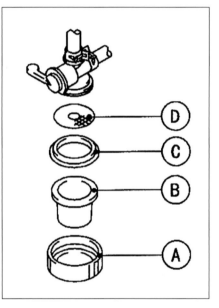

BRIGGS & STRATTON ENGINES LOOK ALIKE BUT...

TO PROVIDE THE CORRECT PART FOR YOUR ENGINE AN AUTHORIZED SERVICE CENTER MUST HAVE THE MODEL, TYPE, AND CODE NUMBER... MANY PARTS LOOK ALIKE BUT ARE NOT INTERCHANGEABLE.

The illustrations on this sheet show the standard locations for identification numbers on Briggs & Stratton engines

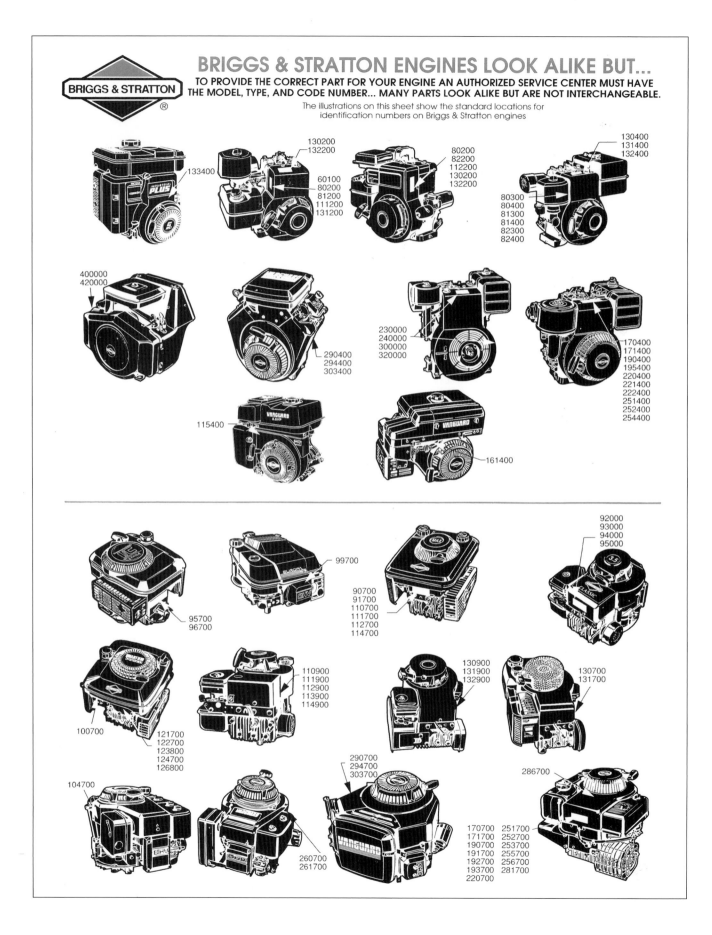

THE FUTURE OF LAWNMOWER ENGINES

▶ **Popular Briggs & Stratton engines.**

Briggs & Stratton engines

From 2012 Briggs & Stratton produced their 'E' Series Engine Initiative, covering the whole of the European vertical crankshaft range. The Initiative placed reduced exhaust emissions at the heart of all their engine performance improvements, by surpassing emission standards by at least 25%, as well as focusing on evolving standards for sound, tonal quality and reliability. They also boast 'first-time starting' with their 'Ready Start' engines. There are five basic 'E' engines, *ie* two displacements delivering three torque options: 125cc (model 450E1) delivering 6.1Nm, 140cc (model 500E) delivering 6.8Nm, and 140cc (550E, 550EX, 575EX, Eco Plus) delivering 7.5Nm, the last including a nylon-based fuel tank with CIC carbon in the fuel cap and low permeation fuel lines.

Kawasaki engines

Although designed for the more professional machines, the latest generation of engines from Kawasaki, developed for the 2013 season FJ180D and FJ220D, demonstrate increased power, smoother, low-vibration operation and improved fuel efficiency, and are more environmentally friendly, and, along with other small engine manufacturers, are improving in design all the time.

This Kawasaki engine features the unique K-twin balancing system, which reduces engine vibration significantly, giving the user a more pleasant and comfortable experience when operating the machine. There are several advantages of this feature over conventional engines, which may not normally be considered by users: (a) it enables the user to work for longer periods without any ill effects; (b) less design input on stiffening and rigidity is required on the machine when low-level vibration engines are used, which results in lower weight and production costs; and (c) lower vibration causes less stress and fatigue on the machine and the engine's powering, increasing the life expectancy of the entire piece of equipment, not just the engine.

▲ **Kawasaki FJ180D engine. Hot off the production line, the next-generation Kawasaki engine.**

▶ **Kawasaki K-twin balancer system.**

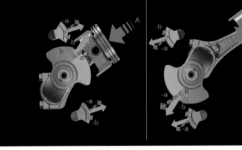

■Kawasaki's K-Twin Balancer System will reduce vibration by maintaining balance among the forces.

Chapter 13

Lawnmower racing – the alternative motor sport

During the early 1970s, when author Brian Radam could be found testing his modified garden tractor around his Lancashire back garden, hoping to enter it into *The Guinness Book of Records* as the fastest lawnmower. Meanwhile, an Irishman called Jim Gavin returned from a car rally in the Sahara. Soon afterwards he was chatting to some mates in a Sussex pub, bemoaning the huge cost of motor racing, and said, 'Isn't there another way of motor racing without the enormous expense, but with just as much excitement?'

So the lads in the pub started talking about the alternative sport of bar stool racing, which soon escalated to wheel barrow racing. After a few beers, careful consideration and debate, they ended up deciding on racing combine harvesters, the only minor problem being that there were only three in the county, and the farmers were very reluctant to lend them. So they finally finished up by saying, 'Everyone's got a lawnmower, so let's race them!'

In 1973 the first Grand Prix race for lawnmowers was held at Wisborough Green in Sussex, England. The sport attracted numerous excited lawnmowerists, and 35 types of mower of all shapes and sizes turned up on the starting grid. The machines ranged from a 1923 vintage ride-on lawnmower to run-behind mowers and garden tractors. Nowadays if you get 50 bucking racing lawnmowers revving up next to each other on a starting grid, it's an awesome sight and can be quite frightening.

Remembering that lawnmowers have been designed to travel only up to a top speed of 6mph, once they're

> 'Lawnmower racing doesn't cost an arm or leg unless you mow over yourself, but it's really great fun and very British.'
> *Sir Stirling Moss, 1976*

▶ A gaggle of Group 2, grass-roots-level racing lawnmowers.

◀ The world's fastest lawnmower.

▲ Group II racing lawnmower. A racing Atco 20in.

▲ Group II racing lawnmoo-er – only for the brave!

▲ Group II racers. A gaggle of racing lawnmowers cutting a dash.

▼ Group II duel – twin-cutters racing at the cutting edge.

▼ Group II orange. All you need to mow!

▲ **Flymo-ing, a common lawnmower race manoeuvre.**

▲ **The *Gadget Show* TV team finding out that 'it's a lot more bovver than a hover!'**

pushing over 30mph they can have a mind of their own, and can be a bit of a sod to handle. Add to this that most lawnmower racing drivers are at the cutting edge of being absolute lunatics with nerves of steel, equates to a motor sport unequalled in providing a unique and exciting concoction of extreme excitement, fun and skill.

After that very first race, the present-day classifications and regulations were drawn up, and lawnmower racing is governed by a simple but strict set of rules that includes a thorough scrutineering check of each mower before it's allowed to compete, very similar to the system followed in Formula One. Anyone not adhering to the rules is turfed out.

Unbelievably, lawnmower racing isn't yet recognised as an Olympic sport,

▲ **'Cool Cuttings' in Finland.**

▼ **The British 'Upper-Cut', cutting a swathe.**

▼ **Cutting a dash in the Le Mans-start 12-hour race!**

▲ Group III Westwood Racing Lawnbug. Many attain over 50mph.

▲ 'Let's kick grass!' Another Lawnflight.

but they're working on it...we hope. Certainly it's often the star attraction at all sorts of sport and charity events, as well as being great fun to watch – although after an event people may have a different opinion, when they find they're covered in grass, mud and any other substance that's been churned up, depending on what was deposited in the field prior to the event (especially when the racing's on farmland...).

There are three racing classes:

■ Class I – Run behind: This class is the grass roots of lawnmower racing. Mainly cylinder lawnmowers with a powered rear metal roller and smaller rollers at the front. The machines are modified to go just a bit quicker than you can run and are often raced by relay teams – particularly amusing to watch, especially when drivers try to swap over without losing control and falling flat on their face or losing engine speed. This class is ideal for the budding enthusiastic athlete. The speeds of these machines are governed by the ability of the perspiring runner to keep up with the lawnmower without doing themselves serious injury.

■ Class II – Sit behind: This class uses cylinder lawnmowers with a trailing seat. The geometry of these machines is modified to achieve the lowest centre of gravity, with the handlebar and steering lowered to match and balance the rest of the machine. Once adapted, the driver has more control, creating faster cornering and stability. The class is a creative engineer's dream, and it's a soul-stirring sight to see a full field of Class II sod-stomping machines, grassbox to grassbox, exhausts bellowing, powering round a tight circuit at 50mph. When competing, this class is definitely not for the faint-hearted, especially when on full lock your brakes are starting to wane, and the machines in front, alongside and to your rear are almost out of control whilst dicing on the fastest corner of the circuit, with an unavoidable hay bale looming ahead with an already up-turned lawnmower beached on top of it, its engine bellowing smoke while still on full throttle!

■ Class III – Sit-on: This class uses the common ride-on domestic garden tractor. Once attention is given to tweaking the gearing and steering geometry these machines are the fastest class, and the best fun you'll have without your eyeballs dropping out. It was a member of this class of mower that in 2010 attained the accolade for the world's fastest lawnmower, at over 95mph.

Upon official inspection the machines should be able to revert to their original grass-cutting capabilities.

And how fast can they go? Well, scary speeds of 60mph are often achieved, but once driven above 30mph they can become a bit of a handful and a sod to control. However, on 23 May 2010, on Pendine Sands in South Wales, Donald Wales – grandson of Sir Malcolm Campbell and nephew of Donald Campbell (who between them broke over 20 land and

THE GRASS ROOTS REGS

1 The mower must originally have been designed, manufactured and sold to mow lawns, and not the rolling prairies of America or the steppes of Russia.
2 The blades must be removed (for safety).
3 The machine must be self-propelled and petrol-powered (as mains cables aren't long enough).
4 You can't fit a bigger engine than the manufacturer intended (like a V8).
5 The mower must still look like a mower, and not like a Ferrari.

Murray Walker, the famous Formula One commentator, has occasionally done the race commentary, and the celebratory Champagne for the winner is always Moët.

water speed records) – attained the amazing speed of 87.833mph and mow-tored into the *Guinness Book of Records* with the world's fastest lawnmower, at a speed only 49mph slower than the first land speed record achieved by his grandfather Sir Malcolm in 1926 – in a vehicle that didn't even cut grass (Don's mower, codenamed 'Project Runningblade', was filmed cutting grass before its record attempt). Before Don attempted the speed record, the course, being next to an army training ground, had to be cleared of live ammunition, otherwise the speed attempt might also have achieved the Guinness World Record for the first person to blow himself up on a lawnmower.

Later the same year, on 25 September, Bobby Cleveland set a new world lawnmower land speed record of 96.529mph on a Snapper Racemower on Bonneville Salt Flats, USA. Who knows what the record will be by the time you're reading this? In 2013 Honda engineers were racing to build another world's fastest lawnmower, called 'Mean Mower', at a cost of £50,000 and capable of attempting a speed of 130mph plus (209kph). The machine was derived from a Honda HF2620 garden tractor, fitted with a 1,000cc Honda Firestorm superbike engine, resulting in a lawnmower that can accelerate from 0–60mph in four seconds – almost a second faster than a Porsche 911. One of the test drivers was 'The Stig', from BBC's *Top Gear* programme.

Amongst the many lawnmower races that take place all over the country each year, one annual event that draws huge crowds is the sod-stomping bladeless Mow-down at Wisborough Green in Sussex, normally around midsummer's day, starting at 10pm on a Saturday night and ending 12 hours later at 10am Sunday morning. With a thrilling Le Mans-type start, this famous endurance race often attracts over 50 entries. Famous racing champions such as Sir Stirling Moss, Derek Bell and Tony Hazelwood teamed up to win one race, with Tony Hazelwood knocking up 276 miles and thereby establishing another Guinness World Record (for the greatest distance covered in a bumpy muddy lawnmower race) during the 1980 event. During one thrills-and-spills-packed

▲ **Donald Wales (right) and author Brian Radam in 2010, with the world's then fastest lawnmower, a Countax A Series model assembled 90% from standard Countax components and powered by a 999cc Kawasaki FX1000V twin-cylinder engine and cutter deck – truly a cut above the rest. Don holds nine UK land-speed records.**

race night there was one unfortunate incident when an out-of-control machine demolished one of the ladies' toilet tents. Shocked witnesses of the event – among them famous movie star Oliver Reed – described seeing a lady speed into the night screaming like a banshee; to this day she remains unidentified.

Other big events on the international lawnmower race calendar include the Two-Day World Championships, which attracts teams from all over the world, from New Zealand to Zimbabwe, with a Hong Kong team entry winning a superb marble trophy in an early race in 1980.

Lawnmower racing has often been described as 'an enjoyable insanity', with truly insane rules, but it could

well be the answer for many would-be motor sports competitors who've been deterred by the huge cost of the many other forms of motor racing. We're not saying it's a perfect substitute, but once you're sat behind a screaming, bucking and almost out of control lawnmower at speeds of over 50mph, while in close contact with a dozen similar machines roaring around a bumpy, muddy, stubble field, you can't argue that it's not a bad alternative.

For further information on lawnmower racing see the useful contacts appendix. A comprehensive guide and manual called *Build your own Racing Lawnmower* is also available for speedy lawnmowerists.

APPENDIX 1

Fault finding

NOTES
- It's assumed that starting procedures were correct.
- It's assumed that the starter is turning the engine over smartly. If it isn't, it should be removed and the starter fault rectified.
- Always have a fire extinguisher to hand.
- Don't work in a confined or enclosed space.

MOWER WON'T START
- Check that the on-off switch is 'on'.
- Check that the fuel tap is on.
- Check the choke position.
- Check the condition and operation of the throttle cable.
- Check the condition and operation of the presence control cable.
- Check that the shorting-out strip is not touching the top of the plug.
- If the shorting-out connection is at the carburettor, check this doesn't foul any part and provide a way to earth.
- Check, remove and inspect the spark plug: if it's wet, petrol's getting in there.
- Hold spark plug with screw portion against engine and spin with starter. If no spark, remove the lead and hold it about 1.5–2.0mm (0.06–0.08in) from a clean part of the top of the cylinder head, and spin again. If there's a spark, the plug is faulty and needs renewing.
- If no spark, check the contacts in the contact breaker for correct gap, and make sure points are clean.
- Check the connections through the ignition system, for loose wires or screw fittings.
- If the mower still won't start, change the capacitor.
- If the plug is dry and there's a spark, check that there's petrol in the tank, check the fuel filter isn't blocked and check the petrol line right through.
- If the plug is wet and there's a spark, check that the air cleaner isn't choked.

NOTE: *Never run the engine without the air cleaner, even for a few moments.*

- If the air cleaner is clear, check the choke setting.
- Check the carburettor adjustments.
- Check exhaust muffler isn't blocked, especially on two-stroke engines.

ENGINE STARTS, BUT THEN STOPS
- Fuel contamination or restricted fuel pipes.
- Blocked fuel cap vent.
- Faulty spark plug.
- Faulty coil or capacitor.
- Sticking valves, or valve-seat fault.

MOWER STARTS, BUT GIVES LOW POWER
- Dirty air filter.
- Governor sticky or movement blocked.
- Fuel restricted.
- Throttle or mixture controls incorrectly set.
- Blocked exhaust ports (two-strokes) or carbon in exhaust muffler.
- Mower parts clogged with grass etc.
- Badly adjusted chains or belts, and/or clutch out of adjustment, causing drag – tight chains and belts consume power.
- Poor crankcase seal (two-strokes).
- Faulty reed valve, or dirty reed valve (two-strokes).

MOWER RUNS UNEVENLY
- Incorrect mixture setting, probably too rich.
- Loose dirt in fuel line.
- Sticky carburettor controls.
- Blocked exhaust system.
- Loose hand controls or cables that move with the movements of the mower.
- Reed valve choked (two-strokes).
- Faulty spark plug.
- Carburettor fault.
- Sticking valves, or carbon build-up.

ENGINE MISSES WHEN DRIVING MOWER

- Dirty spark plug: clean and then reset gap. Renew if in poor condition.
- Pitted contact breaker points: file smooth or renew points, and reset gap.
- Contact breaker moving point arm is sticky: remove and clean pivot, lubricate with one drop of machine oil.
- Valve clearance incorrect, or weak valve springs (four-strokes).
- Carburettor adjustment incorrect, probably richer mixture needed.
- Reed valve choked (two-strokes).

ENGINE KNOCKS

- Carbon in combustion chamber.
- Flywheel loose: remove starter and check that the key in keyway of shaft is correctly located. Check Belleville washer has domed side uppermost and retighten securing nut.
- Check for wear on main and connecting rod bearings.

ENGINE EMITS DARK GREY SMOKE

- Engine overfilled with oil.
- Choke applied.
- Worn piston rings.
- Valves not seating properly.

ENGINE EMITS LIGHT GREY SMOKE

- Has the machine been tipped?
- Engine overfilled with oil.
- Air filter contaminated.
- Fuel contamination.

ENGINE EMITS BLACK OIL FROM THE SILENCER

- Has the machine been tipped?
- Engine overfilled with oil.

ENGINE EMITS OIL FROM THE AIR FILTER

- Has the machine been tipped?
- Engine overfilled with oil.

NOTE: *If, after checks, performance still seems poor, the engine may need overhauling. A quick check on compression is as follows:*

Two-strokes
Turn the engine slowly, one complete revolution. Repeat several times. There should be a distinct resistance to turning, but much more resistance during one half-turn than during the other half-turn.

Four-strokes
Spin the engine the opposite way to normal running (anticlockwise when viewed from the flywheel end in the case of Briggs & Stratton engines). There should be a sharp rebound.

QUICK TROUBLESHOOTING GUIDE

Engine won't start or has low power:	
Symptom	**Cause and remedy**
No fuel in combustion chamber (spark plug is dry).	Check fuel level. Fuel tap. Blocked fuel filter or pipe. Blocked tank cap vent. Blocked or faulty carburettor. Clean and retry.
Spark-plug fouled by fuel (spark plug wet).	Over-rich fuel-air mix. Stale or incorrect fuel. Water in fuel. Faulty carburettor. Clogged air filter. Spark plug. Change fuel and spark plug. If no spark, check on-off switch and ignition coil.
Low compression.	Faulty head gasket, piston rings, cylinder bore or valves, loose spark plug or head bolt. Tighten loose bolts. Replace gasket and seals. If replacing any major parts check the spares price first.
Weak or no spark.	Spark plug faulty, fouled or incorrect gap. Engine switch in off position. Ignition coil fault. Check oil level and refill to correct level if necessary. Note that the ignition system is automatically disabled if a red warning light is activated.
Overheating engine.	Clogged air filter. Cooling fan, cooling fins and air ducts blocked. Low oil level. Carbon build-up in combustion chamber. Poor ventilation around the engine. Check cutters and drive aren't clogged and are free-moving. Clean blocked cooling system. Change or refill the oil. **NOTE:** *If your engine has been overheating, for whatever reason, the oil viscosity quality will have deteriorated, especially if a multigrade has been used.*

APPENDIX 2

Exploded views of popular lawnmowers

This appendix comprises various exploded views covering Allett, Atco, Qualcast, Suffolk, Balmoral, Kensington, Classic, Punch, Windsor and Webb machines, both 12-, 14-, 17- and 20-inch.

Note that the figures in the exploded views are positional reference numbers – refer to the owners' handbook for the actual part numbers when ordering spare parts.

▶ **Chassis exploded view – electric Windsor/Kensington/Classic.**

▶ **Heavy-duty Allett Buckingham and Atco Royal Professional 20-, 24- and 30-inch lawnmowers transmission exploded view.**

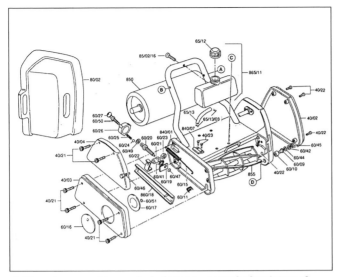

▲ Chassis assembly exploded view – petrol Classic/Punch.

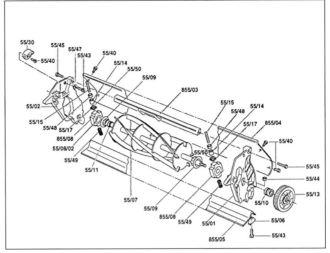

▲ Cutter assembly exploded view – Balmoral/Kensington/Classic/Punch.

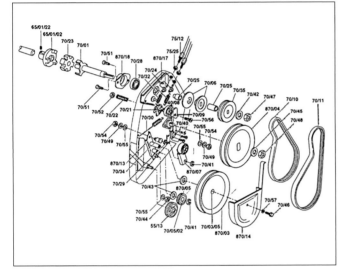

▲ Petrol transmission exploded view – Balmoral/Kensington.

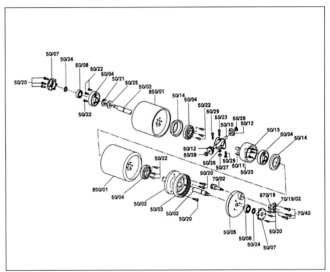

▲ Rear roller exploded view – Balmoral/Kensington.

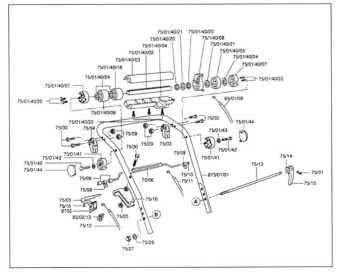

▲ Handle assembly exploded view – Balmoral/Kensington.

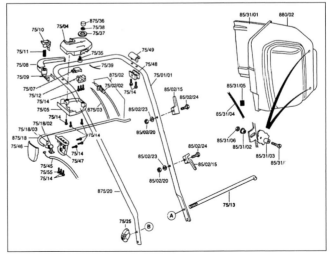

▲ Switch handle assembly exploded view – electric Windsor/Kensington.

APPENDIX 3

Glossary

This is an A–Z of grass-cutting machinery, parts and related words, some of which may have different definitions in other applications. Though it mainly refers to garden machinery in the UK, it will come in handy when ordering or Googling spare parts.

ABS – Acrylonitrile butadiene styrene. A copolymer or strong type of plastic material used in mower chassis and police riot shields.

AC – Alternating current, as from a mains supply.

Actuator – A device in a strimmer that allows the nylon line to feed out.

Aerator shoes – A pair of clamp-on soles with spikes to aerate a lawn.

AH – Amp hour. Measurement of the power capacity of a battery.

Air gap – A precise gap measurement between a coil and flywheel magnet.

Air vane – A device worked by airflow that governs engine speed, to ensure smoothness.

Alternator – An electrical device that generates alternating current.

Ampere – An amp. A unit for measuring electrical current.

Antisiphon – Valve inserted in a pipe to prevent backflow.

Anvil – A flat blade, against which a sharp blade is pressed to cut. Used in secateurs and loppers.

API – American Petroleum Institute, formed circa 1930.

Armature – The copper wire windings on the rotating shaft of a brush motor. Also describes an electronic coil on a garden machine petrol engine.

Back lap – Turning blades backward and applying grinding paste to sharpen a cutting cylinder.

Banjo – A banjo-shaped carburettor fitting, which the fuel pipe attaches to.

BBC – Blade brake clutch, also Roto-stop. A device for stopping rotary blades without stopping the engine.

Belleville washer – A domed spring-steel washer used as a locking device.

Belt drive – A V-belt or tooth belt that transfers power from a power source to blades, wheels, roller or drive.

Big end – The part of the connecting rod that fits around the crankshaft.

Bi-metal strip – Two joined strips of thin metal, designed to bend when heated.

Blade boss – An adaptor that fixes the blade to a drive shaft.

Blower housing – An engine cover over the flywheel. American term for an engine cowling.

Bottom blade – Bottom plate or sole plate. The fixed blade on a cylinder lawnmower.

Breather valve – A valve that equalises crankcase pressure and prevents oil being expelled from the engine.

Broadcast – To spread fertiliser, weed killer, seed etc.

Broadcast spreader – A rotary spreader that throws and spreads granulated products. Also used to spread salt to melt ice.

Brush – A carbon conductor found in electric motors that presses against the commutator.

Bump feed – A spring-loaded cup, fitted on the head of a grass trimmer.

Allows the nylon line to be fed out when tapped on the ground.

Bush – A tube used to form the outside of a plain bearing to improve the shaft life.

Butterfly – An oval or round plate in a carburettor, which pivots on a shaft to control airflow and thus the speed of the engine.

Cam – A pear-shaped projection on a shaft that moves an adjacent part.

Cam followers – Tappets. Shaped metal levers that fit between the cam lobes of the camshaft and the valve stems, to open the inlet and exhaust valves.

Camshaft – A rotating shaft with cams attached.

Capacitor – An electrical component that stores electrical energy for starting an electric motor.

cc – Cubic centimetres. An engine capacity measurement of the total volume of space a piston displaces when moved from the top to the bottom of a cylinder.

Chain brake – A chainsaw device that immediately stops the rotation of a saw chain.

Chain drive – A bicycle-type chain that transfers power to the blades, wheels or roller.

Chain skate – A nylon or metal slipper to aid the smooth running of a chain, normally fitted on a chain adjuster.

CIC – Carbon in cap. A fuel cap designed to produce lower emissions.

Circlip – A round, sprung steel clip located in a groove that can be widened by special pliers to fit in a slot on a shaft.

Clam shell – A housing, usually in pairs (left- and right-hand), which covers and mounts the motor on an electric trimmer.

Clearance – A space between two moving parts, or between a moving part and a stationary one.

Clutch – A device that's connected to a drive shaft, which can be engaged or disengaged.

Coil – Ignition coil. Wire wrapped around a core. Provides high voltage to the spark plug.

Commutator – Insulated copper bars around the rotating shaft of an electric motor, where the brushes conduct current.

Condenser – An electrical component that stores electrical energy. Used on a petrol-engine magneto.

Con rod – Connecting rod. The rod that joins the crankshaft to the piston.

Copper slip – A type of grease, copper in colour, designed to prevent seizure of a component *in situ*.

Cotter pin – A pin with a split end that when put through a hole can be spread, to hold parts together.

Cow-horn handle – A two-handed, U-shaped handle often fitted on brush cutters.

Crank – Short for crankshaft.

Crankcase – The main body of an engine. Houses the crankshaft and most internal engine components.

Crankshaft – A rotating shaft driven by a piston, which delivers power to the gears or drive.

Cup and cone – An open bearing race that runs on a cone-shaped shaft, which can be adjusted by tensioning the cone on the bearing.

Cutter bar – The blade on a rotary mower in the UK. The bottom blade of a cylinder mower in the USA.

DC – Direct current, as in power from a battery.

Decal – A sticker or transfer depicting a manufacturer's model name, instructions or diagrams.

Deck – The main part of a rotary chassis or tractor cutter housing.

Decompressor – A device on an engine to lower the compression, to make it easier to pull over.

Dia – Abbreviation of diameter.

Diaphragm – A flexible oscillating membrane found in mower, chainsaw and petrol trimmer carburettors.

Dipstick – Device that measures the oil level in an engine.

Direct collect – Term used to describe a garden tractor where the grass is thrown directly into the grassbox.

Double insulated – Electrical machines designed not to require a safety connection to electrical earth. Designed to prevent electric shock to the user.

Dowels – Close-fitting pegs used to accurately align engine parts.

Drop spreader – A tool for dropping seed or fertiliser to the exact width of the machine.

Dump valve – The lever on a hydrostatic gearbox, which when pushed or pulled disengages the drive into neutral.

E clip – A round sprung steel clip, similar to the shape of a letter 'e', which fits in a slot on the outside of a shaft.

Electrode – A conductor, such as the tips on a spark plug.

Electrolyte – The liquid in a lead acid battery, consisting of sulphuric acid and distilled water.

Electronic ignition – A solid-state component coil that requires no points or condenser.

Element – A paper air filter.

Engine knock – A noise made by an engine, caused by too much carbon in the combustion chamber, a loose flywheel or blade boss, a worn big end, or the engine running on a poor grade of fuel.

ES – An electric start engine.

Estimate – An approximation of the final cost, which may subsequently vary up or down – unlike a quotation, which should be the final cost.

Feeler gauge – Metal finger strips of specified thickness used for setting or measuring narrow gaps, as on spark plugs, points, electrodes and electronic coil air gaps.

Ferrule – A metal cup that secures the outer sleeve on a control cable. The metal cover on the end of a tool handle.

Flexible drive – A rope-like flexible wire that transmits power in a curved shaft, as on a bent-shaft grass trimmer.

Float – A floating device that stops or allows the flow of fuel in a carburettor.

Float bowl – A bowl-like container that houses the float.

Flooded – Where the carburettor or engine have been overfilled with fuel.

Flywheel key – A metal key that locates the flywheel to the crankshaft.

If the flywheel is strained the key will break, preventing the flywheel or shaft from being damaged.

Four-mix – A four-stroke engine that runs on a petrol and oil mixture. Mainly found in hand-held machines.

Friction disc – A device that lets a blade slip when under impact.

Galvanised – Zinc coating on steel or iron to prevent rust.

Gear – A round transmission drive part, which has teeth meshing with and is driven by another gear.

Governor – A device coupled with the throttle. Limits engine maximum speed, stops over-revving and aids smooth running. There are two main types: a mechanical governor, located inside the crankcase, with centrifugal force moving weights to control the carburettor via a rod; and an air vane governor, located over the flywheel cooling fins, that controls the carburettor according to the generated airflow.

Governor spring – A spring that controls the speed and smoothness of an engine.

Grease nipple – A fitting shaped like a body nipple. Allows grease to be pumped one way into a machine part such as a bearing or shaft.

Grind and balance – Term for resharpening a rotary blade.

Grind and set – Term for resharpening and readjusting the set on the cutting cylinder of a lawnmower.

Grinding compound or paste – A paste made for grinding in blades or valves.

Gudgeon pin – Metal pin that fits in the piston that connects the little end of the con rod.

Gum – A varnish-like substance left in an engine when fuel goes stale.

Hand wheel – A nut and bolt, where the nut can be undone or tightened by hand.

Hollow tine aerator – A tool that takes a plug of soil from the ground without compressing the soil around it.

hp or bhp – Horsepower or brake horsepower. Measurement of the power of an engine. Ransomes Lawnmowers say they invented the term. Measured in Watts produced at the crankshaft of an engine: 1hp = 745.7W.

HT lead – High tension lead that conveys high voltage. Connects the coil to the spark plug.

Hydro – Hydrostatic. A hydraulic variable-speed gearbox.

Hydrometer – A device that checks the condition of a lead acid battery by measuring the specific gravity of the electrolyte.

Idler pulley – Moving pulley that tensions a drive belt.

Ignition coil – An induction coil that supplies the high voltage to the spark plug.

Impellor – A disc with fins that creates the airflow required to cool motors. Used to create the lift on hover-type mowers.

in – Inch. Imperial measurement traditionally used for the width of cut on a lawnmower.

Induction motor – A brushless mains electric motor. Requires less maintenance and is quieter than a brush motor. Fitted on many wheeled electric rotary mowers.

Interlock switch – A safety switch in an electrical circuit that prevents operation unless a component is properly engaged. Often found on garden tractors when engaging reverse gear.

Kevlar – Space age material for high-stress applications, five times stronger than steel. Used in garden tractor belts, tyres, cables, body armour, skis etc.

Keyway – A slot in a shaft, which houses a locating key to stop a pulley or sprocket from turning.

Kissing – Term used to describe the correct setting on a lawnmower, when the cylinder cutter just touches the bottom blade.

KS – A key-start engine.

Laddering – Effect left on the lawn by an incorrectly set or blunt cylinder cutter.

LCD – Liquid crystal display. An instruction or information screen.

Lead acid battery – A battery that contains lead, sulphuric acid and distilled water. Often used in tractors and cars.

Leak down tester – Device to test the sealing capability of compression components.

LED – Light emitting diode. A semiconductor light source, used as indicator lamps in control panels.

Little end – The part of the con rod that fits around the gudgeon pin in the piston.

Lithium ion – A rechargeable high-energy battery, lighter and more powerful than others and with no memory effect.

Magneto – A combination of coil and flywheel magnets and components that converts mechanical energy into electrical energy to fire the spark plug.

Manometer – Instrument for measuring vacuum in a crankcase.

Meat – Measurement between a cylinder spider and the cutting edge of a blade, to determine the lifespan of the cutter.

Micron – Unit of length equivalent to a millionth of a metre.

Mills pin – A solid pin wider in the centre, to grip when it's fitted into a shaft.

mm – Millimetre.

Motor brake – Magnetic device fitted on an electric motor that stops the motor as soon as a switch is released.

Muffler – American word for an engine silencer or exhaust.

Mulching – The process of recycling grass clippings by finely cutting and recutting the grass. Concealing cuttings within standing grass, where they decompose into fertiliser.

n/a – Not available. Term used when a spare part can't be obtained, especially found in listings of budget, foreign, or obsolete lawnmowers.

Nickel cadmium – A rechargeable battery that uses nickel oxide hydroxide and metallic cadmium as electrodes.

Nm – Newton metre. A measurement of power.

Not true – Term used to describe an eccentric cylinder cutter. Remedied by a regrind.

Nylotron washer – A plastic washer designed by Briggs & Stratton.

Obsolete – Term used in the garden machine industry to indicate a part that's no longer made.

Offset – Term used to describe a cylinder cutter that isn't touching the bottom blade.

OHC – Overhead cam. A camshaft that drives the valves, and is situated above them.

OHV – Overhead valve. Engine valves positioned on top of the piston. Promotes more efficient running than a side-valve engine.

Oiler – A fitting with a hinged cap to keep debris out. Allows access for oil to lubricate parts like bearings and shafts.

Oilite bearing – A bearing made of phosphor bronze with microscopic holes, which holds lubricant within it.

Oil seal – A rubber ring, often with a coil spring inserted, to fit on a shaft next to a bearing, to stop oil seepage.

Oil splasher/dipper – A bar fitted on to the big end to disperse oil from the sump around the inside of the crankcase and cylinder.

OPC – Operator presence control. A handgrip that, when released, will stop the machine. Often called a 'dead man's handle'.

O-ring – A rubber or neoprene sealing ring.

Pawl – A pivoted lever shaped to engage with a ratchet to prevent motion in a particular direction, as in a recoil or rear-roller gears.

PD – Suffix that describes a 'power drive' or 'self-propelled' (SP) machine.

PDI – Pre-delivery inspection in the garden machine and car industry. Fully-assembled machine with oil and fuel is run, tested, ready to use and demonstrated to the customer.

PH – The relative acidity or alkalinity of soil.

Pinion – A small round gear that normally engages a larger gear.

Piston ring clamp – A steel band that's tightened to compress the piston rings around the piston for assembly purposes.

Pitted – Depressions in metal parts caused by corrosion, rust or improper combustion.

Points – Contact breaker points. A pair of opening and closing electrodes, operated by a cam on the crankshaft, that controls the ignition of the fuel at the correct time.

Points gap – A precise measurement between the two contacts on the contact breaker points.

Powered sweeper – An attachment to a tractor that sweeps up the grass by means of a revolving brush, driven by a PTO drive.

Primer bulb – A neoprene bulb that, when pushed, draws fuel into the carburettor.

PTO – Power take-off. A facility found on garden tractors to attach auxiliary powered tools via a drive shaft or belt, such as a grass sweeper, shredder, chipper, chemical spreader, sprayer, etc.

Push-on retainer – Washer with sharp tangs that, when pushed over a shaft, can't slip back.

QR code – A square code scanned by a web-enabled smart phone to deliver moving pictures and information.

Quill housing – A bearing housing, often complete with bearings and shaft, to which the blade is attached on a garden tractor cutter deck.

RCD – Residual current device. An inexpensive lifesaver that reduces the risk of electrocution. Monitors current in the live and neutral wires, which should be equal; when residual current is present due to a fault or short, the RCD cuts the power. Test the RCD each time it's used by pressing the test button.

R-clip – A quick-release fixing clip in the shape of the letter R, often used instead of a nut where tightness or tools aren't required.

Reciprocating knife – Blades that cross over each other back and forth, as fitted on powered hedge-cutters, scythe mowers and barbers' trimmers.

Recoil starter – A rope-based engine-starting device fitted on to a crankshaft. When the rope is pulled a ratchet engages drive to the engine. After pulling the rope retracts into a housing via a flat coil spring.

Rectifier – A solid-state component that converts alternating current (AC) to direct current (DC).

Reed valve – Thin metal plate mounted between the crankcase and carburettor on a two-stroke engine.

Reel mower – American name for a cylinder lawnmower.

Regrind and balance – Resharpen and adjust the balance on a rotary cutter blade.

Ring gear – A gear that's on the inside or outside of a circumference.

Roll pin – Hollow tubular pin, with a split along its length, that can be fitted tightly in a hole.

ROS – Reverse operation system. A switch device that allows a garden tractor to cut in reverse.

Rotavator – A brand name for a cultivator.

Roto-stop – A name used by Honda to describe a mechanism that stops the blade from turning but keeps the engine running. Also known as a blade brake clutch (BBC).

rpm – Revolutions per minute. A measurement that describes the speed of a shaft.

SAE – Society of Automotive Engineers. Specified oil grade.

Shanks' pony – A pony-drawn lawnmower made by Alexander Shanks of Arbroath in the mid-1800s.

Shim – A thin washer or strip of metal for adjusting the clearance or play between parts.

SIF – Suffolk Iron Foundry.

Sod – An American term for turf.

Solenoid – A coiled wire that when electrified operates a mechanical function electromagnetically. Often used as a heavy-duty switch on garden tractors and older battery electric models as part of an electric start.

Sole plate – The bottom blade on a cylinder lawnmower.

SP – Suffix that describes a 'self-propelled' or 'power drive' (PD) machine.

Spark plug gap – The space between the electrodes on a spark plug.

Spherical bush – A ball-shaped phosphor bronze bush, able to rotate to compensate for and match the direct angle of a shaft.

Spider – Part of a cylinder cutter, to which the blades are attached.

Split pin – A wire pin with an eye at one end and two parallel shafts. When fitted the legs are bent to retain the pin in position.

Spring washer – A split spring steel washer that when compressed prevents nuts and bolts from vibrating loose.

Sprocket – A wheel with teeth driven by a chain.

Stator plate – The mounting plate, to which the coil, condenser or points are fixed.

Stimpmeter – A device for measuring the speed of a golf putting green.

Stolon – Runner. A creeping grass stem growing on the surface.

Strimmer – A Black & Decker trademark name for an electric nylon-line grass trimmer.

Sub seal – A seal that fits next to a bearing to stop the ingress of debris.

Suppressor cap – Cap on top of a spark plug that stops radio interference.

Tachometer – Device for measuring the speed of an engine or the rpm of a shaft.

Tap'n'go – Grass trimmer head that feeds nylon line when tapped on the ground. Also called a 'bump feed'.

Tappet – Cam followers. A rod in an engine that's moved by a cam. Used to open the inlet and exhaust valves.

Thatch – Dead grass and clippings that form a mat at the base of grass.

Thingamajig – Popular term used to describe a complicated or unknown spare part. Often heard at spare-parts counters.

Tickler – A spring-loaded rod that depresses the float to allow fuel to flow into a carburettor. Found on many pre-1980s lawnmowers.

Too hard-on – A term used to describe a cylinder cutter that's set too hard on to the bottom blade.

Top dead centre – TDC. Moment when the piston is at the highest point of its travel. It occurs twice in one cycle of a four-stroke engine, at the top of the compression stroke when the spark ignites the fuel, and between the inlet and exhaust cycles.

Torque – Pulling or turning power, rotating force of an engine produced by a rotating shaft. Many engines are now rated in torque instead of horsepower.

Torque wrench – A tool with a gauge indicating the force applied to tightening a bolt, measured in foot-pounds (ft/lb).

Towed sweeper – A grass-collecting accessory with revolving brushes, powered by the forward motion of its own drive wheels. Normally pulled by any non-collecting tractor.

Transaxle – A combined gearbox and drive axle found on manual or hydrostatic tractors.

Trunnion nut – Tubular threaded nut that can move around an axis.

Two-stroke – An engine that has one power stroke for every two piston strokes.

Ultrasonic bath – Machine for cleaning carburettor parts by creating millions of bubbles.

Vapour lock – A condition caused by overheating of fuel, where bubbles obstruct fuel flow and cause the engine to stall.

Venturi – Part of a carburettor that forces air through an inlet tube.

Weedwhacker – The original American brand name for a nylon-line grass trimmer. Invented after watching an automatic car-wash mechanism.

Whatsit – An all-encompassing term used to describe a mower spare part. A more common term than thingamajig.

Woodruff key – A semicircular key that sits in a slot of the same profile in a shaft, to prevent a pulley, gear, wheel or roller from moving.

APPENDIX 4

Useful contacts and suppliers

AL-KO
Wincanton Business Park, Wincanton
Somerset BA9 9RS
Tel 01963 828000. *Fax* 01963 828001
Email sales@al-kogarden.co.uk
Internet www.alkogarden.co.uk

Allett
Hangar 5, New Road, Hixen
Staffordshire ST18 0PJ
Tel 01889 271503. *Fax* 01889 271321
Email sales@allett.co.uk
Internet www.allett.co.uk

Allen
Spellbrook, Bishop's Stortford
Hertfordshire CM23 4BU
Tel 01279 723444. *Fax* 01279 723821
Email sales@hayter.co.uk
Internet www.hayter.co.uk

Ariens
Countax House, Great Haseley Trading Estate,
Great Haseley
Oxfordshire OX44 7PF
Tel 01844 278800
Email sales@countax.com
Internet www.countax.com

Aspera
Tecnamotor
Internet www.tecumsehpower.com

Atco (pre-2011 models)
Broadwater Park
North Orbital Park
Uxbridge UB9 5HJ
Tel 01895 838883. *Fax* 08447 360146
Internet www.boschgarden.co.uk

Atco (post-2011 models)
Global Garden Products
Bell Close, Newnham Industrial Estate
Plympton, Plymouth PL7 4JH
Tel 01752 231500. *Fax* 01752 231645
Internet www.atco.co.uk

Atco Car Owners' Club
British Lawnmower Museum
106–114 Shakespeare St, Southport
Merseyside PR8 5AJ
Tel 01704 501336. *Fax* 01704 500564
Email atcocar@lawnmowerworld.com
Internet www.lawnmowerworld.com

Autolawnmow
28 Church Lane, East Carlton
Leicestershire LE16 8YA
Tel 01536 210216
Internet www.ambrogiorobots.com

Barrus
Launton Road, Bicester
Oxfordshire OX26 4UR
Tel 01869 363636. *Fax* 01869 363618
Internet www.lawnflight.co.uk

Black & Decker
210 Bath Road, Slough
Berkshire SL1 3YD
Tel 01753 574277. *Fax* 01753 551155
Internet www.blackanddecker.com

Bosch
Broadwater Park,
North Orbital Park
Uxbridge UB9 5HJ
Tel 01895 838883. *Fax* 08447 360146
Internet www.boschgarden.co.uk

Briggs & Stratton
Road Four
Winsford Industrial Estate
Winsford, Cheshire CW7 3QN
Tel 01606 868276. *Fax* 01606 862180
Email service@briggsandstratton.co.uk
Internet www.briggsandstratton.com

Brill
Wincanton Business Park,
Wincanton
Somerset BA9 9RS
Tel 01963 828000. *Fax* 01279 723821

British Agriculture & Garden Machinery Association
Middleton House, 2 Main Road
Middleton Cheyney, Banbury
Oxfordshire OX17 2TN
Tel 01295 713344. *Fax* 01295 711665
Email info@bagma.com
Internet www.bagma.com

British Lawnmower Museum
106–112 Shakespeare St
Southport
Merseyside PR8 5AJ
Tel 01704 501336. *Fax* 01704 500564
Email info@lawnmowerworld.com
Internet www.lawnmowerworld.com

British Lawnmower Racing Association
Hunt Cottage, Wisborough Green
Billingshurst,
West Sussex RH14 OHN
Internet www.blmra.co.uk

Castel Garden
Internet www.castelgarden.com

Champion Spark Plugs
Federal-Mogul Corporation
Internet www.federalmogul.com

Countax
Countax House
Great Haseley Trading Estate
Great Haseley,
Oxfordshire OX44 7PF
Tel 01844 278800.
Fax 01844 278792
Email sales@countax.com
Internet www.countax.com

John Deere
Harby Road
Langer
Nottinghamshire NG13 9HT
Tel 01949 860491. *Fax* 01949 860490
Internet www.deere.co.uk

Dennis
Ashbourne Road, Kirk Langley
Derbyshire DE6 4NJ
Tel 01332 824777. *Fax* 01332 824525
Email sales@dennisuk.com
Internet www.dennisuk.com

Draper
Hursley Road, Chandlers Ford, Eastleigh
Hampshire SO53 1YF
Tel 02380 494333. *Fax* 02380 494201
Email sales@drapertools.com
Internet www.drapertools.com

DR Products
Wincanton Business Park, Wincanton
Somerset BA9 9RS
Tel 01963 828000. *Fax* 01963 828001
Internet www.drproducts.co.uk

Efco
Unit 8, Zone 4, Burntwood Business Park
Burntwood, Staffordshire WS7 3XD
Tel 01543 687660. *Fax* 01543 670721
Email info@emak.co.uk
Internet www.emak.it

Etesia
Greenway House, Sugarswell Business Park
Shenington, Oxfordshire OX15 6HW
Tel 01295 680120. *Fax* 01295 680852
Email sales@etesia.co.uk
Internet www.etesia.co.uk

Flymo
Preston Road, Aycliffe Industrial Park
Newton Aycliffe
County Durham DL5 6UP
Tel 0844 2435263. *Fax* 01325 302530
Internet www.flymo.com/uk

Gardena
Preston Road, Aycliffe Industrial Park
Newton Aycliffe, County Durham DL5 6UP
Tel 0844 8444558
Internet www.gardena.com/uk

GGP
Internet www.mountfieldlawnmowers.co.uk

Hayter
Spellbrook, Bishop's Stortford
Hertfordshire CM23 4BU
Tel 01279 72344. *Fax* 01279 600338
Internet www.hayter.co.uk

Honda
470 London Road, Slough
Berkshire SL3 8QY
Tel 0845 2008000
Internet www.honda.co.uk

Husqvarna
Preston Road, Aycliffe Industrial Park
Newton Aycliffe,
County Durham DL5 6UP
Tel 0844 2435263. *Fax* 01325 302530
Email husqvarna@husqvarna.co.uk
Internet www.husqvarna.co.uk

Jerram & Pearson
Ashbourne Road, Kirk Langley
Derbyshire DE6 4NJ
Tel 01332 824777. *Fax* 01332 824525
Internet www.dennisuk.com

Jonsered
Preston Road, Aycliffe Industrial Park
Newton Aycliffe, County Durham DL5 6UP
Tel 0844 8444558
Internet www.husqvarna.co.uk

Kawasaki
1 Dukes Meadow, Millboard Road
Bourne End, Buckinghamshire SL8 5XF
Tel 01628 856600. *Fax* 01628 856799
Email engines@kawasaki.eu
Internet www.kawasaki-engines.eu

Kohler
Unit 1, Europark, Watling St
Clifton upon Dunsmore, Rugby
Warwickshire CV23 0QA
Tel 01788 861150. *Fax* 01788 860450
Internet www.hardi-uk.com

Kubota
Dormer Road, Thame, Oxfordshire OX9 3UN
Tel 01844 214500. *Fax* 01844 216685
Email service@kubota.co.uk
Internet www.kubota.co.uk

Lawnflight
Launton Road, Bicester
Oxfordshire OX26 4UR
Tel 01869 363636. *Fax* 01869 363618
Internet www.lawnflight.co.uk

Lawn-Boy
Railway Rd, Downham Market
Norfolk PE38 9EB
Tel 01366 38204/388540
Fax 01366 384204

Lawn King
Dove Fields, Uttoxeter
Staffordshire ST14 8HU
Tel 01889 565155. *Fax* 01889 563140
Email enquiries@trenchex.com
Internet www.lawn-king.co.uk

Lawnmowerworld
106–112 Shakespeare St, Southport,
Liverpool, Merseyside PR8 5AJ
Tel 01704 501336/535369
Fax 01704 500564
Email info@lawnmowerworld.com
Internet www.lawnmowerworld.com

Lloyds & Co
Birds Hill, Letchworth
Hertfordshire SG6 1JE
Tel 01462 683031. *Fax* 01462 481964.
Email sales@lloydsandco.com
Internet www.lloydsandco.com

MacAllister
Brand name – refer to original supplier or
B&Q stores

Makita
Michigan Drive, Tongwell, Milton Keynes
Buckinghamshire MK15 8JD
Tel 01908 211678. *Fax* 01908 211400
Internet www.makitauk.com

McCulloch
Preston Road, Aycliffe Industrial Park
Newton Aycliffe, County Durham DL5 6UP
Tel 0844 2435263. *Fax* 01325 302530
Email husqvarna@husqvarna.co.uk
Internet www.husqvarna.co.uk

Mitsubishi
Master Farm Services Ltd (GB)
Bures Park, Colne Rd, Bures
Suffolk CO8 5DJ
Tel 01787 228450. *Fax* 01787 229146
Email masterfarm@btconnect.com
Internet www.masterfarm.co.uk

Mountfield
Unit 8, Bluewater Estate, Bell Close,
Plympton, Plymouth PL7 4JH
Internet www.mountfieldlawnmowers.co.uk

MTD
Launton Road, Bicester, Oxfordshire OX26 4UR
Tel 01869 363636. *Fax* 01869 363620
Internet www.lawnflight.co.uk

Murray
Road Four, Winsford Industrial Estate
Winsford, Cheshire CW7 1SZ
Tel 01606 868276. *Fax* 01606 862180
Internet www.murray.com

NGK Spark Plugs
Maylands Avenue, Hemel Hempstead
Hertfordshire HP2 4SD
Tel 01442 281000. *Fax* 01442 281001
Internet www.ngkntk.co.uk

North West Lawnmower Racing Association
Internet www.nwlmra.org

Old Lawnmower Club
PO Box 5999, Aspley Guise, Milton Keynes,
Buckinghamshire MK17 8HS
Internet www.oldlawnmowerclub.co.uk

Partner
Preston Road, Aycliffe Industrial Park
Newton Aycliffe, County Durham DL5 6UP
Tel 0844 8444558
Internet www.partner.co.uk

Qualcast (pre-2011 models)
Gipping Way, Stowmarket, Suffolk IP14 1EY
Tel 01449 742031. *Fax* 01449 742214
Internet www.boschgarden.co.uk

Qualcast (post-2011 models)
Argos/Homebase stores

Ransomes Jacobsen
West Road, Ransomes Europark
Ipswich, Suffolk IP3 9TT
Tel 01473 270000. *Fax* 01473 276300
Email enquiries@tip.textron.com
Internet ransomesjacobsen.com

Robin
Fuji Industries Ltd Group
905 Telser-Road, Lake Zurich
Illinois 60047, USA
Tel (847) 540 7300
Internet www.robinamerica.com

Robomow
Unit 11, Westminster Industrial Estate
Station Road, North Hykeham
Lincolnshire LN6 3QY
Tel 01522 690005. *Fax* 01522 690004
Internet www.robomow.com, www.
robomow.eu

Rover
Launton Road, Bicester Oxfordshire OX26 4UR
Tel 01869 363636. *Fax* 01869 363618
Internet www.lawnflight.co.uk

Ryobi
Medina House, Fieldhouse Lane
Marlow, Buckinghamshire BL7 1TB
Tel 01628 894400. *Fax* 01628 894401
Email sales@ryobipower.co.uk
Internet www.ryobipower.co.uk

Sanli
Unit 200, Milton Park Estate
Abingdon, Oxfordshire OX14 4TB
Tel 01235 861640. *Fax* 01235 835055
Email info@sanli.co.uk
Internet www.sanli.co.uk

Shanks
Launton Road, Bicester
Oxfordshire OX26 4UR
Tel 01869 363636. *Fax* 01869 363620
Internet www.barrus.co.uk

Snapper
Road Four, Winsford Industrial Estate
Winsford, Cheshire CW7 3QN
Tel 01606 868276. *Fax* 01606 862180
Email service@briggsandstratton.co.uk
Internet www.briggsandstratton.com

Stiga
Bell Close, Newnham Industrial Estate
Plympton
Plymouth PL7 4JH
Tel 01752 231500. *Fax* 01752 231645
Internet www.stigalawnmowers.co.uk

Stihl
Stihl House, Stanhope Road,
Camberley
Surrey GU15 3YT
Tel 01276 20202. *Fax* 01276 670510
Email postmaster@stihl.co.uk

Sisis
Ashbourne Road,
Kirk Langley
Derbyshire DE6 4NJ
Tel 01332 824777. *Fax* 01332 824525
Email info@sisis.com
Internet www.sisis.com

Suffolk (pre-2011 models)
Gipping Way, Stowmarket
Suffolk IP14 1EY
Tel 01449 742031. *Fax* 01449 742214
Internet www.boschgarden.co.uk

Suzuki
Steinbeck Crescent, Snelshall West
Milton Keynes,
Buckinghamshire MK4 4AE
Tel 0500 011959. *Fax* 0870 6081305
Email customerservices@suzuki.co.uk
Internet www.suzuki.co.uk

Tecumseh
Tecnamotor
Internet www.tecumseh.com

Toro
1 Station Road, St Neots
Cambridgeshire PE19 1QH
Tel 01480 226800. *Fax* 01480 226801
Email toro.sales.uk@lely.com
Internet www.torouk.com

Turfmech
Hangar 5, New Road, Hixon
Staffordshire ST18 0PJ
Tel 01889 271503. *Fax* 01889 271321
Email sales@turfmech.co.uk
Internet www.turfmech.co.uk

USLMRA
USA Lawnmower Racing Association
Internet www.letsmow.com/uslmra

Victa
Launton Road, Bicester
Oxfordshire OX26 4UR
Tel 01869 363636. *Fax* 01869 363620
Internet www.barrus.co.uk

Viking
Stanhope Road
Camberley
Surrey GU15 3YT
Tel 01276 20202. *Fax* 01276 670510
Internet www.vikingmowers.co.uk

Villiers
Meetens Ltd, Far Furlong
Blackleach Lane, Catforth, Preston
Lancashire PR4 0JA
Tel 01772 691604. *Fax* 01772 691602
Email pchild@meetens.co.uk
Internet www.meetens.co.uk

Warrior
Farrell House, Orchard Street
Worcester, Worcestershire WR5 3DW
Tel 01905 763027. *Fax* 01905 354241
Email sales@midlandpower.co.uk
Internet www.midlandpower.co.uk

Webb (pre-2011 models)
Gipping Way, Stowmarket, Suffolk IP14 1EY
Tel 01449 742031. *Fax* 01449 742214
Internet www.boschgarden.co.uk

Webb (post-2011 models)
Hobley Drive, Swindon, Wiltshire SN3 4NS
Tel 01793 333212
Email customerservice@handydistribution.
co.uk
Internet www.handydistribution.co.uk

Westwood
Freepost 3376
Plymouth, Devon PL7 5ZY
Tel 0800 0720127. *Fax* 0800 0720132
Email sales@westwoodtractors.com
Internet www.westwoodtractors.com

Wolf Garden Ltd
E.P. Barrus Ltd, Launton Road, Bicester
Oxfordshire OX26 4UR
Tel 0845 2707603. *Fax* 01871 4291498
Email wolf-garten@barrus.co.uk
Internet www.wolfgarten-tools.co.uk

Yamaha
Sopwith Drive, Brooklands, Weybridge
Surrey KT13 0UZ
Tel 01932 358000. *Fax* 01932 358030
Internet www.yamaha-motor.co.uk